The concept "diaspora" is an enduring one that reverberates within a mosaic of academic and public landscapes. This book adumbrates the missiological currents, perspectives, implications, and significance of Africa as two tales of a continent – Africans in diaspora and diasporas in Africa. Historically, both diasporas, that is, Africans sojourning outside the continent and non-Africans settling on the continent, have made their mark in their respective "host contexts," or rather "new homes," economically, politically, culturally, socially, and demographically. The contributors in this book hone missiological and theological imaginations; plural narratives of co-presence and absence; the exigencies of diaspora missions; the complex iterations of home; belonging, identity, and hospitality; and what these portend for imagining world Christianity historically and in the contemporary global era. This book is a must-read.

Afe Adogame, PhD
Maxwell M. Upson Professor of Religion and Society,
Princeton Theological Seminary, New Jersey, USA

This compendium of enriching perspectives from authentic voices is a compelling call to a new paradigm in mission engagement. It brings together – quite admirably – the biblical, historical, political, and contemporary worldviews to make the point that this is not a time for diasporas to lament lost grounds. Here we find a firm foundation from which to launch mission into today's new worlds. As beneficiaries and proclaimers of the transforming gospel, this is an indispensable resource.

Most Rev. Emmanuel A. S. Egbunu, PhD
Bishop of Lokoja, Anglican Communion, Nigeria

This volume starts a very good conversation. Africans are now recognized as participants in all kinds of global cosmopolitan milieus, not least, Christianizing organizations. Our reverse impact at home as supporters of a wide variety of missional initiatives cannot be underestimated either. As the mother continent gets more deeply immersed in a variety of demographic, economic, and political transformations, reflective diaspora Christians ought to be aware of each other, to strategize, network, collaborate, and ultimately make our presence felt wherever we are scattered. This volume is like a hearty village feast where a full spread meets the ready appetites of people who have been away. It can only be good for the challenges that belie our boisterous comings and goings amongst other strangers and aliens in this world.

Wanjiru M. Gitau, PhD
Assistant Professor of World Christianity and Practical Theology,
Palm Beach Atlantic University, Florida, USA

Africans in Diaspora and Diasporas in Africa is a magnificent work of scholarship. The writers come from different backgrounds and have firsthand accounts and experiences of migration and displacements. What is unique about this book is its global breadth, diverse contributors, scholarly engagement, accessible writing, and convincing arguments. The authors are concerned with the contribution of migratory movements to God's mission not only in Africa, but also around the world. The world has come to Africa, and Africa has gone to the world. This is a book to have on your desk; pick it up and read it.

David Tarus, PhD
Executive Director, Association for Christian Theological Education in Africa

The story of God's work in the world is linked to the scattering of humans across it. In *Africans in Diaspora and Diaspora in Africa* readers catch glimpses of this reality. A useful contribution to the ongoing conversations on God's work through dispersed ordinary human agents.

Tite Tiénou, PhD
The Research Professor of Missions, Dean Emeritus,
Trinity Evangelical Divinity School, Illinois, USA

Africans in Diaspora and Diasporas in Africa

Africans in Diaspora and Diasporas in Africa

Editors

Bulus Galadima and Sam George

GLOBAL LIBRARY

© 2024 Bulus Galadima and Sam George

Published 2024 by Langham Global Library
An imprint of Langham Publishing
www.langhampublishing.org

Langham Publishing and its imprints are a ministry of Langham Partnership

Langham Partnership
PO Box 296, Carlisle, Cumbria, CA3 9WZ, UK
www.langham.org

ISBNs:
978-1-83973-984-2 Print
978-1-78641-021-4 ePub
978-1-78641-022-1 PDF

Bulus Galadima and Sam George hereby asserts their moral right to be identified as the Author of the General Editor's part in the Work in accordance with sections 77 and 78 of the Copyright, Designs and Patents Act 1988.

All rights reserved. No part of this publication may be reproduced, stored in a retrieval system or transmitted, in any form or by any means, electronic, mechanical, photocopying, recording or otherwise, without the prior written permission of the publisher or the Copyright Licensing Agency.

Requests to reuse content from Langham Publishing are processed through PLSclear. Please visit www.plsclear.com to complete your request.

Scripture quotations marked (NIV) are taken from the Holy Bible, New International Version®, NIV®. Copyright © 1973, 1978, 1984, 2011 by Biblica, Inc.™ Used by permission of Zondervan.

Scripture quotations marked (NASB) are taken from the New American Standard Bible®, Copyright © 1960, 1962, 1963, 1968, 1971, 1972, 1973, 1975, 1977, 1995 by The Lockman Foundation. Used by permission.

Scripture quotations marked (ESV) are taken from The Holy Bible, English Standard Version®, copyright © 2001 by Crossway, a publishing ministry of Good News Publishers. Used by permission. All rights reserved.

British Library Cataloguing-in-Publication Data
A catalogue record for this book is available from the British Library

ISBN: 978-1-83973-984-2

Cover & Book Design: projectluz.com

Langham Partnership actively supports theological dialogue and an author's right to publish but does not necessarily endorse the views and opinions set forth here or in works referenced within this publication, nor can we guarantee technical and grammatical correctness. Langham Partnership does not accept any responsibility or liability to persons or property as a consequence of the reading, use or interpretation of its published content.

Dedication

Bulus: To my African diasporic family
Rose, Atsen and Janna, Abi and Tim, Arum and Justine, Atu,
Ezra, Josiah, Na'omi, Vitani, Azi, Motara and Ayisa

Sam: To my Indian diasporic family
Mary, Daniel and Joshua

Contents

Foreword xi

Acknowledgements xv

Introduction 1
Bulus Galadima

1 Beyond Empire: Global Migrations and New Approaches to Christian Mission 9
Jehu J. Hanciles

2 African Christian Diaspora in the UK: A Story of Hope and Despair in Three Congregations 25
Harvey Kwiyani

3 Ghanaian Diaspora Christians in North America: Reflections on Challenges and Opportunities for Mission and Ecumenism 35
Moses O. Biney

4 Diasporas in North Africa and North Africans in Diaspora 45
Tharwat Wahba

5 Africans in Brazil and Brazilians in Africa 55
André Jonas Chitlango

6 Mobilizing African Christian International Students for Global Missions 63
Yaw Perbi

7 Indians in East Africa and Africans in India 75
Harshit Gudka and G. John Daniel

8 Chinese Diaspora Missions in Africa 93
Wenhui Gong

9 African Diaspora and New Horizons in Theological Education in Africa 103
Bulus Galadima and Elizabeth Mburu

10 A Postcolonial Evangelical Approach to Theology: A Rerouting of Mission 119
Godfrey Harold

11	Sub-Saharan Migration Transit Patterns from Africa and into Europe 131
Mitch Hamilton	
12	Human Trafficking in Africa and Beyond...................... 145
Anne Abok	
13	Trauma Healing for Refugees: Building Resilience and Restoring Dignity.. 159
Clene Nyiramahoro	
14	Eucharistic Hospitality: A Brief Postcolonial and Missional Reading 169
Mabiala Justin-Robert Kenzo	
15	Hospitality as a Platform for African Urban Migratory Theology... 177
Afolabi Ghislain Agbèdè	
16	Engaging African Diaspora Communities with Media............ 187
Rudolf Kabutz	
	Conclusion: Africans in Diaspora and Diasporas in Africa........ 197
Sam George	
	Author Profiles 209	
	Index... 215	

Foreword

Africa looms large on the international horizon today. For years, it was considered as the forgotten part of our planet. However, it is an intriguing and captivating continent. In my multiple ministry trips over the last four decades to various regions, I have been fascinated by the massive transformative changes in Africa and the impact of Africans around the world.

Vast and Complex

Africa is a continent stretching between the latitudes of 35 degrees north and 35 degrees south of the equator. No other continent provides us with the diversity and complexity it does.

- The continent is home to a rich animal, plant, and marine biodiversity.
- Africa is recognized as a storehouse of natural resources.
- Some 1.5 billion people live on the continent, and they form the largest single block in the United Nations with fifty-four sovereign nation-states.
- Africa is home to a multiplicity of ethnic groups with over eighteen hundred languages and diverse art, music, and literature.
- Africa is the least urbanized of the inhabited continents. Hence, the urban/rural compositions of the nation-states vary drastically.
- Africa's population is the youngest anywhere in the world. It has many more people aged fifteen to thirty-five than any other continent.

Emerging Resilience

Africa was the most colonized of all the continents and the last to be decolonized. Most of the African nation-states owe their territorial identity to their colonial histories. The Second World War ended the high noon of colonialism in Africa. The liberation of Africa from colonial rule made the second half of the twentieth century a triumphant period for the peoples of Africa.

Suffering has been a part of the African experience – whether it arose from harsh struggles with nature or the cruelty of fellow human beings. The process of decolonization was long and difficult. In the first forty years of independence, many African countries experienced missed opportunities for development. With a lack of responsible leadership and good governance, Africans found themselves mired in rampant corruption, destructive civil wars, genocide, and military coups and plagued with periodic large-scale famines and the spread of diseases. The living standards of citizens declined, including educational attainments and modern social advances. Africa contains the world's largest concentration of least developed countries and fragile states.

The dawn of the twenty-first century provides grounds for optimism almost across the continent. Africans have begun to face their deficits and deficiencies squarely with courage, endurance, and resilience. Africa is taking greater responsibility for its destiny adhering to the injunction to seek "African Solutions to African Problems." Many countries have learned from their past mistakes and now face huge new opportunities with domestic vision and renewed vigour. There is mounting evidence of stronger leadership, deepening democracy, successful policies for sustainable economic improvement, and a peaceful future. With various stakeholders becoming increasingly conscious of the need to work together, regional development cooperation is being pursued. The prevailing condition across Africa suggests a revitalization. Resurgence and Renaissance are becoming the operative watchwords.

Africa and Migration: Internal, Outbound, and Inbound

Migration is not a recent phenomenon in Africa as it has a long history of interconnections with Asia, Europe, and the Americas. This has allowed for the free movement of people and the development of transnational trade routes over the centuries. It is often seen as a region of mass migration for economic and educational opportunities as well as displacement caused by poverty, conflict, and environmental crises.

In the pre-colonial century and the colonial period, industrial Europe needed Africa's raw materials and was a magnet for outward labour migration even with low wages and limited legal rights. Therefore, outbound migration appears to be a secondary offshoot of industrialization. Colonial histories are marked by forced displacement to the plantations and mines of European companies or for the construction of transport infrastructure to exploit its natural resources. With the improvement of many travel routes, migration from villages to cities was inevitable.

Over forty million Africans are migrants, a 30 percent increase since 2010. This trend is only expected to surge in the coming decades. From the global migration statistics, Africa only accounts for 14 percent compared to 41 percent from Asia and 24 percent from Europe. African migration is being propelled by a varied combination of push-pull factors in each country. Push factors include conflict, repressive government, and limited economic opportunity. The pull factors are proximity, established diasporas, educational pursuits, and economic opportunity. Most of the migrants go to other African countries which are developing as regional economic hubs like South Africa, Kenya, Uganda, Nigeria, and Cote d'Ivoire.

It is estimated that 15 percent of African migrants travel without an official document. They are vulnerable to exploitation and trafficking, either along the way or in the country of destination. Deterioration of the economic situation or change in government policies could result in the mass expulsion of such people. Increasingly bilateral partnerships and migration control measures have been formulated to address irregular immigration or to stop fake asylum seekers. However, Africa has a stronger share of forced migration rather than economic migrants. The continent also is the largest destination of refugees only second to Asia and accounts for one-third of the United Nations High Commissioner for Refugees (UNHCR) refugees. Climate change is accelerating rural-to-urban migration. National disasters such as droughts and floods are displacing a record number of Africans.

Africa has also experienced inbound migration. The Arabs first came to North Africa as traders; then a huge wave of Arabs arrived in the eleventh century. Today, Arabic is the official language of eleven of the continent's countries. The Portuguese entered Africa in the fifteenth century and the Dutch followed. In the second half of the seventeenth century, the Danish, English, French, German, and Swedish came to trade. Under the British Empire, Indians were brought to Africa. Today, some three million members of the Indian diaspora reside in forty-six countries of Africa. Most of the Lebanese immigration to Africa occurred between the World Wars and Lebanese number a quarter million. In recent decades, there has been a rapidly growing number of Chinese economic migrants who now number about a million. Koreans and Japanese are also beginning to invest in the continent.

Africans who moved off the continent largely went to Europe, the Middle East, and some to North America. Most of them are thriving in their new environments and making significant contributions to their host communities. The good news story is about the African Christians and churches. They are writing an exciting chapter in modern missions. They are growing in numbers and multiplying through church planting. They are bold in their Christian witness to their neighbours. Their worship services are colourful and joyfully exuberant. They are vibrantly and massively reshaping contemporary World Christianity.

The Global Diaspora Network of the Lausanne Movement hosted the Diaspora Consultation in partnership with Cape Town Baptist Seminary, South Africa from 25–29 August, 2022. The theme of the consultation was *Africans in Diaspora and Diasporas in Africa*, and participants came from over thirty countries. We were stimulated by the papers presented by scholars and practitioners, and the robust interactions. I heartily commend Dr. Bulus Galadima and Dr. Sam George for editing and making this volume available to the global church.

Rev. Dr. T. V. Thomas
Chairman, Global Diaspora Network

Acknowledgements

The journey of this book has been long. The Global Diaspora Network was launched at the Third Lausanne Congress in Cape Town, South Africa in 2010. Lausanne held its first congress in 1974 in Lausanne, Switzerland and the second in Manilla, Philippines in 1989. We planned a consultation in Cape Town in 2020 to commemorate the tenth anniversary of the network. However, due to the COVID-19 pandemic, the event was postponed. We are grateful to God because this delay proved providential, allowing many who would not have attended in 2020 to join us. He indeed led us at each stage of this journey.

We express our gratitude to each author for their dedication in writing, presenting, and editing their chapters for publication. We also thank all the participants of the consultation; their feedback greatly enhanced the quality of each chapter and the book as a whole.

The success of our meetings worldwide depends heavily on local hosting teams. A Hausa proverb states, "You can conquer a city with an indigene." Our global meetings have consistently relied on the invaluable support of local hosting teams, whose contributions have been instrumental to our success. The goodwill and extensive network of the Lausanne Movement further bolstered our efforts. We extend our deepest gratitude to Cape Town Baptist Theological Seminary, our local academic partner, and especially to Professor Godfrey Harold, the principal of the seminary. Professor Harold, along with his dedicated faculty and staff, provided us with exceptional support and coordinated the involvement of key Christian leaders in South Africa.

We are profoundly thankful to the members of the local hosting team comprised of Professor Godfrey Harold, Bishop Cyril Pillay of Peoples Church of God in Durban, Dr. Jacob Igba, Dr. Paul Pookkattu, Emma Brewster, and Rev. Dr. Sipho Zondi. Their efforts enabled us to "conquer" Cape Town with grace and effectiveness. We also acknowledge the contributions of Athlone Church, Claremont and Gleemor Baptist, and Dr. Sipho Zondi, Senior Pastor of Langa Baptist Church, along with his congregation, Rev. Jaegee Lee, Pastor of Cape Town Korean Church, and his congregation for their exceptional hospitality in hosting us, worshipping with us and providing dinner each evening.

We are immensely grateful to Langham for their unwavering support for this project. Luke Lewis, the director of Langham Publishing, embraced this project with enthusiasm from the start. He connected us with Mark Arnold, editorial and contracts coordinator of Langham Literature, who ensured the project continued seamlessly. We also thank Megan Lowe, production coordinator, for her expert guidance and patience throughout this process.

We express our appreciation to various volunteers like Mary Thomas, Karen Medina, and others who helped with many aspects of registration and hospitality to the consultation participants.

We acknowledge the support of the Global Diaspora Network executive team: Rev. Dr. T. V. Thomas, chair; Rev. Barnabas Moon, vice chair; Rev. Art Medina, treasurer; Professor Godfrey Harold; Dr. Hanna Hyun; Dr. Elizabeth Mburu;Rev. Dr. John Park, Rev. Dr. Paul Sydnor, Rev. Joel Wright, and Dr. Jeanne Wu.

Finally, we owe a debt of gratitude to our wives, Dr. Rose Galadima and Dr. Mary George, for their immense support during our travels and work on this book.

Introduction

Bulus Galadima

Africans have been in diaspora and diasporas have been in Africa throughout recorded history. This trend has continued to the present and is accelerating. Growing up as kids in Nigeria, we were always reminded of the relationship between our tribe and the neighbouring tribes. Some were our "playmates" and others were our distant relatives. We were told the story of how we migrated and how these other tribes moved from away from us and became new tribes. In order to strengthen this relationship with these new tribes, an association was established called JIKKA – a name with a double entendre. First, the name stands for Jarawa, Irigwe, Kagoro, Kaje, and Anaguta, picking the first letter of the names of these tribes. Second, the word is pronounced to communicate the familial term *jika* in Hausa which means a grandchild. Many tribes in Africa talk about the movement of their people. These stories are deeply embedded in the identity of the people.

In the Scriptures, we read about the movement of people from Africa to Israel and back. Diasporas have been fascinated by Africa because of its natural resources and civilization. North Africa, particularly Egypt, has been a major ancient civilization for several millennia with many of its structures still in existence today. It has attracted ancient civilizations because of the Nile River which made it fertile and the bread basket of the ancient world. Egypt also conquered other kingdoms sending its people to occupy them and bringing some of those people to settle in Egypt. The Bible tells of the patriarchs of Israel going to Egypt to find food during a time of famine. Joseph was sold as a slave in Egypt along with other people showing that people from other cultures had been coming to Egypt. The famine led to the Israelites sojourning in Egypt for four centuries before they were freed.

Alexander the Great conquered Egypt and established a new metropolis, Alexandria, in 332 BC. It was the centre of the spread of Hellenization in the ancient world. It was a prominent centre of education and culture for nearly a thousand years, also becoming an important commercial centre and the largest city in the world. When the Romans conquered the city around 47 BC, they allowed its three large ethnic groups – Greeks, Egyptians, and Jews – to coexist.

There was a strong Jewish community residing in Alexandria. This community was instrumental in giving us the Septuagint (the Greek Old Testament). Seventy-two Jewish leaders from this community are said to have translated the Jewish Old Testament into Greek in the second century BC. Probably because of the strong Jewish community in Egypt, God instructed Joseph and Mary to flee to Egypt in order to save the life of Jesus Christ. Therefore, the idea of Africans in diaspora and diasporas in Africa is not a new phenomenon.

In the gospels, Simon of Cyrene carried the cross of Jesus (Mark 15:21). Cyrene is located in Libya. On the day of Pentecost, there were several Jewish African people present, from Egypt and parts of Libya near Cyrene (Acts 2:9). In Acts chapter 9 we read of the conversion of the Ethiopian eunuch. Christianity flourished significantly in North Africa with Alexandria becoming an important theological centre. As Thomas Oden says, African Christianity shaped the Christian mind and bequeathed the global church many of its orthodox beliefs.[1] During this time, it was not uncommon for people to travel from Africa to Rome and Greece, and into Asia. Saint Augustine in his *Confessions*, while discussing his conversion, talked about listening to Saint Ambrose of Milan (modern Italy) preach. His travel to Europe is an example of such mobility. Africans have always moved voluntarily for trade, education, and adventure.

Alexandria continued to be a prominent city until it fell to the Arabs in 641 AD. Over the centuries, the Arabic and Islamic conquest brought to Egypt a significant change and domination of the region but did not halt the movement of people. Within the continent, people migrated to find better farmlands and pastures. They were also moved by the powerful empires and kingdoms that emerged like the Aksum, Benin, Borno, Dahomey, Ethiopia, Ghana, Kongo, Mali, Mutapa, Oyo, Songhai, Zimbabwe, and Zulu to mention a few. These kingdoms fought each other. At their heights, they controlled large swathes of land comprising several modern African countries, and they moved people.

The story of the king of the ancient kingdom of Mali gives a glimpse of the movement within and outside the continent and its impact. In the fourteenth century, Mansa Mūsā of the Mali Empire was immensely wealthy and deeply pious. Though he was not the first ruler to travel to Mecca to perform the Hajj,

---

1. Thomas Oden, *How Africa Shaped the Christian Mind: Rediscovering the African Seedbed of Western Christianity* (Downers Grove: InterVarsity Press, 2007), 9.

his trip was legendary. He had an entourage of sixty thousand people and a personal retinue of twelve thousand people wearing brocade and Persian silk. This is significant because it showed that his kingdom had contact with Persia. On this trip, there were five hundred slaves ahead of him each carrying a gold-adorned staff along with eighty camels each carrying three hundred pounds of gold. He made a stop in Cairo to visit the Sultan.

The historian al-ʿUmarī, who visited Cairo twelve years after the emperor's visit, found the inhabitants of this city, with a population estimated at one million, still singing the praises of Mansa Mūsā. So lavish was the emperor in his spending that he flooded the Cairo market with gold, thereby causing such a decline in its value that the market some twelve years later had still not fully recovered.[2] This visit caused many Muslim kingdoms in North Africa and European countries (diasporas) to desire to come to Africa.

Slavery has been one of the ways by which Africans have been moved from the continent. Different kingdoms within Africa moved people from one part of the continent to another as new kingdoms and alliances were formed. The trans-Saharan slave trade and transatlantic slave trade had drastic effects on the continent because they involved the movement of a large number of people outside of the continent. The infamous transatlantic slave trade of the sixteenth century moved a large number of Africans involuntarily to different parts of the world, where they planted deep roots.

The African Union in 2003 recognized the contribution of the African diaspora to the development of the continent and made it the sixth region of Africa. African Heads of State passed a resolution "to invite and encourage the effective participation of Africans in the diaspora, as an important part of our continent, to the construction of the African Union."[3] This has resulted in the formation of the State of the African Diaspora, an organization with a constitution, ministers, and seat on the African Union.[4]

This volume does not address the place of the African diaspora in politics, media, technology, music, sports, non-religious education, science, economics, etc. Africans in the diaspora have played and continue to play significant roles in politics both in Africa and in the diaspora. For example, Kofi Anan was Secretary General of the UN, Ayaan Hirsi Ali is a former politician in the

---

2. John Coleman de Graft-Johnson, "Mūsā I of Mali," *Encyclopedia Britannica*, https://www.britannica.com/biography/Musa-I-of-Mali.

3. State of the African Diaspora Constitution, https://thestateofafricandiaspora.com/wp-content/uploads/2023/04/Constitution-2.pdf.

4. https://thestateofafricandiaspora.com/media/.

Netherlands, and Yemi Mobolade was recently elected mayor of Colorado Springs, Colorado in the United States. In global public health, the current director general of the World Health Organization is Tedros Adhanom Ghebreyesus who played a vital role during the recent COVID pandemic. African diasporas have also returned to Africa to occupy significant political positions, such as Ngozi Okonjo-Iweala, the current Director-General of the World Trade Organization, who was finance minister twice in Nigeria with two different administrations; Ellen Johnson Sirleaf, a former Minister of Finance, who worked in the World Bank and later became President of Liberia; and George Weah, a former FIFA Footballer of the Year who is now President of Liberia.

Africans in diaspora and diasporas in Africa are inevitable phenomena. This book explores the effect of this on the continent, and global implications, from multiple Christian religious perspectives. Christianity has had a significant impact in the past which still continues today. Africans are characterized by values like spirituality, religiosity, communality, and hospitality. Wherever they go, they carry these values with them. These values are often what they miss the most and what they want to establish as quickly as possible anywhere they resettle even if it is temporary. The phenomenal growth of Christianity in Africa asserted by Andrew Walls,[5] and the projection that Africa will comprise 38 percent (from the current figure of 24 percent) of the global Christian population by 2050,[6] makes this volume valuable for the study of global Christianity.

Book Outline

The consultation in Cape Town, South Africa brought together pastors, practitioners, and scholars to discuss various aspects of the modern African movement of people under the topic of Africans in diaspora and diasporas in Africa. The following chapters are a compilation of some of the presentations. In chapter 1, Jehu Hanciles, who is originally from Sierra Leone, then lived in England and now lives in the US, asserts the inevitability of global migration. He then focuses on African migration and shows how this has shaped global

---

5. Andrew F. Walls, *The Missionary Movement in Christian History* (Maryknoll: Orbis Books, 1996), 85.

6. "The Future of World Religion: Population Growth Projections, 2010–2050," Pew Research Center, Washington, DC (2015), https://www.pewresearch.org/religion/2015/04/02/christians/.

Christianity. Chapters 2 to 6 cover Africans in diaspora in different parts of the world. In chapter 2 Harvey Kwiyani, who is from Malawi and lives in England, discusses the experiences of Africans in the United Kingdom and how they are changing the demography of Christianity. It ends with a reflection on the future of Christianity among second-generation Africans. Moses Biney, originally from Ghana and now living in the US, in chapter 3 examines the church planting work of Ghanaian Presbyterians. He examines their relationship with the Presbyterian church in the United States. Chapter 4 by Tharwat Wabha, an Egyptian who studied in the UK, describes the status and the challenges facing African diasporas in North Africa, often in transit, and how the church can reach them. He also talks about church planting efforts among North African diasporas in Europe and North America. In chapter 5 Andre Chitlango from Mozambique, who lived and studied in South Africa, scrutinizes what is the largest African population outside of Africa – Brazil. It is not well known that during the nefarious transatlantic slave trade, more Africans were taken to Brazil than anywhere else. He explains how many of these former slaves have made efforts to return to Africa, and their impact on Christianity in Mozambique today. Chapter 6 shines a light on African international students. Yaw Perbi, a Ghanaian who lived in Canada and recently returned to Ghana, laments the under-engagement of this group in missions and proposes what the church in Africa could do to harness this incredible force.

The next two chapters deal with diasporas in Africa. Indians have had a long history in Africa, particularly in South Africa and more recently in East Africa. Chapter 7, by Hash Gudka, an Indian-Kenyan studying in the US, and John Daniel, an Indian who studied in the UK, begins with Indian diasporas in Kenya and their contribution to nation-building. The second half talks about the experience of Africans in India and how the church can engage these as effective witnesses of Christ. In chapter 8, Wenhui Gong, a Chinese working in Kenya, who studied in the US, analyzes the ministry of a missionary organization among the Chinese diasporas in Kenya and how the church in Kenya can partner with the organization to reach the Chinese diaspora in Kenya and beyond.

The following two chapters examine the role of the African diaspora in the task of the development of theology. In the first part of chapter 9 Bulus Galadima, a Nigerian now residing in the US, and Elizabeth Mburu, a Kenyan who studied and worked in the US, reveal the contributions of ancient African diasporas in the development of theological education in Christian African antiquity and the global Christian mind. They also show how modern African diasporas are influencing theological education today. In the second part, they show how theological education can be reformed by being "glocal" drawing from the example of Paul's ministry in Athens in Acts 17. Next, in chapter 10, Godfrey Harold, a South African of Indian descent, analyzes how missionaries as diasporas in Africa shaped evangelical theology's approach to diaspora missions in South Africa, revealing its blind spots that hinder it from being holistic. He concludes with suggestions on how it can be rehabilitated.

The last 6 chapters focus on practical issues related to diaspora missions. Beginning with chapter 11, Mitch Hamilton, originally from the US and residing in the Middle East, draws attention to the harrowing experience of a few Sub-Saharan African migrants crossing North Africa to Europe. He describes the four major travel routes through North Africa and the risks and rewards of migration. Most studies focus on the points of origin or the destination. He argues that transitional spaces between origin and destination are fertile grounds for missions because of the hopelessness and disillusionment of the journey. He mentions how the church can bring hope to this situation. In chapter 12, Anne Abok, who is originally from Nigeria and resident in the UK, describes how endemic human trafficking is today in Africa among women and children. She discusses the different ways people are lured into trafficking and trapped as modern slaves in its different permutations. The chapter ends with several practical suggestions on how the church can actively participate to stem human trafficking.

Inarguably, the greatest loss experienced by people on the move is their loss of home and sense of belonging. For refugees, it is also often a loss of their identity at a profound level. Africans feel this sense of loss very heavily because they are communal and hospitable people. The next three chapters deal with belonging and hospitality. In chapter 13, Clene Nyiramahoro – from Rwanda and now living in Kenya – recounts the experience of refugees living with trauma, its effect on them, and how the church can walk with them. She describes the powerful impact of the process of trauma healing and illustrates this with the changes that have occurred among refugees in East Africa resulting in thriving and flourishing communities.

The following two chapters concentrate on the issue of hospitality. In chapter 14, Mabiala Kenzo – originally from the Democratic Republic of Congo and now residing in Canada – lays the theoretical and theological foundation of hospitality. He discusses how the Christian Eucharist is an act of hospitality one of the key African values. He shows how radical the idea of hospitality is, and how contrary to human nature. He reasons that it is grounded in the Trinity, exhibited in nature, the incarnation, and is an expression of Christian life. He says it is a difficult concept to practice. He makes a case for how this should be extended to the *Other*. In chapter 15, Ghislain Agbede – from Benin, studied in the US – argues that hospitality is part of the African culture. He roots this in the African concept of *Ubuntu* and demonstrates how it can be practiced in the African urban context hosting Africans from different countries and from Asia, particularly China and Korea. He also uncovers the biblical basis of hospitality and says that the church in African cities can reach the growing number of African migrants and Asian diasporas in Africa, a form of Christian witness to Jesus Christ.

Finally, in chapter 16, Rudolf Kabutz – a South African of German descent – explores how people on the move have the powerful tool of the cellphone to communicate with their homelands, their fellow travelers, and their families wherever they are. They also use it to access media to consume and relay information. In this chapter, he describes the significance of media to people on the move and how it can be used to reach them with the gospel in Africa and Europe. The chapter offers illustrations and practical suggestions on how this can be accomplished.

There are several issues among African diasporas that this volume does not address which are worthy areas of further research. For example, this study did not cover the substantial impact that the mercy ministries of African diasporas are having on the continent in the area of medical missions and other social and humanitarian efforts. There is also the huge impact of the remittances by African diasporas on the continent. African diasporas have had a significant influence on Christianity in Europe and the Americas. They have planted vibrant and flourishing churches there. African diasporas are also active in every area of life in their new homelands, such as arts, education, entertainment, etc. For example, African music is becoming part of mainstream music globally. The African movie industry, especially Nollywood (Nigerian) is growing in influence and many African actors and actresses are playing significant roles in Hollywood. No discussion of sports today will be incomplete without a mention of African diasporas who are playing professionally in Europe, Asia, and America and even representing their new homelands.

All of this notwithstanding, the issues addressed in this volume paint a fairly accurate picture of Africans in diasporas and diasporas in Africa. There is a plurality and diversity of voices as the authors are comprised of practitioners and scholars from different parts of the continent. We pray that you will be enriched, encouraged, challenged, and called to action as you read and see the situation of Africans in diaspora and diasporas in Africa.

References

"The Future of World Religion: Population Growth Projections, 2010–2050." Pew Research Center. Washington, DC (2015). https://www.pewresearch.org/religion/2015/04/02/christians/.

Graft-Johnson, John Coleman de. "Mūsā I of Mali." *Encyclopedia Britannica*, 11 Oct. 2022. https://www.britannica.com/biography/Musa-I-of-Mali.

Oden, Thomas. *How Africa Shaped the Christian Mind: Rediscovering the African Seedbed of Western Christianity*. Downers Grove: InterVarsity Press,, 2007.

State of the African Diaspora Constitution. https://thestateofafricandiaspora.com/wp-content/uploads/2023/04/Constitution-2.pdf.

State of the African Diaspora. https://thestateofafricandiaspora.com/media/.

Walls, Andrew F. *The Missionary Movement in Christian History*. Maryknoll: Orbis Books, 1996.

1

Beyond Empire: Global Migrations and New Approaches to Christian Mission

Jehu J. Hanciles

This chapter addresses the issue of global migrations and the interconnection between missions and Christian witness. It looks at human migration, its implication for Christian mission within the African context against the backdrop of global realities, and concludes with some implications for missions.

Human migration is a fact of history. As long as humans have inhabited the planet, relocation, displacement and population transfers have always marked the human condition. Migration has always been crucial for human development, and it accounts for major transformations in our world. In fact, perhaps most significantly, the global religious landscape that we see today is largely the product of complex migration movements. There is a vital link between wide-ranging human mobility and the worldwide spread of religious beliefs and ideas. All the world's major religions are uniquely formed by extensive migrations of people groups. However, Christianity provides the most exemplary model of this connection. This is because the emphasis within the Christian story and tradition towards human migration is not simply incidental, it is *intrinsic* to the faith. Migration is integral to the concept of Christian mission and is ingrained in its theological heritage.

There is no time or space here to attempt a biblical theology of migration. We can only do a quick survey. In the Scriptures we encounter every major form of migration. The theme of migration is in fact encountered so much so in the Bible, that the very biblical narrative and its message would be *meaningless* without it. The link between migration and mission is shown throughout the whole of Scripture in the stories of the Hebrew Bible, as well as the Gospels and the entirety of the New Testament. God's purposes and designs repeatedly unfold within the experience of migration and human dislocation. As Timothy Smith puts is, migration is "a theologizing experience" for most of the characters we encounter in the biblical story.[1] The Gospel narratives are also permeated with migrant movement and relocation. Indeed, some of the most remarkable encounters take place in that intersection of culture and geography. In the Book of Acts and beyond, migration often provides the central impetus for missionary action. Paul was an incessant migrant; you cannot fully grasp or make sense of his theology without understanding that fact. From a historical perspective, a significant proportion of the letters of the New Testament were written to predominantly immigrant congregations.

In acknowledging that the Scriptures portray migration as intrinsic to faith, one would understand that God has a profound predilection for migrants. The Scriptures often present the vulnerability and relative powerlessness of the migrant as a badge of identity for the people of God. This is not to advocate use of the Bible as a narrow ideological tool for migrant study. Quite the contrary. Understanding the Bible (in its larger context of migration) can expose our own ideological blindness and offer us a fresh lens or a new way of thinking. This is because from the very beginning the cross-cultural expansion of the Christian movement has been inseparable from migration, migrant action, and migrant networks.

Interestingly, the role of migration as a driving force of global religious expansion and transformation is often viewed as a matter of recent history. It was partly the need to address this misconception that motivated me to take on the research that led to the publication of the book *Migration and the Making of Global Christianity*, which covers the first fifteen hundred years of the history of Christianity.

Migration and Christian Expansion: The Causal Link

Every foreign missionary is a migrant. But even more important from a biblical perspective is the recognition that every Christian migrant is a potential missionary. Migrants have always been a minority of humanity. But this

---

1. Timothy L. Smith, "Religion and Ethnicity in America," *The American Historical Review* 83, vol. 5 (December 1978): 1155–85.

minority has always punched well above its weight in terms of historical impact and development. Unequivocally our missionary ancestors (those who had gone before us in missions) were predominantly migrants. These people – most of them unknown and unrecorded – who account for the shape of Christianity today were individuals and communities whose lives were defined by mobility and displacement. Their experiences reflect every form of migration and every category of migrant: traders; soldiers; refugees; exiles; captives; spies; defectors; evacuees; smugglers; antigens; pilgrims; monks; and so on. In most of these contexts these migrant missionaries were the face of poverty and powerlessness, of suffering and rejection, of marginalization, and vulnerability. Very seldom were these migrants associated with political power or institutional authority and favored status. Even those whose original status was that of affluence and wealth experienced loss and outsider status when they became migrants.

It is therefore bewildering to note the vast literature on the history of Christianity and Christian missions have almost completely overlooked perhaps the *most significant element* in the spread and transmission of the Christian faith: namely, the crucial role of migration and migrant movement. There are a few exceptions. Renowned mission historian, Andrew Walls, briefly assessed the role of migration in global Christian expansion in a 2002 article.[2] Some sixty years ago Mennonite theologian John H. Yoder explained that.

> Throughout the history of the Christian faith, migrant Christians who settle in new areas and form settled fellowships that provide long term witness have formed the main thrust of cross-cultural expansion: not the few gifted specialists serving in distant lands, dependent on the superior resources of their church and country.[3]

My recent work, *Migration and the Making of Global Christianity*, establishes the thesis that migration has played a pivotal role in the global spread of Christianity from the earliest beginnings. The book examines the first fifteen hundred years of Christian history – a period in which Christianity spread both within and throughout the Roman Empire and beyond, into Western and Northern Europe, throughout the former Persian Empire, into Africa and the Arabian Peninsula, and across the vast reaches of Asia, all the way to India and China. I conclude with the argument that:

---

2. Andrew Walls, "Mission and Migration: The Diaspora Factor in Christian History," *JACT* 5, vol 2 (2002): 3–11.

3. John H. Yoder, "Christian Missions at the End of an Era," *Christian Living*, August 1961, 14.

> [i]nstitutional authority and agents, that are commonly considered indispensable for global Christian expansion . . .p layed a minimal role. [That] when all is said and done, the rise of Christianity as a world movement [was] predominantly through the agency and activity of migrants – individuals and communities living as strangers and outsiders in foreign lands.[4]

This conclusion goes against the grain of centuries of thinking and historical interpretation. But it establishes a fundamental truth: namely that migration is an indispensable tool or analytical concept for the historical study of Christianity and missiological thinking and historical assessment of Christianity. Consider this: Christians are now found in every nation on the planet; but with very few exceptions, the community of believers in every society and culture first heard the gospel from migrants. The United States, to cite a prominent example, is a nation whose very existence epitomizes the powerful interaction between migration and Christian mission. Like its peoples, the earliest American churches of any denomination or tradition, Protestant or Roman Catholic, began as an immigrant congregation. This is also true for the Christian communities in Korea, England, Norway, India, Australia, Nigeria, and so on. To cite one more example, the oldest Christian community in sub-Saharan Africa dates to the arrival of one thousand one hundred Black Christians, in what is today Sierra Leone, in 1792. And the first missionaries in many parts of "modern" Africa were not European, but Black Christians from the United States. Many came to Africa not as missionaries, but as migrants and repatriates.

All of this raises two important questions. First, what accounts for the profound neglect of the significance of migration and diaspora networks in missiological scholarship for the study of global Christianity? Secondly, what are the implications of this migrant factor for contemporary Christian ministry and missionary engagement? To address the first question requires a recognition that the primary approach to historical interpretation is shaped by a "top down" view of history that I term the "empire argument." This is because analysis is often inspired by the conviction that major social transformations in history – including the spread of religion – are best understood in terms of hegemonic power. This is a view that emphasizes the role of the powerful motivated by political ambition or economic self-interest, as well as the efforts

---

4. Jehu J. Hanciles, *Migration and the Making of Global Christianity* (Grand Rapids: Eerdmans, 2021), 420.

of institutional elites. So, regardless of the region or social context in history – from medieval Europe to Persia, Central Asia to the Tang Dynasty in China – historical scholarship often fixates on structures of power.

Inevitably, this emphasis on institutional agents and political action fosters an almost exclusive focus on male agents. As well-known historian Phillip Curtin puts it:

> Western historians have often concentrated on the doings of great men. Top nations or great civilizations unconsciously keep setting aside the activities of women in the ordinary run of men or societies whose achievements failed to attract western admiration.[5]

This explains why females are so often missing or remain invisible in historical accounts. However, once the migrant factor is brought into focus, a very different image emerges regarding the role of women in the spread of global Christianity.

The point at issue is that the pervasiveness of the empire argument helps to explain the inattentiveness to migration in mission history literature. In the recent past, however, many shifts have taken place in missiological studies, including a strong emphasis on indigenous agencies. Yet the vast literature on the globalization of faith, including many of the books we have in our libraries, emphasizes the exploits of the individual. Formal organizational structures and planned initiatives made possible by Western economic resources also remain central to assessments. While these details are part of the story, they do not offer a full explanation of events as they unfolded and can even distort understanding. It is not that the empire argument lacks merit. The problem is that it seeks to explain everything using a single lens and leaves much unaccounted for.

Global Migrations and the Mission of the Twenty-First-Century Church

The Western missionary movement was dominated by an empire mentality. But that does not mean that an empire approach provides us with a grasp of what transpired. To better grasp historical realities, we must recognize that a preoccupation with structures of power and dominant processes leaves out a lot of what transpired in the world of Christian missions. Indeed, uncritical

---

5. Philip D. Curtin, *The World and the West* (New York: Cambridge University Press, 2002), xii.

dependence on the empire framework is liable to distort missiological understanding. Thankfully this is changing. A new generation of missionary thinkers and practitioners have begun to grapple with the primary importance of global migrations for Christian ministry and mission. But there is still much work to be done, for this new emphasis calls for new models and approaches. More on this below.

Having stated the limitations of the empire framework, we must now turn to our second question: "How does migration impact the witness and mission of the church today?" What are the implications for Christian ministry and missionary engagement?

This topic is too large to adequately address in this chapter. But it is important to start with the recognition that we are living in a new era of global migrations. Never in the history of humanity have migrant movements been as voluminous, unrelenting, and extensive as they are today. There are more people on the move today globally than at any other time in the history of humanity. By 2020, according to the latest estimates, there were over two hundred and eighty million international migrants – people living outside their country of birth – in the world. This is the highest number of people living abroad in recorded history. In 2019, according to UN data, nearly one person was forcibly displaced every two seconds as a result of conflict or persecution. By May 2022, over one hundred million people were displaced worldwide.[6] It is important to recognize too in this regard that 85 percent of the world's displaced peoples are hosted in developing countries – that is, countries with significant economic challenges of their own.[7]

When the catastrophic COVID-19 pandemic erupted in a global environment already marked by a tidal wave of international migrants, an extraordinary number of displaced peoples and a record number of refugees and asylum seekers were stuck. Within a matter of months, 90 percent of the world's population were living in countries with unrelenting social issues.[8] But not even a global pandemic could change the overall force and calculus of migrations for humanity. Indeed, the COVID-19 pandemic impacted global migrations in ways that have far-reaching implications for any analysis of migration from a missiological perspective. Among other things, it reinforced

---

6. UNHCR, "Figures at a Glance," https://www.unhcr.org/about-unhcr/who-we-are/figures-glance.

7. UNHCR, "Figures at a Glance."

8. "Globalisation Unwound: Has Covid-19 Killed Globalisation?," *The Economist* (May 14, 2020).

two interrelated global trends: the building of walls and the inequities of international migration.

The Building of Walls

The pandemic galvanized pre-existing anti-immigrant sentiments around the world and intensified suspicion of foreigners. We might point to countless painful examples in developing countries, from Asia and Latin America to the Middle East and the Pacific. The recurrent violence and hatred towards African foreigners in South Africa comes immediately to mind. But the rise of *anti*-immigrant attitudes and policies in many wealthy Western nations has arguably been the most prominent indication of unprecedented antipathy to global migration flows. This is perfectly illustrated by the proliferation of border walls in the last two decades.[9] Just over thirty years ago the fall of the Berlin Wall (in 1991) was celebrated as marking the end of an era of fixed orders. The sentiments at that time were towards a new mobility and a new world order, one marked by international movement and the free flow of goods, money, and people. Yet, the proliferation of border walls around the world is a new fact of our time. By March 2022, according to one assessment, some seventy-four border walls existed around the globe – most of them erected this century; and at least fifteen more were in some stage of planning or construction. Significantly, some 32 percent of these border walls are aimed at halting unwanted immigration. There may be more people on the move globally than ever before; in many contexts, this has also triggered unpresented efforts to restrict migrant movement.

The Inequities of Migration

The COVID-19 pandemic also exposed the deep injustices and discriminatory practice that characterize responses to international immigrants among Western nations. The hardening hostility to African immigrant populations and intensified effort by many EU countries to expel and exclude African refugees or asylum seekers is a prominent case in point. Since this book is specifically devoted to African diasporas and migrant movement, it presents me with a good opportunity to address the widespread misconception that Africans – who are regularly depicted in the Western media as the face of migration and

---

9. See Élisabeth Vallet, "The World Is Witnessing a Rapid Proliferation of Border Walls" (MPI, 2022).

its perils – are overrepresented among the tide of desperate migrants that seek refuge in Europe and North America. The prominence of Africans in media coverage, and the drastic measures by Western governments to stem the flow of African migration, paints an inaccurate or quite misleading picture of African migration. Not only does Africa contribute a smaller percentage of international migrants than the rest of the world – just 2.5 percent of the African population are international migrants – also, less than half (about 42 percent) of African migrants leave the continent. In other words, most of these African international migrants remain on the continent as they move to other African countries.[10]

Most important, the African migrant experience provides the most alarming illustration of the inequities of global migration, as vividly demonstrated by recent examples. We all mourn the Russian invasion of Ukraine and the massive catastrophe in its aftermath. This has been the fastest and largest migration in recent European history; one also marked by innumerable acts of human compassion and remarkable hospitality towards the displaced. Yet, refugees of colour fleeing the same calamity, including thousands of foreign students, were often treated very badly. The mistreatment of many African migrants who were abused, prevented from leaving, or faced violent threats from local Ukrainian authorities, caused quite an outrage. Tedros Ghebreyesus, the head of the World Health Organization, asked publicly in April 2022 whether the world gives equal attention to Black and White lives.[11]

Strikingly, the Ukrainian catastrophe coincided with efforts of the British government to deport non-European asylum seekers to Rwanda in the face of widespread condemnation; including by UK church leaders, who denounced the initiative as immoral. About the same time (February, 2022), a new study in the US concluded that Black immigrants "have been denied more citizenship more often than any other racial or ethnic group."[12] Meanwhile the resurgence

---

10. United Nations International Organization of Migration, *World Migration Report 2020*, https://publications.iom.int/books/world-migration-report-2020, 54. See also Phillip Connor, *At Least a Million Sub-Saharan Africans Moved to Europe since 2010* (Washington, DC: Pew Research Center, 2018), 3.

11. "WHO chief blames racism for greater focus on Ukraine than Ethiopia," *The Guardian* (April 13, 2022).

12. Emily Ryo and Reed Humphrey, "The Importance of Race, Gender, and Religion in Naturalization Adjudication in the United States," *PNAS* 119, vol. 9 (February 22, 2022).

of White nationalism (in church and society) has inflamed xenophobic hostility and increased the likelihood of violent attacks against African immigrants.[13]

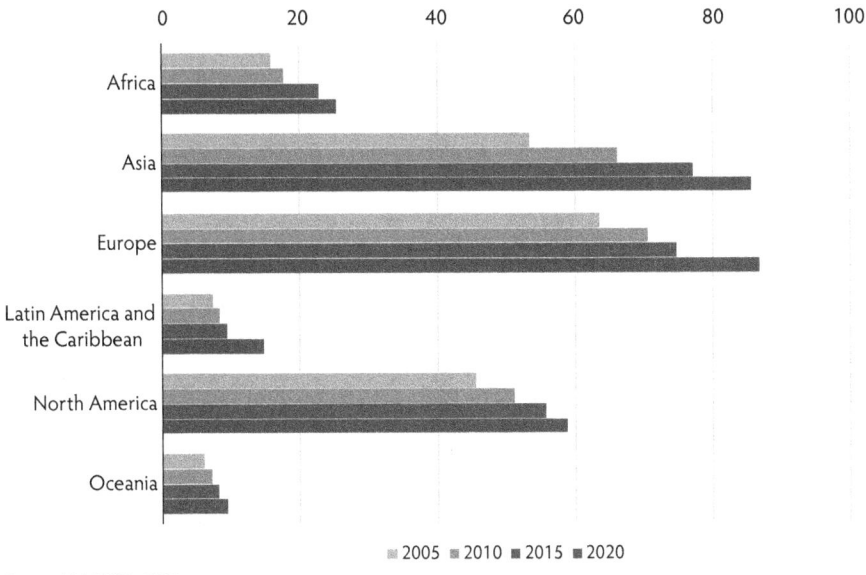

Figure 1. International Migrants, in millions (2005–2020)[14]

On this note, it is my personal conviction that one of the greatest threats to Christian missions or the witness of the church for our time is White Christian nationalism. This movement or phenomenon is amorphous to a certain degree and adherence occurs on a spectrum from tacit accommodation to fervent belief. By and large it conflates Christian identity with whiteness, territorial control, and a specific cultural heritage, it views Christian beliefs as markers of belonging, and considers nonWhite immigrant (and multiculturalism) a threat.

---

13. "The Escalating Terrorism Problem in the United States," Center for Strategic and International Studies (June 17, 2020), https://www.csis.org/analysis/escalating-terrorism-problem-united-states.

14. International Organization of Migration, *World Migration Report 2022*, https://publications.iom.int/books/world-migration-report-2022.

Migration and Missions

This broad overview of the fraught nature of global migrations is not intended to discourage or indict, but rather to invite a clear-eyed appreciation of the challenges and dilemmas confronting the global church. Indeed, it is important to note that on the issue of migration, statistical data and official figures never tell the whole story; and we must never lose sight of the fact that these numbers point to tremendous pain, human loss, and suffering. Attentiveness to global migrations will remain crucial for Christian ministry and witness well beyond our lifetime for many critical reasons. Not least the fact that this new age of migration coincides with the transformation of Christianity into a predominantly non-Western and nonWhite faith movement.

In this regard, it is striking to note, based on 2010 figures, that close to a majority of international migrants are Christian (see figure2).[15] Though it is now somewhat dated, there is no compelling reason to doubt the data's continued significance. More to the point, the religious landscape in many nations – especially in Europe and North America – cannot be fully analyzed without reference to massive nonWhite immigration, which brings a great influx of practicing Christians. The 2010 data indicates that more of the immigrants who originate from outside the EU (some 56 percent) are Christian.[16] The situation in the US, which receives more Christian migrants than any other nation, is even more eye-catching. From 1992–2012, close to thirteen million Christian immigrants gained permanent residency (green cards).[17] In all, Christians account for roughly 65 percent of the entire foreign-born population.[18] By even the most conservative extrapolation, some 25–30 million Christians were added to the American church in the half-century following the Immigration Act of 1965.

---

15. "Faith on the Move: The Religious Affiliation of International Migrants," Pew Research Center Washington, DC (2012), https://www.pewresearch.org/religion/2012/03/08/religious-migration-exec/. See also Phillip Connor and Catherine Tucker, "Religion and Migration around the Globe: Introducing the Global Religion and Migration Database," *International Migration Review* 45, vol. 4 (2011), 985–1000, 994.

16. Compared to 30 percent who are Muslim.

17. "The Religious Affiliation of US Immigrants: Majority Christian, Rising Share of Other Faiths," Pew Research Center, Washington, DC (2013). Among unauthorized immigrants – who primarily originate from Mexico and the Caribbean – the percentage of Christians is even higher: 83 percent.

18. See Connor and Tucker, "Religion and around the Globe," 11f.

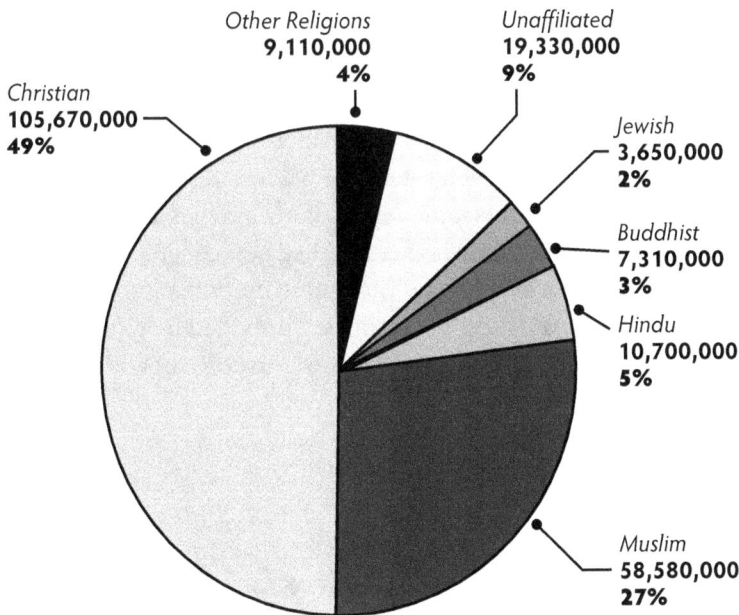

Figure 2. Religious Composition of International Migrants, 2010[19]

Africans constitute a prominent element in this Christian migrant movement. In major cities in Northern America and Europe, churches and ministries established by African Christian immigrants continue to multiply rapidly. In the city of London, people of African descent account for only 14 percent of the population, but reportedly make up 60 percent of church attendance.[20] It is reported that Black immigrants are the main reason for the "50 percent rise in the number of churches in the capital city" between 1979 and 2012.[21] As would be expected, a significant percentage of new immigrants from sub-Saharan Africa in the US are Christian – possibly as high as 70 percent.[22]

---

19. "Faith on the Move: The Religious Affiliation of International Migrants," Pew Research Center, Washington, DC (2012), https://www.pewresearch.org/religion/2012/03/08/religious-migration-exec/.

20. Harvey C. Kwiyani, "Blessed Reflex: African Christians in Europe," *Missio Africanus* 3, vol. 1 (2017): 41–49, 45.

21. Madeleine Davies, "Is London More Religious Now Than It Was in the Days of Margaret Thatcher?," *Church Times* (2018), https://www.churchtimes.co.uk/articles/2018/7-december/news/uk/is-london-more-religious-now-than-it-was-in-the-days-of-margaret-thatcher.

22. Monica Anderson, "African Immigrant Population in US Steadily Climbs," Pew Research Center, Washington, DC (2017), https://www.pewresearch.org/short-reads/2017/02/14/african-immigrant-population-in-u-s-steadily-climbs/. See also, Jie Zong and Jeanne Batalova, "Sub-

African immigrants are also among the most religious of America's new foreign-born population. Research has long confirmed that Black people in the US are more religious than other races. It turns out that new African immigrants are even more religious than American Black people and attend religious services at a much higher rate (54 percent versus 32 percent).[23] Not only have African immigrants joined American churches and denominations in significant numbers they have also established new congregations (including French speaking ones) at a rapid rate. The church needs to respond well to these new opportunities for mission and ministry provided by global migration. Diaspora mission requires new models, new perspectives and new tools for better assessment.

Conclusion

The significance and impact of global migration has three major implications for missionary thinking. First, it exposes the limitations of the "empire construct." While we are already moving in this direction, more work needs to be done. Today we often use the phrase "from anywhere to everywhere." We are getting over the older paradigms where the major metropolitan centers were the main sending centres for the church. Now the immigrant influx is inverting the story, reshaping cities with new ethnic and creative sources for global mission. We need a new framework of missions that does not privilege any culture, nation or race. Not only that, we also need a new framework that speaks with a prophetic voice *to* the church as well as *from* the church. The emphasis on structures of power and dominant processes actually weakens our ability to speak prophetically to the church itself and blinds us to the missionary action or potential of marginalized groups. In this sense, the "empire construct" undermines the very witness of Christian fraternity that it celebrates and represents. The church needs to frame its missionary endeavors and missiological constructs around repentance and renewal and embrace what Roman Catholic historian, Robert Schreiter describes as "mission from the ground-up" – which entails "listening before speaking; contemplation before

---

Saharan African Immigrants in the United States," Migration Policy Institute (2017), https://www.migrationpolicy.org/article/sub-saharan-african-immigrants-united-states-2015.

23. See David Masci, "5 Facts About the Religious Lives of African Americans," Pew Research Center Washington, DC (2018), https://www.pewresearch.org/short-reads/2018/02/07/5-facts-about-the-religious-lives-of-african-americans/.

action."²⁴ This is because only by a greater focus on the larger *movements* of peoples in our world, can we hope to participate in God's *reconciling* work in the world.

Second, global migrations point to the need for new research tools and analysis. Mission studies have long been dominated by anthropological study of a distant peoples in unfamiliar cultures, statistical evaluation of growth or success, or visiting missionary archives to wade through mountains of correspondence, policy papers, statistical accounts, and missionary reports. The missional significance of global migrations calls for tools of ethnographic study and sociological analysis – tools or methods, in other words, that are better designed to explore lived experience and investigate the largely unstructured, often clandestine, nature of missionary movement. In the old order, trained or self-identified Christian missionaries became migrants. In this new dispensation, Christian migrants (of all types) become unidentified missionaries.

Third, attentiveness to global migrations in missionary thinking invites an approach that is more "bottom up." This involves a more expansive understanding of the missionary task that gives primary significance to the voices, experiences, and actions of ordinary people. It is an outlook that pays closer attention to how the underlying, often hidden, structures truly embody the outworking of the *missio Dei* within the global order. A "bottom up" approach seeks to understand how the frontiers of missionary engagements are often occupied by marginalized peoples; drawing inspiration from the fact that the gospel invariably spreads from the margins. In essence, a "bottom up" perspective in missiological analysis will help us to rediscover how the powerlessness and vulnerability of displaced peoples, as well as the faith and fragility of migrants, often makes them effective agents of God's purpose; and therefore, holds important clues to his redemptive presence. Ultimately, we must never lose sight of the fact that it is God's mission, and that the church is the participant. If nothing else, the link between migration and missions reminds us that the entirety of what God is doing in the world is more than we can measure; often less spectacular than we hope for but always somehow centered on acts of mobility.

---

24. Robert Schreiter, "Mission from the Ground Up: Emergent Themes in Contemporary Mission," in *Mission after Christendom*, eds. Ogbu Uke Kalu, Peter Vethanayagamony and Edmund Chia (Louisville: Westminster John Knox Press, 2010), 12–24, 22.

References

Anderson, Monica. "African Immigrant Population in US Steadily Climbs." Pew Research Center (2015). https://www.pewresearch.org/short-reads/2017/02/14/african-immigrant-population-in-u-s-steadily-climbs/.

Connor, Phillip. *At Least a Million Sub-Saharan Africans Moved to Europe since 2010.* Washington, DC: Pew Research Center, 2018.

Connor, Phillip and Catherine Tucker. "Religion and Migration around the Globe: Introducing the Global Religion and Migration Database." *International Migration Review* 45, vol. 4 (2011): 985–1000.

Curtin, Philip D. *The World and the West: The European Challenge and the Overseas Response in the Age of Empire.* New York: Cambridge University Press, 2002.

Davies, Madeleine. "Is London More Religious Now Than It Was in the Days of Margaret Thatcher?" *Church Times* (2018).

"The Escalating Terrorism Problem in the United States." Center for Strategic & International Studies (June 17, 2020). https://www.csis.org/analysis/escalating-terrorism-problem-united-states.

"Faith on the Move: The Religious Affiliation of International Migrants." Pew Research Center. Washington, DC (2012). https://www.pewresearch.org/religion/2012/03/08/religious-migration-exec/.

"Globalisation Unwound: Has Covid-19 Killed Globalisation?" *The Economist* (May 14 2020).

Hanciles, Jehu. *Migration and the Making of Global Christianity.* Grand Rapids: Eerdmans, 2021.

———..*Beyond Christendom: Globalization, African Migration and Transformation of the West.* Maryknoll: Orbis, 2008.

Kwiyani, Harvey. "Blessed Reflex: African Christians in Europe," *Missio Africanus* 3, vol. 1 (2017): 41–49.

Masci, David. "5 Facts About the Religious Lives of African Americans." Pew Research Center. Washington, DC (2018). https://www.pewresearch.org/short-reads/2018/02/07/5-facts-about-the-religious-lives-of-african-americans/.

"The Religious Affiliation of US Immigrants: Majority Christian, Rising Share of Other Faiths." Pew Research Center. Washington, DC (2013). https://www.pewresearch.org/religion/2013/05/17/the-religious-affiliation-of-us-immigrants/.

"Religious Composition of Migrants 2010." Pew Research Center. Washington, DC https://www.pewresearch.org/religion/2012/03/08/religious-migration-exec/.

Ryo, Emily, and Reed Humphrey. "The Importance of Race, Gender, and Religion in Naturalization Adjudication in the United States." *Proceedings of the National Academy of Sciences* 119, vol. 9 (February 22, 2022).

Schreiter, Robert. "Mission from the Ground Up: Emergent Themes in Contemporary Mission." Pages 12–24 in *Mission after Christendom: Emergent Themes in*

Contemporary Mission. Edited by Ogbu Uke Kalu, Peter Vethanayagamony and Edmund Chia. Louisville: Westminster John Knox Press, 2010.

Smith, Timothy L. "Religion and Ethnicity in America." *The American Historical Review* 83.5 (December 1978): 1155–85.

United Nations High Commissioner for Refugees (UNHCR). "Global Trends." https://www.unhcr.org/global-trends.

United Nations International Organization of Migration. *World Migration Report 2020*. https://publications.iom.int/books/world-migration-report-2020.

———. *World Migration Report 2022*. https://publications.iom.int/books/world-migration-report-2022.

Vallet, Élisabeth. "The World Is Witnessing a Rapid Proliferation of Border Walls." Migration Policy Institute (2022).

Walls, Andrew. "Mission and Migration: The Diaspora Factor in Christian History." *Journal of African Christian Thought* 5, vol. 2 (2002): 3–11.

"WHO chief blames racism for greater focus on Ukraine than Ethiopia." *The Guardian* (April 13, 2022).

Yoder, John H. "Christian Missions at the End of an Era," *Christian Living* (August 1961, 14).

Zong, Jie, and Jeanne Batalova. "Sub-Saharan African Immigrants in the United States," Migration Policy Institute (2017). https://www.migrationpolicy.org/article/sub-saharan-african-immigrants-united-states-2015.

2

African Christian Diaspora in the UK: A Story of Hope and Despair in Three Congregations

Harvey Kwiyani

This chapter explores the history of African diaspora Christians in the United Kingdom. It argues that Africans have lived in the UK for many centuries even though where their history often starts is too closely connected to the era of the Trans-Atlantic slave trade. It suggests that many Africans who ended up in the UK during this era were Christians and practised their faith in various UK cities. However, it is in the twentieth century that African Christianity exploded in the UK to a point where it can be argued that London Christianity is increasingly an African phenomenon and that it is shaped, to a great extent, by the revivals happening in Africa. It ends by presenting three key challenges faced by African Christians in the UK, namely racism, tribalism, and failure to disciple their own children, and proposes that these challenges can be mitigated by intentional mission training being provided to African Christians before they migrate.

African Christians in Britain: An Historical Overview

People of African heritage have lived in the UK for centuries. Some of the earliest records locate Black people in York and in Bristol during Roman times.

A great deal of their history, however, is not recorded until the eighteenth century when, due to Britain's part in the Trans-Atlantic slave trade,[1] many Africans ended up in such places as London and Liverpool. David Killingray and Joel Edwards note that by 1750, there were about ten thousand Africans in London and another five thousand outside the city.[2] They came to Britain for various reasons: some of them were sea merchants, while others were students.[3] Some of them had already converted to Christianity before coming to Britain, especially those who came from the plantations in the West Indies and the Americas. Citing church historian Stephen Tomkins, Paul Nzacahayo notes, for instance, the presence of freed slaves, Olaudah Equiano (Nigerian), and Ottobah Cugoano (Ghanaian) in 1780s London, along with "hundreds of former slaves" in Britain.[4] Another African man, a preacher by the name John Jea, born 1773 in Old Callabar, Nigeria, had an evangelistic ministry that reached the UK and Ireland. Jea might have planted a church in Portsmouth in 1805 after settling down in the city.[5] David Killingray mentions a few other African ministers leading White congregations in Britain in the nineteenth century.[6] Mention has to be made as well of Samuel Ajayi Crowther who was educated in London and consecrated as a bishop in Canterbury Cathedral in 1864 before being sent back to lead the Anglican church in West Africa.

It was not up until 1906 that the first known Black Pentecostal church was established in London by the Ghanaian businessman and schoolmaster Thomas Kwame Brem-Wilson (1855–1929).[7] It was called the Sumner Road Chapel and it was located in Peckham. The church continues today under its new name, Sureway International Christian Ministries.[8] Later, in 1922, a Nigerian man,

---

1. Kwame Bediako, *Christianity in Africa: The Renewal of a Non-Western Religion* (Edinburgh: Edinburgh University Press, 1995), 75.

2. David Killingray and Joel Edwards, *Black Voices* (England: Inter-Varsity Press, 2007), 21.

3. Hakim Adi, "Pan-Africanism and West African Nationalism in Britain," *African Studies Review* 43, vol. 1 (2000): 70.

4. Paul Nzacahayo, "A Biblical and Historical Theology of Mission," in *African Voices: Towards African British Theologies*, ed. Israel Oluwole Olofinjana (Carlisle: Langham Global Library, 2017), 49–62, 54.

5. See more in John Jea, *The Life, History, and Unparalleled Sufferings of John Jea, the African Preacher* (University of North Carolina, 2001), https://docsouth.unc.edu/neh/jeajohn/jeajohn.html.

6. David Killingray, "The Black Atlantic Missionary Movement and Africa (1780s–1920s)," *Journal of Religion in Africa* 33, vol. 1 (2003): 3–31.

7. Babatunde Aderemi Adedibu, *Coat of Many Colours* (UK: Wisdom Summit, 2012), 26.

8. Adedibu, *Coat of Many Colours*, 26.

Daniels Ekarte (1890–1964), started a ministry near the Liverpool docks[9] which he moved to the Toxteth area of Liverpool and renamed the African Churches Mission (ACM) in 1931.[10] An extension of that church was later turned into an orphanage for Black children on the south side of Liverpool. Further on, during the period between the two World Wars, many more Black Christians came to Britain, especially from the West Indies. Three years after the Second World War, Britain invited Black people, most of them Christians, from the West Indies to help with the labour shortage. On 22 June 1948, the first group of four hundred and ninety-two people from the Caribbean Islands arrived in England as the SS *Empire Windrush* docked at Tilbury.[11] They came as citizens of the British Commonwealth to help the "mother country" but were greeted with hostility. In some areas of London, they were welcomed by protest signs saying, "No Irish, No Blacks, No Dogs," often making access to rental property difficult. Most of them were practising Christians and were members of British mainstream denominations (Methodists, Anglicans, Baptists) back home. They expected to settle down in these churches but unfortunately they faced the same discrimination as they did on the streets. Hence, it became necessary for them to form their own congregations.[12] The first of these was the Calvary Church of God in Christ, which began in London in 1948. Shortly after, in 1953, both the New Testament Church of God and the Church of God of Prophecy were established. Five years later, in 1958, the Wesleyan Holiness Church emerged. In 1961, the New Testament Assembly was also incorporated.[13]

Following the collapse of European colonization of Africa in the 1960s, many Africans began to come to Europe. Access to Western education as well as the general European life was a major factor. Longstanding migration patterns that saw Europeans migrate to the new world for four hundred and fifty years

---

9. After observing some documents from Nigerian National Archives in Ibadan though, Thomas Higgins inferred that Ekarte began his ministry in 1922 near the Liverpool docks. See more in Thomas Winfield Higgins, "Mission Networks and the African Diaspora in Britain," *African Diaspora* 5, vol. 2 (2012). I must note the obvious here that Ekarte and his work are of particular interest to this study, having sprouted in Liverpool – the specific setting of this research, so I have explored his story a little more in a later section.

10. Marika Sherwood, *Pastor Daniels Ekarte and the African Churches Mission, Liverpool, 1931–1964* (London: Savannah Press, 1994).

11. Nzacahayo, "A Biblical and Historical Theology of Mission," 54. The Windrush generation gets its name from the SS *Empire Windrush* ship. See more in Matthew Mead, "Empire Windrush," *Journal of Postcolonial Writing* 45, vol. 2 (2009).

12. Gerrie ter Haar, *Halfway to Paradise: African Christians in Europe* (Fairwater, Cardiff: Cardiff Academic Press, 1998), 92.

13. Christian Enquiry Agency, "Contributions of the Black Majority Church," https://www.christianity.org.uk/article/contributions-of-the-black-majority-church.

began to slow down and, within a short time, started to reverse as people from the colonies and the wider rest of the world found their ways to the West. With these, many more African churches emerged in Britain.[14] These congregations were particularly grounded in "the social and religious traditions of the African communities from which they draw most of their members."[15] In 1964, the first African Independent Church, the Church of the Lord, *Aladura*, emerged in the UK, led by the late Primate Adeleke Adejobi.[16] Since then, thousands of African congregations have mushroomed across the UK. Every major town and city in the UK will have more than a handful of African congregations – Nigerian, Ghanaian, Zimbabwean, and many other nationalities.[17]

By the 1980s, the migration of Africans to the UK was beginning to grow steadily. As a result, African Pentecostal denominations also started to establish their congregations in the country. A good example of those is the Redeemed Christian Church of God (RCCG), a Nigerian Pentecostal church, that was registered in the UK in 1989. It has two hundred thousand members in one thousand congregations scattered across the UK. Three in four of these congregations are in England, and half of them are in the Southeast, with a special concentration in London. When they gather in London Excel for prayer vigils, which they do at least two times every year, more than fifty thousand people show up. They attempt to plant fifty new churches every year. Another Pentecostal denomination from Ghana, the Church of Pentecost, also registered in 1989, has grown in its presence in the UK, having around one hundred and sixty congregations (largely concentrated in England as well). These two are just the largest among the numerous smaller denominations, networks, and associations of African churches in Europe and North America; Christ Apostolic Church (Nigeria), Winners' Chapel (Nigeria), Living Waters (Malawi), Deeper Life (Nigeria), Light House Chapel (Ghana), and the Apostolic Faith Mission (South Africa), to mention but a few. In addition, there are thousands of independent non-denominational congregations of African origin in the UK. For example, Kingsway International Christian Centre (KICC), one of the largest churches in the UK, was established in 2022 and is led by a Nigerian, Matthew Ashimolowo, and claims to have over twelve thousand members.

---

14. Israel Olofinjana, *Partnership in Mission: A Black Majority Church Perspective on Mission and Church Unity* (Watford: Instant Apostle, 2015), 26.

15. Haar, *Halfway to Paradise*, 94–95.

16. Olofinjana, *Partnership in Mission*, 26.

17. Nzacahayo, "A Biblical and Historical Theology of Mission," 55.

London Christianity is Becoming Black

Here in Britain, for example, it seems plausible that 20 to 40 percent of church-going Christians in the UK are Black.[18] Thus, any faithful discussion of contemporary British Christianity must reflect a real awareness of thousands of Black and Brown Christian denominations that have emerged in the past five to six decades. Christians from around the world, of various ethnicities and theological traditions, are, by the thousands, living in Britain today, and their presence in many British cities is changing the appearance, beliefs, practices, and hopefully, the self-understanding of British Christianity. Many of them are not White, they are fluent in other languages besides English, and were raised in cultures of peoples far away from Europe. They understand the Christian faith and shape their lives in ways that make them perpetual religious strangers in a land that should be home. Despite the many challenges they face, they continue to prop up the presence of Christianity in some fast-secularizing European cities. For instance, it is a well-established fact today that African and Afro-Caribbean churches in London drive church attendance in the city. In the early years of the twenty-first century, a riddle emerged in Britain that says, "London Christianity is a Black religion." Others joke that, in terms of Christianity, "as Lagos goes, so does London," meaning the *christianisation* of Lagos inevitably leads to an increase of Nigerian (or African) Christian presence in London. This also leads to a general increase in Christianity in London even when mainline White-British Christians continue their exodus from the church.

There is some truth in these riddles: African Christians make British Christianity what it is today. It is not too far-fetched to argue that London Christianity as a whole, not only migrant congregations in London, depends on migration, especially the migration of Christians from other parts of the world. Without the migration of Christians from the current Christian heartlands of Africa, Asia, and Latin America, the decline in European Christianity would be more pronounced. Studies exploring African Christianity in the UK, including the works of Babatunde Adedibu,[19] Israel Olofinjana,[20] and Andrew Rogers,[21]

---

18. David Voas, "A Less Christian Future for England and Wales," British Religion in Numbers (February 2023), https://www.brin.ac.uk/a-less-christian-future-for-england-and-wales/.

19. Adedibu, *Coat of Many Colours*.

20. Israel Olofinjana, ed., *African Voices: Towards African British Theologies* (Carlisle: Langham Global Library, 2017).

21. Andrew Rogers, *Being Built Together: A Story of New Black Majority Churches in the London Borough of Southwark* (London: University of Roehampton, 2013).

reveal the presence of thousands of independent African churches in London. The Old Kent Road alone in southeast London is home to two hundred African churches and ministries. Altogether, these denominations of Black Pentecostals make up a huge proportion of diaspora Christians. It is estimated that 75 percent of diaspora Christians in London are of African and Afro-Caribbean heritage. In 2011, African and African Caribbean Pentecostals represented 50 percent of church attendance in London.[22] In 2020, that percentage has gone up to around 65 percent even though only 14 percent of the city's population is Black.[23] Without Black Christians in London, church attendance would be down by at least 50 percent. Essentially, when we talk about "British Christianity," it is necessary that we include in our definition the many African Christians living, working, and being the church in many British cities up and down the country. Many of them are Christians and are contributing to the British Christian landscape of this century. They, too, are British Christians. Without them, British Christianity, most certainly London Christianity, would look different.

The Experience of African Churches in the UK

It is impossible to pinpoint the number of African congregations in the UK. Many of them, especially those of independent and non-denominational nature, are always changing. Some are emerging while others are closing or moving locations or cities. However, anecdotal estimates say there are between five and ten thousand African congregations scattered around the UK. A majority of these churches have been started in the twenty years between 1990 and 2010. A small percentage of them are growing, albeit slowly through the migration of their fellow nationals to Europe and the evangelistic efforts of other Africans, especially by their fellow nationals already resident in their cities. Most of them are struggling to grow though their target audience is limited. The experience of African Christians in the UK is shaped by several factors such as national/cultural exclusivism, anti-Black racism (not only by peoples of other races but by Africans too), the discipling of their children (the so-called second generation), and lack of theological/missiological education. Let us look at these in turn.

African Christians in Britain tend to segregate according to national identities. A great deal of this happens because of the colonial legacy of the

---

22. Peter W. Brierley, *London's Churches are Growing!* (London: ADBC Publishers, 2013).
23. Harvey C. Kwiyani, *Multicultural Kingdom: Ethnic Diversity, Mission and the Church* (London: SCM Press, 2020).

partitioning of Africa for easy European subjugation and governance that took place in the 1880s. Thus, we have Nigerian churches for Nigerians, Ghanaian churches for Ghanaians, Zimbabwean churches for Zimbabweans, and so forth. If the leader is of a certain nationality, the flock will be from that nationality. The distrust of fellow Africans runs deep. As a matter of fact, these lines go further; African churches in the UK can easily be identified according to their ethnic origins. The RCCG is Yoruba, the Church of Pentecost is Akan, and so forth. As a result, it is difficult even for African Christians to belong together.

African Christians in the UK have to make a living in a world that is generally unwelcoming to Black people. The racist nature of the British Christian landscape is well-documented.[24] This means that for congregations to gain access to worship buildings is not easy. It also means that some of their beloved practices are inhibited. For example, the loud overnight prayers have to be quiet, they cannot preach on the street as much as they want, and their extra-long services have to be cut short. It also means that, as much as they would like to have White British people as members, they will have to wait a long time before this can happen. While it is common to see African Christians follow White British leaders, it is almost impossible to find White British Christians following an African leader. The legacy of White superiority continues. In addition, of course, the foreignness of African Christianity is over-emphasised to justify the disconnect between African congregations and their White counterparts.

Every African congregation in Britain must think about the discipleship of their children, the second generation. These young Africans are evidently losing their faith just like their White British counterparts. The only difference is that they are walking away from Christianity at an older age, after high school, when they go to college or move away from their parents' homes.[25] This secularisation of the second generation often causes problems with continuity among migrant churches. Many of them end up being around for only one generation. As a result, there is a general anxiety among African church leaders in the UK about the faith of their children. They find it difficult to disciple their own children, and they realise that there is nobody out there who can do this for them.

---

24. Ben Lindsay, *We Need To Talk About Race: Understanding the Black Experience in White Majority Churches* (London: SPCK, 2019). Also see Azariah D. A. France-Williams, *Ghost Ship: Institutional Racism and the Church of England* (London: SCM Press, 2020).

25. White British children generally secularize in later primary school years.

Conclusion

It seems plausible to me that all these challenges can be resolved if African pastors and church leaders in the UK have access to good missiological training for the context of the diaspora. Many realise rather late that what worked in Lagos does not necessarily produce results in London. The evangelism and church growth strategies used in their churches in Africa do not translate to success in Britain. Their preaching styles are, generally speaking, out of context and they lack the skills to contextualise effectively. As a result, it is a challenge for them to connect with British people in a manner that could make their congregations multicultural. It is for this reason that diaspora missiology needs to be embedded in African Christianity, to prepare their people for when they migrate to the West and other parts of the world. The African church will do well to think of migration as an avenue for mission and, therefore, prepare their young people to be effective in God's mission wherever they migrate to. This type of mission training ought to start long before the migration itself takes place.

References

Adedibu, Babatunde Aderemi. *Coat of Many Colours*. UK: Wisdom Summit, 2012.
Adi, Hakim. "Pan-Africanism and West African Nationalism in Britain." *African Studies Review* 43, vol. 1 (Apr 2000): 69–82.
Bediako, Kwame. *Christianity in Africa: The Renewal of a Non-Western Religion*. Edinburgh: Edinburgh University Press, 1995.
Brierley, Peter W. *London's Churches are Growing!* London: ADBC Publishers, 2013.
Christian Enquiry Agency. "Contributions of the Black Majority Church." https://christianity.org.uk/article/contributions-of-the-black-majority-church.
France-Williams, Azariah D. A. *Ghost Ship: Institutional Racism and the Church of England*. London: SCM Press, 2020.
Haar, Gerrieter. *Halfway to Paradise: African Christians in Europe*. Fairwater, Cardiff: Cardiff Academic Press, 1998.
Higgins, Thomas Winfield. "Mission Networks and the African Diaspora in Britain." [In English]. *African Diaspora* 5, vol. 2 (2012): 165–86. https://brill.com/view/journals/afdi/5/2/article-p165_3.xml.
Jea, John. *The Life, History, and Unparalleled Sufferings of John Jea, the African Preacher*. University of North Carolina, 2001. https://docsouth.unc.edu/neh/jeajohn/jeajohn.html.
Killingray, David. "The Black Atlantic Missionary Movement and Africa (1780s–1920s)." *Journal of Religion in Africa* 33, vol. 1 (2003): 331.
Killingray, David, and Joel Edwards. *Black Voices*. Nottingham: Inter-Varsity Press, 2007.

Kwiyani, Harvey C. *Multicultural Kingdom: Ethnic Divesity, Mission and the Church.* London: SCM Press, 2020.

Lindsay, Ben. *We Need to Talk About Race: Understanding the Black Experience in White Majority Churches.* London: SPCK, 2019.

Mead, Matthew. "Empire Windrush: The Cultural Memory of an Imaginary Arrival." *Journal of Postcolonial Writing* 45, vol. 2 (2009): 137–49.

Nzacahayo, Paul. "A Biblical and Historical Theology of Mission: Reflections on the Flip Side of 'Reverse Mission.'" Pages 49–62 in *African Voices: Towards African British Theologies.* Edited by Israel Oluwole Olofinjana. Carlisle: Langham Global Library, 2017.

Olofinjana, Israel. *Partnership in Mission: A Black Majority Church Perspective on Mission and Church Unity.* Watford: Instant Apostle, 2015.

Olofinjana, Israel, ed. *African Voices: Towards African British Theologies.* Carlisle: Langham Global Library, 2017.

Rogers, Andrew. *Being Built Together: A Story of New Black Majority Churches in the London Borough of Southwark.* London: University of Roehampton, 2013.

Sherwood, Marika. *Pastor Daniels Ekarte and the African Churches Mission, Liverpool, 1931–1964.* London: Savannah Press, 1994.

Voas, David. "A Less Christian Future for England and Wales." British Religion in Numbers (February 2023). https://www.brin.ac.uk/a-less-christian-future-for-england-and-wales/.

3

Ghanaian Diaspora Christians in North America: Reflections on Challenges and Opportunities for Mission and Ecumenism

Moses O. Biney

The growing presence of congregations and ministries in the Western world with roots in Africa has been noted by scholars.[1] This chapter describes and analyzes attempts by Ghanaian protestant churches in North America to engage in mission and ecumenism. Using congregations affiliated or connected with Presbyterian and Methodist denominations in Ghana as examples, it outlines some of the main challenges confronting these churches as they seek to be "international" and at the same time rooted in the United States and Canada, and looks at some existing opportunities for doing effective mission and evangelism. Broadly, it raises issues of ecclesiology, missiology,

---

1. Jacob Olupona and Regina Gemignani, *African Immigrant Religions in America* (New York: New York University Press, 2011); Jehu J. Hanciles, *Beyond Christendom, Globalization, African Migration, and the Transformation of the West* (Maryknoll: Orbis Press, 2008); Biney, *From Africa to America*; Mark R. Gornik, *Word Made Global: Stories of African Christianity in New York City* (Grand Rapids: Eerdmans, 2011); Afe Adogame and James V. Spickard, eds., *Religion Crossing Boundaries: Transnational Religious and Social Dynamics in Africa and the New African Diaspora* (Leiden and Boston: Brill, 2012); and Frieder Ludwig and J. Asamoah-Gyadu, eds., *African Christian Presence in the West: New Immigrant Congregations and Transnational Networks in North America and Europe* (Trenton: African World Press, 2011).

ecumenism, and transnationalism in the North American African diaspora and interrogates the concept of "reverse mission." With so much focus on Pentecostal Christianity in Africa and the African diaspora by scholars, this chapter calls attention to the key role former mission (once mainline) congregations play in diaspora mission.

Ghanaian Immigrants in North America

Ghanaian immigrants remain prominent on the religious landscape in North America, though they are numerically small, constituting only about 0.3 percent of the foreign-born population in America. The Ghanaian population has increased from about ten thousand in 1980 to about two hundred and thirty-five thousand in 2015.[2] In Canada, the Ghanaian population almost doubled from 16,985 in 2001 to about thirty thousand in 2011.[3] This Ghanaian presence must be viewed in relation to the increase in African migration to the United States over the last five decades. This increase is, among other things, attributable to the United States Congress' mandated Diversity Visa Lottery which makes available to persons from countries under-represented in the United States fifty thousand visas per year. Like most immigrants from Africa, Ghanaian immigrants are noted for their engagement and investment in religion and its institutions. In many cities and towns where they reside, such as New York City, Chicago, Atlanta, Worcester, and Toronto, they have formed religious congregations which serve as communities of faith and spaces which provide opportunities for networking, and the maintenance, reproduction and transmission of African religious beliefs and cultural values. These congregations, many of which meet in storefront spaces, converted basements, and borrowed sanctuaries, vary in size, composition of membership and denominational affiliation. They include those affiliated to the once mainline protestant churches such as the Presbyterians, Methodists, Anglicans, Roman Catholics, Pentecostals/Charismatics, and African Initiated Churches. For my current purpose, I will focus on congregations affiliated to two nineteenth-century mission-originated denominations, the Presbyterian Church of Ghana (PCG) and the Methodist Church of Ghana (MCG) which I broadly refer

---

2. "The Ghanian Diaspora in the United States," *Migration Policy Institute Report* (May 2015), https://www.migrationpolicy.org/sites/default/files/publications/RAD-Ghana.pdf.

3. Casely B. Essamuah, "Go Ye into All the West: Models of Mission among Ghanaian Methodists in the Diaspora," in *Communities of Faith in Africa and the African Diaspora: In Honor of Dr. Tite Tienou with Essays on World Christianity*, ed. Casely B. Essamuah and David K. Ngaruiya (Eugene: Wipf & Stock, 2013), 47–69, 55.

to as Ghanaian Presbyterians and Ghanaian Methodists. Both groups have members who have or maintain some level of connection with Presbyterian and Methodist denominations in Ghana.

Ghanaian Presbyterians

Many Ghanaian Presbyterians in North America are either affiliated with or have historical connections with the Presbyterian Church of Ghana (PCG), the Evangelical Presbyterian Church (EPC), or its sister denomination, the Global Evangelical Church (GEC). These denominations have roots in the mission efforts of the Basel and Bremen (North German Mission Society (*Norddeutsche*) missionary societies, respectively. The PCG began in the Gold Coast (now Ghana) in 1828 through the missionary efforts of the Evangelical Mission of Basel (Basel Mission), the Monrovian Church of Jamaica, the United Free Church of Scotland, and the indigenous people of the Gold Coast. Similarly, the Bremen Mission efforts to evangelize the Ewe peoples of Ghana and Togoland began in 1847 led to the formation of EPC of Ghana and later the GEC. Currently, all these denominations are engaged in worldwide missions and have congregations in cities and towns in North America. Most of these Ghanaian Presbyterians who migrate to the United States, like migrants from other parts of the world, primarily came due to reasons other than religious propagation. They left their home country hoping to find better economic, educational, and social opportunities for themselves and their families. Nonetheless, they also carry with them their faith commitments and religious participation. Some clergy and members of these denominations who have migrated to North America in the last five decades have formed congregations and fellowships to provide the spiritual and cultural needs of people in the Ghanaian communities.

In the United States of America, beginning in the early 1980s, Ghanaian Presbyterians in the New York Tri-state area began organizing themselves into a prayer fellowship which eventually became a full-fledged congregation in Manhattan[4] with a membership of Presbyterians, Methodists, and Anglicans from Ghana. The formation in 1985 of the Ghanaian Presbyterian Church in New York (now, Presbyterian Church of Ghana in New York) seems to

---

4. Elsewhere, I have indicated how the formation of this fellowship was precipitated by the mysterious deaths of Ghanaian immigrants in the New York area. See Moses Biney, *From Africa to America: Religion and Adaptation among Ghanaian Immigrants in the United States* (New York: New York University Press, 2011), 68.

have provided the impetus for other Ghanaians to organize themselves into fellowships and congregations. Ghanaian Presbyterian congregations, over the next decade, were formed in Brooklyn (NY), Bronx (NY), Woodbridge (VA), Worcester (MA), Chicago (IL), and Denver (CO). Meanwhile in Canada, a Ghanaian Presbyterian church was inaugurated in July 1994 and another in Ville St. Laurent, Montreal in 2000. There is every indication that this trend of forming Ghanaian Presbyterian congregations will continue. In fact, for this purpose, the PCG has established a North America/Australia Presbytery and has declared the United States a mission field ripe for evangelism.

The exact number of Ghanaian Presbyterian congregations and fellowships in the United States is yet to be determined. In my estimation, however, they number between one hundred and one hundred and twenty. These are affiliated to various Presbyterian denominations both in Ghana and North America. They are either under the ecclesiastical and administrative control of denominations in Ghana or US and Canadian denominations such as the Presbyterian Church of USA (PCUSA), Presbyterian Church in USA (PCA) and Presbyterian Church of Canada (PCC). There are two main organizing bodies for the Presbyterians with roots in PCG. These are the Conference of Ghanaian Presbyterian Churches in North America (CGPC-NA), which is a gathering of congregations and fellowships affiliated to the PCUSA, PCC and PCA and the North America-Australia Presbytery. The North America-Australia Presbytery has about eight districts with sixty-three congregations and fellowships (preaching points) while CGPC-NA has about twenty congregations and fellowships.

Varied reasons such as the desire to worship using Ghanaian language and culture, the need to be independent from Western religious hegemony etc., are given as justifications for being affiliated to "home" rather than host denominations. Those affiliated to the "host" congregations consider collaborating with their previous partners a more effective way of doing mission. However, one critical issue that has created divisions among these congregations is that of the ordination of LGBTQI persons.

Ghanaian Methodists

Like the Presbyterians, the presence of Ghanaian Methodists in North America is highly visible. Ghanaians rooted in the traditions and practices of MCG have over the last fifty years migrated to Europe and North America and have established churches and fellowships.

Ghanaian methodism began in 1835 through the missionary efforts of the Wesleyan Methodist Missionary Society. It has grown to become one of the largest Methodist denominations in the world.[5] Its worldwide mission now extends to Europe and North America with congregations in the Netherlands, Italy, Germany, Canada, and United States of America. These Methodist congregations, worship and operate in ways reflective of the tradition and liturgical practices of MCG. Among them, as is the case of the Presbyterians, there is division in terms of denominational affiliation. While some have affiliated with United Methodist Church (UMC), the largest Methodist denomination in the US, others are under the ecclesiastical authority of the MCG. As pointed out by Casely Essamuah:

> Given the close ties between the UMC of the United States and the British Methodist Conference (the parent church of MCG), one might assume that Ghanaian Methodists would have found in the UMC a cordial family environment. But about half of Ghanaian churches in the United States have kept their association with the homeland denomination to the exclusion of relating to UMC.[6]

It is clear, based on some internal reports I have read, that there continues to be much struggle with the issue of affiliation among these Ghanaian Methodists. Currently, they are organized into two groups – those affiliated to the UMC, and others affiliated to MCG, called the North American Mission Diocese. Attempts are ongoing for the two groups to engage in some level of collaboration or at least recognize each other as siblings in mission. The North American Mission Diocese has thirty-seven congregations grouped into four circuits.

Reverse Mission to Drive Mission

Post-1965 African missionary engagement in the West, particularly in Europe and North America, has been characterized in diverse ways such as: ethnic missions, migrant ministry, transnational mission, return mission, reverse mission, or reverse flow of mission. Of these, "reverse mission" seems to have gained more popularity among scholars of religion, missiology, theology, and World Christianity. For some, "reverse mission" is merely rhetoric as the African mission in the diaspora remains largely among African immigrants.

---

5. Essamuah, "Go Ye into All the West," 48.
6. Essamuah, "Go Ye into All the West," 57.

While this critique may be valid in some respects, reverse mission nonetheless provides a schema or at least a description of the re-evangelizing of the West by churches and missionaries from Africa, Asia, and Latin America.[7] It must be noted however, that the term connotes a reactive rather than progressive mission. It does not fully capture the creative missionary endeavors of Africans in the diaspora.

Theoretically, reverse mission describes mainly the reversal of the geographical trajectory of mission from what used to be a North to South mission in the nineteenth and early twentieth centuries to South to North missions in the late twentieth and early twenty-first centuries. The presence and mission of Ghanaian Christians, such as those described above, provide evidence of this fact. However, it does not provide any specific strategies for mission, nor does it give any clear indication of the reversal of attitudes such as cultural and financial imperialism, and theological dominance associated with nineteenth-century Western missionary enterprise.

Using the image of driving, particularly the gear shifts of a car, I propose the term *Drive Mission* or *Mission Drive* as a heuristic term for reflecting on the mission of Ghanaian Christians in North America and the African diaspora in general. Drive mission reflects a forward motion that has the African missionary (driver) in charge of not only the steering but more so the planning and determination of the course and destination of their mission. A driver of a vehicle must not only drive in reverse but must also be able to drive forward. In other words, this image provides a more progressive and forward-looking view of the African diaspora mission.

Ghanaian Diaspora Christians in Drive Mission

As mentioned earlier, Ghanaian congregations and fellowships in North America vary in denominational affiliation, theological persuasions, and missional focus. The attempt here is to offer a broad overview of some of the missionary strategies employed by the Ghanaian Presbyterians and Methodists who constitute the focus of this chapter. These have three main mission foci: (a) to create spiritual spaces and communities for Ghanaians, particularly first and second-generation immigrant; (b) form new congregations or ministries and undertake social projects back home in Ghan; and (c) engage in mission among non-Ghanaians.

---

7. See Afe Adogame, *The African Christian Diaspora: New Currents and Emerging Trends in World Christianity* (London: Bloomsbury, 2013), 169.

To attain these broad goals, different congregations use different mission strategies. First, church planting, which involves the formation of congregations and fellowships in the US and Canada comprising of membership from a single country or culture. Another type of church planting is Pan-African congregations that attract membership from many different African nations. Examples of these are First Presbyterian Church, Irvington, Texas, US, which has members from Ghana, Nigeria, Malawi, Guyana, and the US (mainly African Americans), and Montreal West, Canada which has a membership of Ghanaians, Cameroonians, Canadians, etc. The second strategy is home mission or transnational mission where the congregations are engaged in health and educational ministries between their host and home countries. These involve the provision of equipment, personnel, and other resources to support the health and educational systems in Ghana. The third strategy is a ministry with "host" denominations through pastoral and other forms of leadership.

Missional Challenges

As all missional endeavors do, African diaspora Christians face some challenges. In my interview with The Rt. Rev. Dr. Emmanuel Y. Lartey, Charles Howard Candler Professor of Pastoral Theology and Spiritual Care at Candler School of Theology who is also the Bishop's Deputy for the North America Mission Diocese of the MCG, he outlined four main challenges. First is the current lack of clarity regarding the nature and direction of the mission.[8] The critical question here is whether their mission must focus on reaching out to Ghanaian immigrants or go beyond to serve the missional needs of non-Ghanaians. At this point, there is a struggle between groups on opposite sides of this issue and others who seek to do both. A second challenge related to this is the use of language. Congregations with mostly Ghanaian immigrants often use one or more Ghanaian languages in addition to English for worship. This makes it difficult to attract non-Ghanaians as well as second and third-generation Ghanaian immigrants who do not understand or speak the Ghanaian languages used in these congregations. A third challenge he mentioned is that of resources – financial and human. According to him, due to the challenges of immigration and asylum-seeking for many Ghanaians in the United States and Canada, many members of their congregations do not have high-paying jobs. Moreover, several of them must work two or three different jobs to take care

---

8. Telephone interview with The Rt. Rev. Dr. Emmanuel Y. Lartey on 11 August 2022.

of themselves and their families. For this reason, they are unable to volunteer much of their time and skills to support the mission of the church. The same challenges face the Ghanaian Presbyterians. An additional challenge faced by both the Presbyterians and Methodists is how to get the second and third-generation Ghanaians and other youths to participate in or show more interest in their churches and their mission.

Ecumenical Issues

A major challenge for these congregations is the lack of clear ecumenical frameworks to guide the relationships between their originating denominations in Ghana and those in their host countries. For this reason, the Ghanaian diaspora Christians, as mentioned earlier, are very divided in terms of affiliation. While some constitute congregations of the PCUSA, PCC, PCA and UMC, others maintain a lukewarm or even antagonistic attitude towards these once partners. On one extreme is the complete severance of relationship and on the other are attempts to work together through various memoranda of understanding. The PCG, for instance, at its eleventh General Assembly held in 2010 took a decision to "sever relationship with any partner church that ordains homosexuals as ministers and allows for same-sex marriages." This decision was reaffirmed though slightly modified at the twenty-first General Assembly to read:

> The Assembly affirmed its previous decision to sever relations with churches that ordain homosexual and allow same-sex marriages. *This notwithstanding, the PCG shall have bilateral relations with communities, faith Groups, and Congregations that share PCG's position against LGBTQUIA+, but belong to national churches that differ in thought with the PCG against the issue of LGBTQUIA+.* (Italics mine)

The MCG, on the other hand, maintains, at the denominational level, a fuzzy relationship with the UMC based on a Memorandum of Understanding that recognizes all Methodists as part of a worldwide communion.

At its 225th General Assembly, the PCUSA in its attempt at creating understandings with other denominations charged the General Assembly Committee on Ecumenical and Interreligious Relations to develop a template for the creation of Global Covenant Agreements. The template will then be used by denominations who wish to formalize partnerships with the PCUSA.

What these examples show, among other things, is the lack of adequate collaboration between these African denominations and their global partners. This has implications for mission at the denominational and congregational levels. Crucial is the lack of a good working relationship between congregations with members who originally belonged to the same denomination. More so, it raises the question about the role of ecumenism in mission and issues of collaboration.

Conclusion

Since the 1970s Ghanaian immigrants have brought to North America, particularly the United States, their own brands of Christianity (which they practice and seek to propagate), and have formed numerous congregations in cities and towns in North America. Through many forms of ministry, some of which have been outlined in the paper, they seek to engage in mission among Ghanaians in North America and Ghana as well as among other nationalities. We must therefore rethink the mission of these congregations as not only "reverse mission" but a drive (forward-moving) mission with different foci and strategies. If these Ghanaian congregations and ministries are to be more efficient in their mission, they will need to find better ways of working together collaboratively with each other and their host denominations.

References

Adogame, Afe. *The African Christian Diaspora: New Currents and Emerging Trends in World Christianity*. London: Bloomsbury, 2013.

Adogame, Afe, and James V. Spickard, eds. *Religion Crossing Boundaries: Transnational Religious and Social Dynamics in Africa and the New African Diaspora*. Leiden and Boston: Brill, 2012.

Biney, Moses. *From Africa to America: Religion and Adaptation among Ghanaian Immigrants in the United States*. New York: New York University Press, 2011.

Biney, Moses. "Singing the Lord's Song in a Foreign Land: Communality and Identity in a Ghanaian Immigrant Church." Pages 259–278 in *African Immigrant Religions in America*. Edited by Jacob Olupona and Regina Gemignani. New York: New York University Press, 2007.

Essamuah, Casely B., and David K. Ngaruiya. *Communities of Faith in Africa and the African Diaspora: In Honor of Dr. Tite Tienou with Essays on World Christianity*. Eugene: Wipf & Stock Publishers, 2013.

Gornik, Mark. *Word Made Global: Stories of African Christianity in New York*. Grand Rapids: Eerdmans, 2011.

Hanciles, Jehu J. *Beyond Christendom, Globalization, African Migration, and the Transformation of the West.* Maryknoll: Orbis Press, 2008.
Ludwig, Frieder, and J. Asamoah-Gyadu, eds. *African Christian Presence in the West: New Immigrant Congregations and Transnational Networks in North America and Europe.* Trenton: African World Press, 2011.
Olupona, Jacob, and Regina Gemingnani. *African Immigrant Religions in America.* New York: New York University Press, 2011.

4

Diasporas in North Africa and North Africans in Diaspora

Tharwat Wahba

Diaspora is used broadly in this chapter. It refers to those who left their countries because of persecution, violence, or war as well as for educational and economic reasons among others.[1] North Africa refers to the geographical area extending from Egypt to Morocco. One of the most important common characteristics of these countries is that Arabic is the most widely spoken language. Most inhabitants of North Africa are Muslims. These countries are members of the Arab League and the Organization of the Islamic Conference. In addition to belonging to Africa, North Africa is the bridge between sub-Saharan Africa and Southern Europe through the Mediterranean. Most North African countries are economically poor, despite the availability of natural resources. These countries, especially Egypt, Libya, Tunisia, and Algeria, were associated with the Arab Spring, the revolutionary movement that contributed to undermining their political stability, leading to an increase of migrants, especially to Europe, the Persian Gulf, and North America.

---

1. Amos Yong and Chandler Im, *Global Diasporas and Mission*, Regnum Edinburgh Centenary Series Volume 23 (Oxford: Regnum Books International, 2014), 3. Also see, Global Diaspora Network, *Scatter to Gather*, 2018; Sadiri J. Tira and Tetsunao Yamamori, *Scattered and Gathered: A Global Compendium of Diaspora Missiology* (Carlisle: Langham Global Library, 2020).

The Church in North Africa

The church in North Africa was God's instrument for carrying out his mission. It began in North Africa as early as the first century and spread throughout North Africa, especially Egypt. It continued in parts of the region, even after the seventh century when Islam invaded the region. Several centers of Christianity in North Africa have played important roles in the history of Christianity worldwide. Chief of these were Alexandria, Carthage, Kairouan, Hippo, and others. These centers contributed to the formulation of Christian thought and laid the foundations of ecumenical theology, which penetrated the Christian world in Europe and Asia during the first six centuries.[2] Furthermore, this region contributed to the formation of orthodox apologetics. North African Christians developed and spread the principles of monasticism to the rest of the Christian world. They also contributed to the development of biblical interpretation and the creation of worship models.[3]

The Nature of the Church in North Africa

We can divide the North African church into two parts – the old church and the new church – based on the beginning and survival of Christianity in the region. Christianity has been in Egypt since the first century AD and continues to the present. On the other hand, it almost disappeared in the seventh century.[4]

The old church is the Egyptian church and the other churches that branched off from it, especially the Protestant churches. The population of Egypt in 2022 was about 104 million, of whom more than ten to twelve million are Christians, 85 percent of whom are Coptic Orthodox, 10 percent are Protestants, and about 5 percent are Catholics and other denominations. The Egyptian church is an important church in Africa due to its size, history, and the spread of its members around the world, which makes it an important contributor to the mission of God globally.[5]

---

2. Nazir-Ali, Michael. *From Everywhere to Everywhere: A Worldview of Christian Mission* (Eugene: Wipf & Stock, 1991), 21.

3. Alan K. Bowman, *Egypt after the Pharaohs: 332 BC–AD 642* (Berkeley: University of California Press, 1990), 19–21.

4. Jason Mandryk, *Operation World: The Definitive Prayer Guide to Every Nation* (Colorado Springs: Biblica Publishing, 2010), 20–21.

5. Tharwat Wahba, *The Practice of Mission in Egypt: A Historical Study of the Integration between the American Mission and the Evangelical Church of Egypt, 1854–1970* (Carlisle: Langham Monographs, 2015), 31.

The new church is the rest of the church in North Africa. It flourished in the first seven centuries and contributed greatly to the Christian theological and ecumenical movement. But with the arrival of Islam in the middle of the seventh century, Christianity almost disappeared until it reemerged in the last two centuries. This church has been revived through mission work of foreign communities that came, whether in the colonial era or before, and are still present. Moreover, recently God has been saving large numbers of peoples in North Africa and creating a new reality for the church that could serve as missionaries in diaspora.[6]

Diasporas in North Africa

The geographical proximity of North Africa to Europe makes it an attractive point for transit migrants. Many from sub-Saharan Africa and West Asia in the form of refugees, migrants and other aspirants arrive here with the hopes to enter Europe, crossing the Mediterranean Sea whether by legal or illegal means. Currently, over nine million international migrants live in Egypt: most are from Sudan (four million), Syria (one and a half million), Yemen (one million), Libya (one million), and others.[7]

According to the United Nations High Commissioner for Refugees (UNHCR), as of March 2023, there are 291,578 refugees in Egypt, though actual numbers may be much more since the statistic does not account for all forcibly displaced.[8] Generally, the unofficial refugees and illegal migrants face many challenges, especially unemployment. North African countries in general already suffer from high unemployment rates, which makes it more difficult for refugees to find jobs. If they do, they work as manual laborers or janitors with low daily wages. Poverty is widespread among these groups. There are a few schools to serve children, but they do not meet the needs of all foreign communities, and the educational quality is poor.

Refugees, especially those who are not taken care of by the UNHCR, have no access to quality health services, so they turn to charities and government hospitals to obtain minimal levels. Many refugees do not have official papers that grant them legal residence, which makes them vulnerable to being chased

---

6. Mandryk, *Operation World*, 24.

7. "Triangulation of Migrants Stock in Egypt," International Organization for Migration (July 2022), https://egypt.iom.int/sites/g/files/tmzbdl1021/files/documents/migration-stock-in-egypt-june-2022_v4_eng.pdf.

8. "Egypt Factsheet," UNHCR, The UN Refugee Agency (2023), https://www.unhcr.org/eg/wp-content/uploads/sites/36/2023/03/Egypt-Factsheet_March-2023.pdf.

and deported by local authorities. Women and children are also exposed to racism and violence.[9] In addition, the process of obtaining asylum in the West is extremely slow and complicated, which causes many refugees to resort to illegal immigration from their host countries in North Africa, which requires taking a range of risks such as travelling long distances through the desert and using rickety boats across the Mediterranean. All of this exposes them to drowning, gang violence, or human trafficking. In addition, they risk being arrested by local authorities and deported or imprisoned.[10]

The Church in the North African Diaspora

The church in North Africa can be divided into two parts: the old church in Egypt, and the new church. In the countries that embrace the new church and receive some immigrants, especially from Africa, Christian ministry among these immigrants is often limited. Foreign communities gather in churches or meeting places that are restricted to members of this community, such as the Coptic Orthodox Church in Libya and Algeria, or the evangelical or Catholic Church in most North African countries. Some of these churches provide limited services to refugees, such as providing in-kind assistance and hosting some spiritual meetings at the premises of these churches.[11]

In addition, some Christian organizations provide relief and spiritual services in coordination with those in charge of Christian service in these countries. Many refugees can be won to Christ, discipled, and equipped to be God's voice to European countries. The newly emerging churches can also direct part of their service towards the refugees, which helps these churches out of the cycle of feeling persecuted, and move to the circle of responding to God's call to the Great Commission and so cultivate a missionary interest among their members.[12]

---

9. "They Call Us Black and Filthy: Sudanese Refugees in Egypt, Trapped between Racism and Violence," Cairo Scene (June 2017), https://cairoscene.com/In-Depth/They-Call-Us-Black-and-Filthy-Sudanese-Refugees-in-Egypt-Trapped-Between-Racism-and-Violence.

10. DW Report, "Migration across the Mediterranean" (14 July 2021), https://p.dw.com/p/3wTEh.

11. Jennifer M. Brinkerhoff and Liesl Riddle, *General Findings: Coptic Diaspora Survey Project* (Washington, DC: George Washington University Press, 2015), 5.

12. Daniel Pipes, "The Perilous Path from Muslim to Christian: More Muslims are converting to Christianity than ever before and at great personal risk. What accounts for the trend?," in *The National Interest* (July 12th 2021), https://nationalinterest.org/feature/perilous-path-muslim-christian-189544.

In Egypt, the service rendered to the diaspora church varies. On the one hand, there are many existing churches that belong to some foreign minorities settled in Egypt. Most of these churches are concentrated in Cairo, Alexandria, and some major cities. Refugee churches include Sudanese, Ethiopian, Nigerian, Eritrean, and some other African communities. These churches depend on their own resources and need some outside assistance to meet the needs of their people. They usually meet in the premises of Egyptian churches, either through partnership with these churches or by paying for the use of the church facilities. Both the Episcopal Church and the Presbyterian Church in Egypt are active in refugee service by providing resources, sponsoring spiritual/community service in these churches, and providing a legal status that grants residency to the pastors of these churches in Egypt.[13]

The diaspora churches in Egypt try to provide some educational, health, and development services to their members. These churches have a profound need for resources to be able to serve these refugees. There is also a need for partnerships between the Egyptian churches and the churches of the diaspora, especially African ones, to work together to serve the needs of the refugees. However, most Egyptian national churches do not have sufficient resources and lack a vision for service and work outside the church walls, especially in missionary and relief work for refugees. Despite the presence of churches in the diaspora, there are millions of refugees, especially from the Arab or Muslim communities, who need all kinds of services. It is relatively easier to work with African refugees, most of whom are Christians, but it is very difficult for Egyptian churches to work in other North African countries among Muslim refugees.

However, some churches and parachurch organizations make efforts to spread the gospel among Arab and Muslim communities of refugees. Although there are fruitful initiatives, the amount of work and involvement is not commensurate with the number of refugees or their needs. One of the most important reasons why the Egyptian church is reluctant to serve refugees from Muslim backgrounds, in addition to the weak capabilities and the absence of missionary awareness, is what missiologists call the "inheritance of fear." Christians in the Middle East in general, and in Egypt particularly, suffer from this barrier of fear that was built within them during more than fourteen centuries of living under Islamic rule. This generated in them a feeling of

---

13. Koh, "Sudanese Christian refugees in Egypt treated as third-class citizens," *Mission Network News* (December 31, 2018), https://www.mnnonline.org/news/sudanese-christian-refugees-in-egypt-treated-as-third-class-citizens/.

isolation from society and led to the formation of the so-called "minority complex." Egyptian churches should cooperate to break this barrier and develop a passion for missions through education and training.[14]

North African Diaspora

Migrants from North Africa are mostly dispersed in Europe, North America, and the Arab Gulf states. They vary between legal and illegal residents, permanent and temporary workers in the Arab nations, undocumented migrants in the form of refugees and asylum seekers.[15] Since the majority of North Africans are Muslims, most migrants are also Muslims. However, a small minority of Christian communities exists comprising of both Muslim background believers and Christians by birth, chiefly from Egypt and a few North African countries.

Christian migrants fall into several categories in terms of their relationship to the church. There are ethnic groups that moved their churches to the diaspora. The Coptic Orthodox Church has established hundreds of churches in many countries in North America, Europe, Australia, in the Gulf nations and other African countries. These churches primarily serve the Egyptian Orthodox communities residing in those countries. The priests come from their ancestral homeland and conduct worship in Coptic and Arabic to preserve religious traditions. Only occasionally do they use the language of the host country.[16]

In terms of mission and evangelism, most of these churches do not communicate with other groups of the host society, whether other immigrants or locals. There are no programs to go outside the church circle unless the goal is to establish another church for the growing numbers of migrants from the same ethnic and religious background. What applies to the Coptic Orthodox churches in the diaspora applies to a lesser extent to Egyptian Protestant churches, as they follow the same practices but with different theological concepts and worship styles. However, diasporic contexts provide better opportunities than what is available in North African countries to share the gospel. While North African diaspora churches are not involved in evangelism, the churches and organizations in the host countries are making efforts to reach

---

14. Wahba, *The Practice of Mission in Egypt*, 128–31.

15. "African Migration Trends to Watch in 2022." Africa Center for Strategic Studies, (January 2022), https://africacenter.org/ar/spotlight/ar-african-migration-trends-to-watch-in-2022/.

16. Brinkerhoff and Riddle, *General Findings*, 6.

North African migrants through social services in the areas of relief, education, health, and legal advice as well as sharing the gospel message through personal interaction and social media.[17]

There are encouraging results of ministry among migrants, particularly in some European countries. New believers from Muslim backgrounds have joined Western and Arab churches. They need education, leadership training, and support to develop self-sustaining and self-propagating communities of faith. Christian organizations aware of this opportunity have organized discipleship and theological education programs for new leaders creating spiritual revitalization and proliferation of ministries among diaspora communities as well as in their countries of origin.[18]

Ministry Needs among Diasporas

There are many areas for ministry and outreach development among the diaspora in North Africa and North Africans in diaspora. There is a need in North Africa for more efforts, especially to serve unofficial refugees. This includes both social services such as education, health, job opportunities, social development, and spiritual ministry, especially in the areas of evangelism, discipleship, and children and family ministries.

Churches and Christian organizations must cooperate to address the needs of the migrants holistically and educate the local church in North Africa to play an active role in leading migrant ministries. Furthermore, there is an urgent need for accurate data on migrants and refugees in North Africa, and human trafficking across the Mediterranean in order to understand the scope of such ministry. Local churches should work closely with international bodies such as the United Nations and local governments to spread awareness of the dangers of human smuggling, provide job opportunities for young people, and creating a free and transparent political climate to reduce illegal migration.

Other areas of research would be to identify the needs of the North African diaspora, where available resources are to meet those needs, and the Christian services most beneficial to them. A study of immigrant second and third generations must be done to help them integrate into their new society while preserving their identity. They are a resource for spreading the gospel message

---

17. Jim Memory, *Europe 2021 – A Missiological Report* (ECM, 2021), https://www.ecmi.org/en/europe-2021-a-missiological-report, 21.

18. Andrew F. Walls, "Diaspora Factor in Christian History," in *Global Diasporas and Mission*, ed. Amos Yong and Chandler Im, (Oxford: Regnum, 2014), 35.

in the new societies using appropriate technologies to effectively minister to young people in diasporic contexts.

Conclusion

This chapter has attempted to provide an overview of the situation of the diasporas in and from North Africa. North Africa is one of the regions that provides refuge from the dangers of war, persecution, and economic difficulties, for people in the sub-Saharan, Arab, and Asian countries. It examined the role of the old church and the new church in North Africa exploring the ministry opportunities and challenges. It is evident that the Holy Spirit is touching great numbers of immigrants and refugees through the diasporic Christian ministry. However, there is still more work to be done among the diasporic communities. The North African church needs to overcome its inherited culture of fear and boldly step into the opportunities that God is providing for ministry.

God's work will not stop. What we see as a curse by worldly standards, can be an opportunity for the spread of the gospel. We need to be open to God's work and collaborate as believers in a spirit of humility and love to spread the gospel and fulfill the Great Commission.

References

Africa Center for Strategic Studies. "African Migration Trends to Watch in 2022." (January 2022). https://africacenter.org/ar/spotlight/ar-african-migration-trends-to-watch-in-2022/.

Bowman, Alan K. *Egypt after the Pharaohs: 332 BC–AD 642*. Berkeley: University of Californa Press, 1990.

Brinkerhoff, Jennifer M., and Liesl Riddle. *General Findings: Coptic Diaspora Survey Project*. Washington, DC: George Washington University Press, 2015.

DW Report. "Migration across the Mediterranean." (14 July 2021). https://p.dw.com/p/3wTEh. [In Arabic]

International Organization for Migration (IOM) Report on Egypt. (July 2022). https://egypt.iom.int/sites/g/files/tmzbdl1021/files/documents/migration-stock-in-egypt-june-2022_v4_eng.pdf.

Koh, Lyndsey. "Sudanese Christian refugees in Egypt treated as third-class citizens." *Mission Network News* (December 31, 2018). https://www.mnnonline.org/news/sudanese-christian-refugees-in-egypt-treated-as-third-class-citizens/.

Mandryk, Jason. *Operation World: The Definitive Prayer Guide to Every Nation*. Seventh Edition. Colorado Springs: Biblica Publishing, 2010.

Memory, Jim. *Europe 2021 – A Missiological Report*. ECM 2021. https://www.ecmi.org/en/europe-2021-a-missiological-report.

Pipes, Daniel. "The Perilous Path from Muslim to Christian: More Muslims are converting to Christianity than ever before and at great personal risk. What accounts for the trend?" in *The National Interest* (July 12th 2021). https://nationalinterest.org/feature/perilous-path-muslim-christian-189544.

Tira, Sadiri J., and Tetsunao Yamamori, *Scattered and Gathered: A Global Compendium of Diaspora Missiology*. Second Edition. Cumbria: Langham Publishers, 2020.

United Nations High Commision for Refugees (UNHCR). Egypt Factsheet 2023. https://www.unhcr.org/eg/wp-content/uploads/sites/36/2023/03/Egypt-Factsheet_March-2023.pdf.

Wahba, Tharwat. *The Practice of Mission in Egypt: A Historical Study of the Integration between the American Mission and the Evangelical Church of Egypt, 1854–1970*. London: Langham Monographs, 2015.

Walls, Andrew F. "Diaspora Factor in Christian History." In *Global Diasporas and Mission*. Edited by Amos Yong and Chandler Im. Regnum Edinburgh Centenary Series Volume 23. Oxford: Regnum, 2014.

Yong, Amos, and Chandler Im. *Global Diasporas and Mission*. Regnum Edinburgh Centenary Series Volume 23. Oxford: Regnum, 2014.

5

Africans in Brazil and Brazilians in Africa

André Jonas Chitlango

Introduction

Africans in the diaspora and diasporas in Africa, is vitally important for the experience of millions of Africans and Brazilians. Many Africans have been captured, sold to Portuguese slave traders, shipped to Brazil, and sold. In the eighteenth and nineteenth centuries, Africans from all over the West Coast of Africa and from the Indian Ocean (Mozambique) were kidnapped, tortured, and forcefully taken to Brazil against their will. Many Africans died resisting kidnapping and some were killed trying to escape or just because they were exhausted; some committed suicide on route to the ports, and some in the sea on their way to Brazil. In the nineteenth century, we start to see Brazilians who chose to migrate to Africa. These dynamics have shaped what Brazil and some African countries are today. Mozambique as a Portuguese colony experienced, devastatingly, the migration of its people to Brazil as slaves for a long time after slavery was abolished.

This chapter discusses the history and present-day impact of African slave migration to Brazil and draws out implications for missions in Brazil by Africans and for the Brazilian diasporas in Africa. It also recognizes the impact of the Brazilian diasporas in Africa with references to Nigeria and Mozambique.

Africans in Brazil

Out of the twelve million African slaves brought to the New World between 1540 and the 1860s, almost half of them (five and a half million people) were forcibly taken to Brazil and came to be called Afro-Brazilians. According to Florentino, almost ten million Africans disembarked in the Americas and four out of ten went to Brazil.[1] In other words, 40 percent of all slaves that went across the Atlantic went to one country, Brazil. Brazil depended more on the slave trade than any other country on the American continent. However, historians say that the history of the slave trade to Brazil is the least known.[2] Brazil received slaves from West Africa, mainly from Guinea Bissau, Cameroon, Nigeria, Congo, Angola, Cape Town, and four ports in Mozambique. But when the slave trade was abolished, the clandestine slave trade continued with Portugal as the only trader, supplying Brazil and the Americas with slaves from Mozambique.

Mozambicans make up a big part of the Africans in Brazil. From 1645 to 1811 slave ships from Mozambique increased by 1,493 percent (from fifteen ships to two hundred and thirty-four ships) to Rio de Janeiro from 1811 to 1830. West Africa was not safe because the British Royal Navy was controlling the clandestine slave trade. But whenever the British captured a Portuguese ship with slaves, they did not take them back to their native land but offered them into slavery in places like South Africa. There is a community of Makua people from Mozambique with two hundred families in Durban whose ancestors were captured by the British on their way to Mauritius.

The Mozambican slaves in Brazil created a community that was called *Mozambiques*. The Mozambican slaves in Brazil were predominantly in Rio de Janeiro, Minas Gerais, and Recife. However, it has to be distinguished from the term *Mozambiques* used for the slaves from Mozambique in Cape Town as they were waiting to be sold to the ships after slavery was abolished elsewhere, but Portugal was permitted to capture slaves from its controlled territories. This was used also as cover for slaves that were captured in today's Zimbabwe, Zambia, Malawi, and Tanzania by the Portuguese. Portugal's Pink Map was a claim of Portuguese domain from Angola to Mozambique (making today's

---

1. Manolo Florentino, "Slave Trade Between Mozambique and the Port of Rio de Janeiro, c.1790–c.1850: Demographic, Social and Economic Aspects," in *Slave Routes and Oral Tradition in Southeastern Africa*, eds. Benigna Zimba, Edward Alpers, and Allen Isaacman (Maputo, Mozambique: Filsom Entertainment, 2005), 63.

2. Florentino, "Slave Trade Between Mozambique and the Port of Rio de Janeiro," 63.

Zimbabwe, Zambia, and Malawi Portuguese territories). This ended with the 1890 British ultimatum.

Rio de Janeiro received more than half of African slaves to Brazil (70 percent to 90 percent). From 1781 to 1810 Rio de Janeiro imported more Africans than the USA, Spanish Americas, Dutch, and Danish colonies of the Caribbean put together; 70 percent of the English traffic and 80 percent of the French traffic. After 1810, it was three to four times over the Cuban traffic. The main slave traders were Zeferino José Pinto de Magalhães who made 10 trips, Fernando Joaquim de Matos, 8 trips, João Alves da Silva Parto and João Rodriques Pereira de Almeida, a deputy of the trade board who was awarded to the knighthood of the Order of Christ for his role in the slave trade.

The intense slave trade between Mozambique and Brazil, combined with the earlier ones from West Africa, started to create big communities of Africans in Brazil in the nineteenth century. In 1799 in Rio de Janeiro the ration was one Black to every three White people. But by 1821, Blacks comprised almost half the population of Rio de Janeiro and in 1849, Blacks were 40 percent of the region.[3]

The Portuguese slave trade in Mozambique became very lucrative because the slaves were bought very cheaply in Mozambique and sold at very expensive prices in Brazil. Even in Brazil they would be bought and resold, like the story of a Mozambican who was bought in Rio de Janeiro for seventy thousand Reais and resold for two hundred and fifty thousand in another place. The slave trade became very attractive to Brazilians for that reason. Brazilians came to Mozambique and became what were called *negreiros Brazileiros* (Brazilian slave traders) before the eighteenth century. According to Capela,[4] on 12th December 1642, the first business license was issued in Mozambique for the Brazilians Gaspar Pacheco, Francisco Firma, Antonio Raiz Figueredo and Ruydo Silva Pereira.

In 1710 and 1713, ten ships were sent to Mozambique from Bahia.[5] By 1758, Pereira and Pacheco sold slaves not only to Brazil but also to Mauritius Island.[6] This business started to attract Brazilian army officers like Captain Jeronimo Jose de Andrade, who came to Mozambique and stayed from 1779 to 1790 selling guns to slave capturers. He made three hundred thousand

---

3. Florentino, "Slave Trade Between Mozambique and the Port of Rio de Janeiro," 64.
4. J. Capela, *O Tráfico de Escravos nos Portos de Moçambique 1733-1904* (Porto: Edições Afrontamento, 2002), 30.
5. Capela, *O Tráfico de Escravos nos Portos de Moçambique 1733-1904*, 31.
6. Capela, *O Tráfico de Escravos nos Portos de Moçambique 1733-1904*, 161.

cruzados in profit and took with him three hundred and fifty slaves back to Brazil, where he was promoted to Brigadier.[7]

The slave trade of Mozambique was attractive to not only army officers but also to government officials like Pedro Miguel de Almeida Portugal, governor of Sao Paulo, and Mory de Ouro, captain-general who was in Mozambique on 22 August 1744 en route to India. The governor wondered why Brazil was not importing only from Mozambique because the slaves in Mozambique cost fifteen to twenty thousand while slaves from other countries cost one hundred and fifty to two hundred thousand. This led Marques de Pombal to change Portuguese policies to favour the trade between Mozambique and Brazil.[8]

As indicated above, Brazilian army officers sold guns to slave catchers so that they could stay at the coast, waiting for slaves captured in the interior to be brought by bands of slave captors under Mozambican warlords. One of these warlords was Kanyemba, born of a Mozambican chief and a Portuguese Goesa mother. He was supposed to be a chief after his father, but he refused to let go of his Portuguese connections and was disqualified and banished from his father's domain. He was also not well integrated with the Portuguese because he was not White enough. He started an ivory business, and bought slaves and trained them to use firearms and hunt elephants. He asked for an inhabited area and settled with his band. He captured young people and the poor into his private army. He was eventually recognized as a chief, and his community and his bands were called Chicundas, young people well-trained to fight with a firearm. The Portuguese recognized him as a Sergeant in the Portuguese army and commander of his bands or private army.

As ivory became scarce, the slave trade became more attractive. Kanyemba started capturing slaves, using his former slaves (who were by then like free people in his private army) to go into villages to buy slaves from chiefs and kings. Kings and chiefs sold their enemies whom they had captured in war. They also sold criminals and people banished for various social offenses. This supply quickly dried up, so Kanyemba ordered his bands to raid villages, capturing at gunpoint all young people, all women, and children. The elderly people were executed by Kanyemba's bands, and their villages set on fire. Several villages were wiped out, leaving behind burned houses and skeletons of the elders. Those who escaped would live in the bush or ask for asylum in

---

7. Capela, *O Tráfico de Escravos nos Portos de Moçambique 1733–1904*, 161.

8. J. Capela, *O Escravismo Colonial em Moçambique* (Porto: Edições Afrontament, 1993), 193–94.

other kingdoms like the Nguni kingdom which was very strong. There was no slave trade in this part of Mozambique under the Gaze empire.

The captured men and women were taken on a three-month journey from as far as Zimbabwe, Zambia, and Malawi to Inhambane, Sofala, Quilimane, or Mozambique Island to be sold and transported across the Atlantic. They traveled with very little food and water. They were chained with the use of logs to lock their feet and necks when sleeping. They would be very dehydrated, and some would starve to death and others would die of dehydration. Those who tried to escape were killed. Those who became too exhausted and could not walk were killed. Those who became ill or developed wounds sustained in the capture fighting or because of the logs used on their legs and necks were also killed. By the end of three months when they reached the coast, many had died on the way and only the strongest survived and reached the port.

After being bought by the Brazilians, the slaves underwent a process of branding. Each trader had his own brand. For example, they could be branded with the letter "R" standing for Rei (king in Portuguese). The irons with these marks were put in the fire and when they became red hot, the traders printed the letter mark on the chest and shoulder of each slave they bought. As the people screamed in pain, they would be laughing. Then they gave them new names and papers to ship them after the mark wounds healed.

African diasporas had a significant bearing on Brazilian demography. The 2020 statistics indicate that 56 percent of Brazilians identify themselves as Black (*preto* or *pardo*).[9] It is the largest population of African descent outside of Africa. One could say that Brazil is an African country outside of Africa. The majority of Africans in Brazil are descendants of slaves forced to go to Brazil against their will. They suffered many forms of discrimination and inhumane treatment. In 2020 only 18 percent were in Congress; they made up 4.7 percent of executives in the five hundred largest companies, 75 percent of murder victims, 75 percent of those killed by the police, and earned 57 percent of what an average White Brazilian earns. During the COVID pandemic Black Brazilians lost their jobs and died at a higher rate. Such systemic racism abounds all over Brazil.

Brazilians in Africa

The Brazilians also had an impact on Africa. The earliest known community of Brazilians in Africa is in West Africa, predominantly in Nigeria. They are

---

9. "How black Brazilians are fighting racism," *TIME* (December 20, 2023).

called *Amaros* or *Agudas*. Of the approximate four million African slaves sent to Brazil, the Gulf of Guinea has contributed three hundred thousand mainly to Bahia. The Brazilians in Africa came voluntarily as freed slaves who wanted to come back to Africa along with some Brazilian expatriates.[10]

In 1830 the Hausa and Yoruba slaves in Brazil staged the Malê Revolt. Brazil wanted to avoid the escalation of revolts and so allowed them to return home. In 1835 the first group of Brazilian freed slaves moved to Lagos. In 1851 sixty Africans put together four thousand dollars and chartered a ship to Badagry. In 1886 and 1888 more freed slaves from Brazil came and settled in Lagos.

These returnees had adopted Brazilian culture, food, dress, and architecture. Some of them were now Roman Catholics and built The Holy Cross Cathedral with Brazilian architecture in Lagos just as one example of Brazilian architecture. Even though they claimed to be Christians, these former slaves from Brazil upon return to Nigeria did not have a mission outlook. Unfortunately, some of them became slave traders themselves. Examples of these are Francisco Felix de Sousa and Domingo Martinez. De Sousa is considered the founding father of the Brazilian communities in Ghana, Togo, Benin, and Nigeria. But he became *chachá* (*já, já*) of the Brazilian community, that is a slave trader.

As seen above, according to Capela, Brazilians had been living in Mozambique before the eighteenth century and established communities of slave traders, *negreiros Brazileiros*. From time to time government and military officers would come and stay in Mozambique for a long time to trade in slaves. The slaves going to Brazil would depart before being baptized into Catholicism.

Another missiological implication of Brazilians in Africa is that the highest number of missionaries in Mozambique are Brazilians. Some of the Pentecostal and Charismatic churches in Mozambique are of Brazilian origin. For instance, the Universal Church of the Kingdom of God (popularly known as Universal) is the most numerous and wealthiest denomination in Mozambique. Most of their pastors and missionaries come from Brazil. Mozambicans in their churches must learn Brazilian. They speak Brazilian, pray in Brazilian, and preach in Brazilian (Brazilian is Portuguese spoken in Brazil).

---

10. See Niyi Afolabi and Toyin Falola, eds. *The Yoruba in Brazil, Brazilians in Yorubaland: Cultural Encounter, Resilience, and Hybridity in the Atlantic World* (Durham: Carolina Academic Press, 2017); Otero Solimar, "'Orunile,' heaven is home: Afrolatino diasporas in Africa and the Americas" (Thesis, University of Pennsylvania, 2002); Mariano Carneiro da Cunha, *From Slave Quarters to Town Houses: Brazilian Architecture in Nigeria and the People's Republic of Benin.* São Paulo: Nobel, 1985.

Mozambique has many Mozambicans in the diaspora in Brazil and many Brazilian diasporas. While Mozambicans, and other Africans, were forcibly and brutally taken to Brazil, the Brazilians in Mozambique and all of Africa came voluntarily. However, there are also many Africans and Mozambicans who are in Brazil voluntarily and for mission.

Conclusion

Reading about Africans in Brazil and Brazilians in Africa brings back memories of injustice, discrimination, and pain. Powerful clans, rich people, and kings with skilled warriors raided and kidnapped fellow Africans, waged wars, and took prisoners of war just to sell them to slave traders or intermediaries who brought them to the coast and resold them to slave trade ships and further resold several times in Brazil.

If that is what Africa has done to the Africans in Brazil, I wonder why Francisco Felix de Sousa came back to Africa. Other questions are, did he not have somewhere else to go? Did the world have a place for him? Did he come back for revenge to inflict his pain upon others so that they could also suffer like he suffered? The history of the African diaspora is one of pain, anger, revolt, freedom and then using the freedom to inflict the same pain and anger on the others. Can diaspora mission help Africa heal from pain, anger, and revolt? Can Africa start learning to use freedom to love?

References

Afolabi, Niyi, and Toyin Falola, eds. *The Yoruba in Brazil, Brazilians in Yorubaland: Cultural Encounter, Resilience, and Hybridity in the Atlantic World.* Durham: Carolina Academic Press, 2017.
Alonge, M. M. D. "Afro-Brazilian Architecture in Lagos State: A Case for Conversation." PhD Thesis, Newcastle University, 1994.
Capela, J. O. *Escravismo Colonial em Moçambique.* Porto: Edições Afrontamento, 1993.
———. *Tráfico de Escravos nos Portos de Moçambique 1733–1904.* Porto: Edições Afrontamento, 2002.
Cunha, Mariano Carneiro da. *From Slave Quarters to Town Houses: Brazilian Architecture in Nigeria and the People's Republic of Benin.* São Paulo: Nobel, 1985.
Florentino, Manolo. "Slave Trade Between Mozambique and the Port of Rio de Janeiro, c.1790–c.1850: Demographic, Social and Economic Aspects." In *Slave Routes and Oral Tradition in Southeastern Africa.* eds. Benigna Zimba, Edward Alpers, and Allen Isaacman. Maputo, Mozambique: Filsom Entertainment, 2005.

Isaacman, A. L., and B. S. Isaacman. *Escravos, Esclavagistas, Guerreiros e Caçadores: A Saga dos Chicundas do Vale do Zambeze*. Maputo: Promédia, 2006.

Jadwat, Z. "Durban's Zanzibari Makua Community Struggles for Identity." *Salaa Media*, July 28, 2002. https://salaamedia.com/2022/07/28/durbans-zanzibari-makua-community-struggles-for-identity/.

Medeiros, E. *As Etapas da Escravatura no Norte de Mocambique: Estudos 4, Arquivo Histórico de Moçambique*. Maputo: NEUEM, 1988.

Nugent, Caira and Thais Regina. "How Black Brazilians are looking to a slavery era form of resistance to fight Racial Injustice Today." *TIME* (December 16, 2020). https://time.com/5915902/brazil-racism-quilombos/.

Otero, S. "Afrolatino diasporas in Africa and the Americas." Thesis, University of Pennsylvania, 2002.

Zimba, B, E. Alper, and A. Isaacman, eds. *Slave Routes and Oral Tradition in Southern Africa*. Maputo: Filsom, 2005.

6

Mobilizing African Christian International Students for Global Missions

Yaw Perbi

Introduction

One of my favourite VeggieTales music videos is *The Pirates who Don't Do Anything*.[1] A group of animated vegetables first appear in the "silly song" and rant about how they never did anything that they wanted to do, like doing pirating. If Larry and his compatriots are *pirates who don't do anything*, then African Christian international students (ACIS) are "missionaries who don't do anything." What makes the comparison apt is the pirates think of themselves as pirates but do nothing that pirates actually do. ACIS look like missionaries, and at least half of them even like to think of themselves as missionaries, yet hardly actually do anything missionaries do.[2]

---

1. Mike Nawrocki, dir., *The Pirates Who Don't Do Anything: A VeggieTales Movie* (United States: Big Idea, Starz Animation, 2008). See https://bigidea.fandom.com/wiki/The_Pirates_Who_Don%27t_Do_Anything.

2. According to "Not All Who Go Are Sent: A Research Report on the Missionary Preparedness of African Christian International Students, Past and Present, from 116 African Nations," Kwiverr (October 2022), https://kwiverr.org/wp-content/uploads/2023/01/Not-All-Who-Go-Are-Sent.pdf. Kwiverr is a consortium of Christian ministries and mission organizations on a mission to drive deep reflection and radical research into paradigms and praxes, and in spaces, that catalyze ministries into movements to leave no people or place unreached. See www.kwiverr.org.

In his book *The African Christian Diaspora*, Afe Adogame claimed, "an unprecedented upsurge, especially in the last few decades, in the number of African immigrants into Europe, North America and elsewhere heralds a new phase in the history of African diaspora."[3] Migration, therefore, must affect "how we think about mission and outreach."[4] This phenomenon heralds a new phase in the missiology of African diaspora.

This chapter highlights the case of the unaware and unprepared ACIS, from both theoretical and missiological perspectives, to propose concrete solutions for immediate implementation by the African church. Some ACIS think of themselves as missionaries but do not know how to be one or what they should do, because they lack the requisite training. The African church also needs to realize the latent missionary potential of their young men and women who have gone abroad for studies to embrace her unique moment in salvific history.

Diasporic Definitions, Demographics and Dynamics

Migrants have always played a critical role in the *Missio Dei*. Samuel Mpereh posits, "Migration is essential for missions ... migration and mission are bedfellows."[5] For African mission to be fully realized, it must leverage the surging Christian outmigration from Africa.[6] Adapting the African Union's definition of African diaspora, Perbi and Ngugi say,

> the African Christian Diaspora consists of Christ-following people of African origin living outside the continent, irrespective of their citizenship and nationality, who are willing to advance the mission of God to build the kingdom of God in Africa(ns) and through that, to the rest of the nations.[7]

---

3. Afe Adogame, *The African Christian Diaspora: New Currents and Emerging Trends in World Christianity* (London: Bloomsbury Academic, 2013), viii.

4. Emmanuel K. Asante, "Keynote Address," in *Migration and the Church in Africa: Facing Up to a Contemporary Challenge in Christian Mission*, eds. David N. A. Kpobi and Emmanel K. Asante (Accra, Ghana: The Missiological Society of Ghana, 2021), 5.

5. Samuel V. Mpereh, "Migration as a Catalyst for the Fulfilment of the Great Commission," in *Migration and the Church in Africa: Facing up to a Contemporary Challenge in Christian Mission*, eds. David N. A. Kpobi and Emmanuel K. Asante (Accra: The Missiological Society of Ghana, 2021), 206.

6. Yaw Perbi and Sam Ngugi, *Africa to the Rest: From Mission Field to Mission Force (Again)* (Maitland: Xulon Press, 2022), 55.

7. Perbi and Ngugi, *Africa to the Rest*, 56.

The growing numerical strength and economic power of the African diaspora "may very well be the most underestimated, unsung, and underutilized resource of the kingdom of God today!"[8]

ACIS form the *crème de la crème* of the African Christian diaspora. There are about half a million ACIS and thousands of them are going to strategic places as far as the Middle East, India and China. With intentionality, International Student Ministry (ISM) could well become "a marvelous feat of African missions in this era."[9] ACIS can move from an unsung force into a *tour-de-force* in the mission of God. This "great blind spot in mission today"[10] largely unexplored[11] is becoming an "emerging strategic direction for the [African] Church."[12]

Over the last hundred years, ISM primarily received students from the global South who were largely non-Christian. But things have changed a lot with students both going to and coming from every continent in the world. Some of these majority world countries have overtaken their Western counterparts in Christian student numbers and in sheer evangelical outlook and missiological fervour. Therefore, the four types of diaspora missions apply to ISM: a) Missions *to* international students, b) Missions *through* international students (but reaching their own; not cross-cultural yet), c) Missions *by and beyond* international students (cross-cultural now), and d) Missions *with* international students (non-diaspora partnering with internationals).[13] It is now time for the Western church to see ACIS as missionaries at their doorstep.

---

8. Perbi and Ngugi, *Africa to the Rest*, 56.

9. Yaw Perbi, "The African International Student Phenomenon: Turning an Unsung Force into a Tour-de-force in Mission Dei," *Journal of African Christian Thought* 24, vol. 2 (2021), 49.

10. Leiton E. Chinn, "International Student Ministry: Blind-Spot to Vision," Unpublished paper presented at the Lausanne Diasporas Strategy Consultation (2009).

11. Bill Dindi, "The Viability of International Student Ministry in Africa," Unpublished paper, International Leadership University (November 2020), ii.

12. Terry Casino and Charles Cook, "Glossary, Appendices and Ministry Resources," in *Scattered and Gathered: A Global Compendium of Diaspora Missiology*, eds. Sadiri Joy Tira and Tetsunao Yamamori (Eugene: Wipf & Stock, 2016), 228.

13. Enoch Wan, *Diaspora Missions to International Students* (Portland: Institute of Diaspora Studies, Western Seminary, 2019), 6.

Double Double Statistics' Impact on the Three ISM Forces

Africa is the most populous Christian continent in the world and will have *double* the numbers of the next two continents combined by 2050.[14] Again, Africa is the continent projected to have the highest youth growth spurt, with 42 percent of the world by 2030 and *doubling* current numbers by 2080.[15] This staggering *double double* statistic makes it imperative to re-imagine, re-define, and re-strategize ISM.

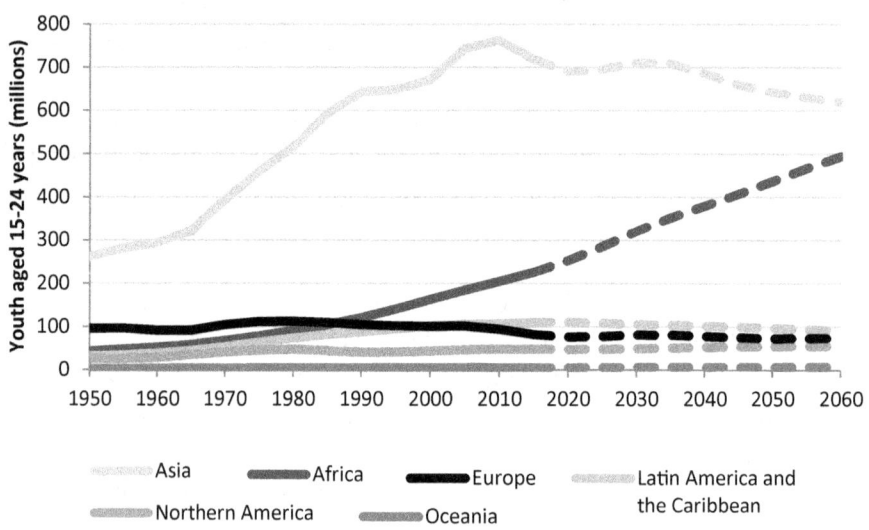

Figure 1. Projected youth demographics by continents (1950–2060)[16]

This *double double* demographic growth implies that there will be an even larger movement of African students within and beyond the continent as they generally aspire for higher quality education and experiences than they are able to get in their homelands.[17] While some see this as "brain drain," in my opinion it is a mission gain because the most Christian continent is the youngest continent, and African Christian youth may be the most powerful

---

14. Johnson, Todd M., et al. "Christianity 2018: More African Christians and Counting Martyrs," *International Bulletin of Mission Research* 42, vol. 1 (2018): 20–28, 3.

15. United Nations, *Population Facts* (May 2015), https://www.un.org/en/development/desa/population/publications/pdf/popfacts/PopFacts_2015-1.pdf, 1.

16. United Nations, *Population Facts* (May 2015), https://www.un.org/en/development/desa/population/publications/pdf/popfacts/PopFacts_2015-1.pdf, 1.

17. Sehoole and Lee, "African Student Flows – Challenging Prevailing Paradigms," *University World News*, 15 June 2018.

force in the mission of God in this century.[18] This *double double* statistic has huge implications on ISM: a) African Christians hosting international students from other parts of Africa and around the world – *"Come and See" mission* (centripetal); b) ACIS sent to other parts of Africa or the rest of the world – *"Go and Tell" mission* (centrifugal); and c) Africans returning from their studies abroad bringing God's kingdom to bear on all societal spheres of their countries of origin as godly, effectual servant-leaders – *"Salt and Light" mission* (centrifocal).[19]

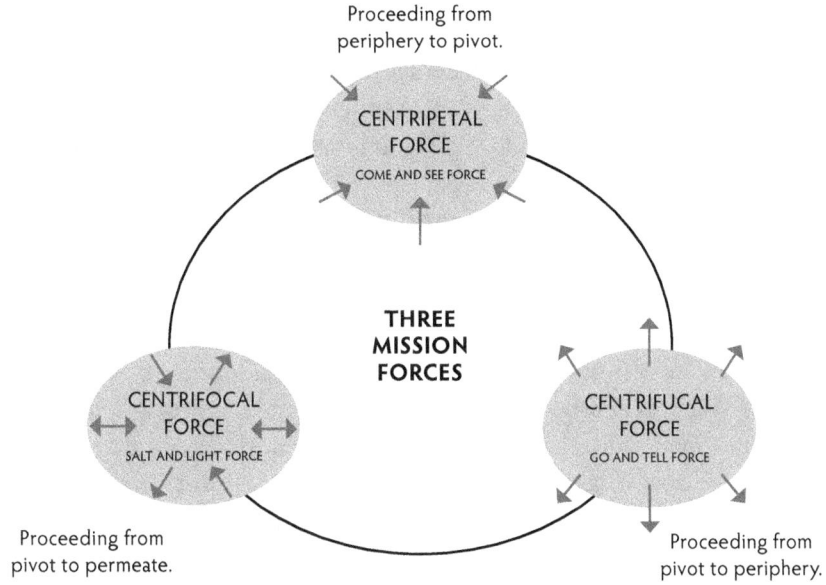

Figure 2. Three Mission Forces of ISM[20]

---

18. Perbi, *Africa to the Rest*, 53.

19. Perbi, "The African International Student Phenomenon," 43–44. The word "centrifocal" was not in the original article and emerged out of author's discussion with Prof. Kofi Saah, former linguistics professor at the University of Ghana in September 2022.

20. Modified from: https://kwiverr.org/the-three-forces-motions-and-dimensions-of-the-triune-gods-three-fold-mission/

ACIS "Go and Tell" Opportunity

Though Africa has a large outbound migration of students, ACIS are not adequately prepared to engage in "Go and Tell" mission.[21] Nearly six percent of African tertiary students enroll in institutions abroad and expected to grow with demographic surge and mismatching educational opportunities. Even if half of the current 500,000 African international students are mobilized, that is a 250,000 mission force!

ACIS are heading to "closed countries" on full scholarships, and to secularized countries that need re-evangelisation, especially in Western Europe. The 100,000 Francophone African international students are the hope of the gospel in secularized France. ACIS are able to rub shoulders with Islamic, Buddhist, Hindu and atheistic colleagues in the course of their studies and be witnesses to Christ's gospel in a way that otherwise would be impossible back in their African cities, towns and villages. It is fascinating that India and China, with the most unreached people groups in the world, have become major destinations for ACIS. China grew its active attraction of African international students twenty-six-fold between 2003 and 2015 and finally overtook the US and UK as the top destination of ACIS in 2017.[22] It appears that God is at work in taking the brightest and the best from the most Christian continent in the world to nations with the most unreached peoples of the world.

These ACIS are "missionaries" who do not have to worry about visas, travel route, finances, decent work, and legal paperwork. They are well-funded "missionaries" relieving the African church of the pressure of raising money to send them to the ends of the earth. If the church in Africa were more alert and intentional, this "Go and Tell" approach to ISM could yield phenomenal results for the kingdom. As it stands, not only are many not seeing the opportunity, but even if they do, they are ill-equipped to take advantage of it.

A Tale of Two Students – Three Decades Back

The following two stories illustrate the potential of ACIS ministry. Sunday Sunkanmi Adelaja became a Christian just before high school graduation and left Nigeria on a scholarship to study journalism at the Belarusian State

---

21. Mary M. Kritz, "International student mobility and tertiary education capacity in Africa," *International Migration* 53, no. 1 (2015): 29–49.

22. Victoria Breeze and Nathan More, "China has overtaken the US and UK as the top destination for anglophone African students," *Quartz Africa*, June 30, 2017.

University in Minsk (former USSR; now Belarus).[23] According to him, he was threatened by authorities for having a picture of Jesus in his house, but nevertheless, he began Christian activities in Belarus during his studies. After graduation and the collapse of the Soviet Union, he moved to Ukraine in December 1993, where he married and took a job. That year with seven others in his apartment, he founded the World of Faith Bible Church (now known as the Embassy of the Blessed Kingdom of God for All Nations). Twenty years later the church claimed twenty-five thousand members in Kyiv, one hundred thousand members in Ukraine, and one thousand churches around the world.[24]

Likewise, Sam Owusu left Ghana for Canada as an international student over three decades ago. He studied at Regent College and obtained a PhD from Trinity Evangelical Divinity School. Later, he planted a church with a multicultural vision in the Greater Vancouver Area of British Columbia, Canada. Today that church, Calvary Worship Centre, is one of the most diverse churches in the world, with one hundred and ten nationalities.[25]

A Tragic Tale

ACIS are found everywhere but they have not been sent by anyone. In different parts of the world, their impact has been largely random and accidental. A 2022 Kwiverr study[26] found that 84.5 percent of the respondents knew that Africa has more Christians than any other continent in the world. Half of the respondents considered themselves as missionaries before leaving their homeland while the other half did not. However, while studying, a slight majority (61.2 percent) considered themselves as missionaries. Some respondents who stated not participating in international missions, acted so because they did not see

---

23. Mark Hutchinson and John Wolffe, *A Short History of Global Evangelicalism* (New York: Cambridge University Press, 2012), 4. See also Robert C. Ostergren and Mathias Le Bossé, *The Europeans: A Geography of People, Culture, and Environment* (New York: Guilford Press, 2011), 203.

24. C. Peter Wagner and Joseph Thompson, eds., *Out of Africa* (USA: Regal Books, 2004); Steven M. Studebaker, *Pentecostalism and Globalization: The Impact of Globalization on Pentecostal Theology and Ministry* (Eugene: Wipf & Stock Publishers, 2010), 60; Adogame, *The African Christian Diaspora*; Allan Anderson, *An Introduction to Pentecostalism: Global Charismatic Christianity* (Cambridge University Press, 2013), 109.

25. Shared by Dr. Sam Owusu himself during a Kwiverr webinar in July 2022, https://calvaryonline.ca/.

26. Kwiverr report, "Not All Who Go Are Sent: A Research Report on the Missionary Preparedness of African Christian International Students, Past and Present, from 116 African Nations" (Accra, Ghana: Kwiverr, 2022), https://kwiverr.org/wp-content/uploads/2023/01/Not-All-Who-Go-Are-Sent.pdf.

themselves as capable of serving as missionaries. Others stated that their host countries were statistically Christian and therefore did not need further missionary work. A handful of participants were indifferent and did not see the need to engage in missions since they traveled for the sole purpose of studying. This response raises concerns about mission awareness of some ACIS.

Participants who considered missions while studying in other countries mainly did so because they had a zeal for Christian missions and had it nurtured by engaging in voluntary missionary work while in their home countries. Some others saw missions as a Christian duty while studying. For the fifty-eight participants (50 percent) who stated their initial zeal for missions as outbound ACIS, only twenty of them (34 percent) had actually taken mission training such as Kairos, Perspectives, Every International, or denominational training. The remaining thirty-eight (66 percent), though passionate and considering themselves as missionaries before leaving Africa as international students, had not participated in any form of mission course.

A number of participants who engaged in missionary activities while studying did so because they had participated in outreaches, crusades and local missionary activities before travelling to study. Some also participated in the activities of Christian missionary societies they were introduced to during school orientations in their host countries. The twenty-nine participants (25 percent) who stated that they had a little training in intercultural missions confessed such training was not of much help, since they experienced the culture shock of a high resistance to the gospel and unfavorable state or school laws on religious activities.

Participants who stated their inability to engage in missionary activity while studying did so because they had an academic work overload and could not afford the time for extracurricular activities which were religious in nature. While acknowledging the reality of academic load, and that excelling academically is a witness to Jesus Christ, a mindset that separates witness from the normal life of a Christian needs to be corrected. A participant mentioned the fear of being ridiculed for sharing her faith since most of her colleagues were completely engaged in academic work. Some respondents who shared this challenge said the presence of Christian support groups would have been a great resource in engaging in missions.

Most of the ACIS researched (66.4 percent) had no general cross-cultural training and a larger percentage (75 percent) had no missionary training whatsoever. This is even more worrying as 78.4 percent have never taken the Kairos or Perspectives course. Only 8 percent had heard about them. This is an indictment on the church as a whole, sending unprepared soldiers to the battlefield. 62.1 percent of ACIS had not established any relationship with a local church in their host lands. Not living in Christian community is as tragic as not sharing the gospel (Hebrews 10:24–25). We have seen and heard many stories of former Christians falling away from the faith after arriving elsewhere, especially in the West, as international students. This is an area requiring a thorough, objective study.

82.9 percent of ACIS alumni wished they had prepared well enough to be missionaries in another country. Some alumni expressed the need for organized training ahead of travelling to study. A participant expressed that prior training would have made her more aware and better prepared for the need of missions. Such training would have enlightened respondents as to the needs and expectations of different cultures. The majority (69.9 percent) were willing to attend cultural and missionary training before departing for their studies.

One-word, Three-step Solution

Samuel Mpereh asserted that "migration *per se* is worthwhile when the migrant has a God-given purpose to accomplish. God-given purpose is to make disciples of all nations."[27] An appropriate response to this tragic tale of the African church is mobilization. Mission mobilization is the process of promoting the mission of God to generate interest and service in mission. The concept of *total* mobilization has three contiguous steps: discovery, development, and deployment. My own local church in Ghana, located on a university campus, keeps sending ACIS missionaries, and recently asked Kwiverr to design a training programme for them. Such a resource, when developed, will be a blessing to the church in Africa and the global South.

The first step in mission mobilization is discovering the ACIS. This involves awareness and envisioning. The church needs to be aware of the critical role of ISM and ACIS in particular in diaspora missiology. They must prayerfully discern and identify who is called to this ministry. The second step is to develop ACIS by empowering and equipping them. ACIS need to depend on the Holy Spirit and be supported by the Christian community in their home countries as well as host cultures.[28] Lesslie Newbigin affirms how missional

---

27. Mpereh, "Migration as a Catalyst for the Fulfilment of the Great Commission," 205.

28. Roswitha Ebner-Golder, "Providing a Spiritual Home away from Home: a Swiss Woman's Way of Witnessing to a Latin American Community in Geneva," *International Review of Mission* 93, no. 368 (2004): 97–104, 99.

this connecting is: "We need their witness to correct ours, as indeed, they need ours to correct theirs. At this moment, our need is greater . . .we imperatively need one another if we are to be faithful witnesses of Christ in our many different cultures."[29] Another element needing development is equipping, which entails training in Bible and cross-cultural skills.[30] The third step is deploying, which entails intentionality on the part of the church and other ministries to commission students who are going abroad for studies. This would provide support, encouragement and oversight.[31]

Conclusion

The mission potential of ACIS to go and tell the nations of the glorious gospel of Jesus Christ is mostly unrecognized and untapped by the church. ACIS themselves are largely unaware and unprepared as missionaries. This chapter has demonstrated how urgently the African church must discover, develop and deploy the students who are going abroad for studies to fulfill the *missio Dei*.

References

Adogame, Afe. *The African Christian Diaspora: New Currents and Emerging Trends in World Christianity*. London: Bloomsbury Academic, 2013.

Anderson, Allan. *An Introduction to Pentecostalism: Global Charismatic Christianity*. Cambridge: Cambridge University Press, 2013.

Asante, Emmanuel K. "Keynote Address" *Migration and the Church in Africa: Facing Up to a Contemporary Challenge in Christian Mission*. Edited by David N. A. Kpobi and Emmanel K. Asante. Accra, Ghana: The Missiological Society of Ghana, 2021.

Bosch, David. "Witness to the World." In *Perspectives on the World Christian Movement: A Reader*. Fourth edition. Chapter 12. Edited by Ralph D. Winter and Steven C. Hawthorne. Pasadena: William Carey Library, 2009.

Breeze, Victoria, and Nathan More. "China has overtaken the US and UK as the top destination for anglophone African students." *Quartz Africa* (June 30, 2017). https://qz.com/africa/1017926/china-has-overtaken-the-us-and-uk-as-the-top-destination-for-anglophone-african-students/.

---

29. Lesslie Newbigin, *Foolishness to the Greeks* (Grand Rapids: Eerdmans, 1986), Chapter 6.

30. Mpereh, "Migration as a Catalyst for the Fulfilment of the Great Commission," 217.

31. Leiton Chinn and Lisa E. Chinn, "Agents of Diaspora Missions in and from the Academic World," in *Scattered and Gathered: A Global Compendium of Diaspora Missiology*, eds. Sadiri Joy Tira and Tetsunao Yamamori (Eugene: Wipf & Stock, 2016), 234.

Casino, Tereso, and Charles Cook. "Glossary, Appendices and Ministry Resources." In *Scattered and Gathered: A Global Compendium of Diaspora Missiology*. Edited by Sadiri Joy Tira and Tetsunao Yamamori. Section eds. Tereso Casino and Charles Cook. Eugene: Wipf & Stock, 2016. 537–65.

Chinn, Leiton E. "International Student Ministry: Blind-Spot to Vision." Unpublished paper presented at the Lausanne Diasporas Strategy Consultation (2009).

Chinn, Leiton, and Lisa E. Chinn. "Agents of diaspora missions in and from the academic world." In *Scattered and Gathered: A Global Compendium of Diaspora Missiology*. Edited by Sadiri Joy Tira and Tetsunao Yamamori. Eugene: Wipf & Stock, 2016. 228–41.

Dindi, Bill. "The Viability of International Student Ministry in Africa." Unpublished paper. International Leadership University (2020).

Ebner-Golder, Roswitha. "Providing a Spiritual Home away from home: a swiss Woman's Way of Witnessing to a Latin American Community in Geneva." *International Review of Mission* 93, no. 368 (2004): 97–104.

Hutchinson, Mark, and John Wolffe. *A Short History of Global Evangelicalism*. New York: Cambridge University Press, 2012.

Johnson, Todd M., et al. "Christianity 2018: More African Christians and Counting Martyrs." *International Bulletin of Mission Research* 42, vol. 1 (2018): 20–28.

Kritz, Mary M. "International student mobility and tertiary education capacity in Africa." *International Migration* 53, vol. 1 (2015): 29–49.

Kwiverr. "Not All Who Go Are Sent: A Research Report on the Missionary Preparedness of African Christian International Students, Past and Present, from 116 African nations." Accra, Ghana: Kwiverr, 2022. https://kwiverr.org/wp-content/uploads/2023/01/Not-All-Who-Go-Are-Sent.pdf.

Mpereh, Samuel V. "Migration as a Catalyst for the Fulfilment of the Great Commission." In *Migration and the Church in Africa: Facing up to a Contemporary Challenge in Christian Mission*. Edited by David N. A. Kpobi and Emmanuel K. Asante. Accra, Ghana: The Missiological Society of Ghana, 2021.

Nawrocki, Mike, dir. *The Pirates Who Don't Do Anything: A VeggieTales Movie*. United States: Big Idea, Starz Animation, 2008.

Newbigin, Lesslie. *Foolishness to the Greeks*. Grand Rapids: Eerdmans, 1986.

Ostergren, Robert C., and Mathias Le Bossé. *The Europeans: A Geography of People, Culture, and Environment*. Second Edition. New York: Guilford Press, 2011.

Perbi, Yaw. "The African International Student Phenomenon: Turning an Unsung Force into a Tour-de-force in Mission Dei." *Journal of African Christian Thought* 24.2 (2021), 41–49.

Perbi, Yaw, and Sam Ngugi. *Africa to the Rest: From Mission Field to Mission Force (Again)*. Maitland: Xulon Press, 2022.

Sehoole, Chika, and Jenny J. Lee, "African Student Flows – Challenging Prevailing Paradigms." *University World News* (15 June 2018). https://www.universityworldnews.com/post.php?story=20180614114114977.

Studebaker, Steven M. *Pentecostalism and Globalization: The Impact of Globalization on Pentecostal Theology and Ministry*. Eugene: Wipf & Stock, 2010.

United Nations. "Population Facts." (May 2015). https://www.un.org/en/development/desa/population/publications/pdf/popfacts/PopFacts_2015-1.pdf.

Wagner, C. Peter, and Joseph Thompson, eds. *Out of Africa*. USA: Regal Books, 2004.

Wan, Enoch Y. *Diaspora Missions to International Students*. Portland: Institute of Diaspora Studies, Western Seminary, 2019.

———. *Diaspora Missiology: Theory, Methodology, and Practice*. Second Edition. Portland: Institute of Diaspora Studies, Western Seminary, 2014.

7

Indians in East Africa and Africans in India

Harshit Gudka and G. John Daniel

This chapter begins with a brief historical overview of Asian migration to Kenya and its socio-religious implications in a foreign culture. It identifies the issue of migrant integration in Kenya against the backdrop of the recent conferral of tribal status to Asians, exploring the themes of migration and identity. It then examines the experiences and challenges confronting recent African migrants to India and the implications facing the Indian and African church for diaspora missions and missiology. It concludes with some missional bridge-building ideas for addressing these complex and challenging issues. Harshit Gudka is of Asian Indian descent, was born and raised in Kenya and is a first-generation follower of Christ. John Daniel is based in Bengaluru, India and has lived, studied and served in Singapore and the UK.

South Asian Indians in Africa: Kenya's Forty-Fourth Tribe

The peoples from the Indian subcontinent are collectively referred to as Asians in East Africa and Great Britain.[1] The term Asian became common in East Africa after 1947 following the partition of India into two nations,

---

1. J. Brown, *Global South Asians: Introducing the Modern Diaspora. New Approaches to Asian History* (Cambridge University Press, 2006), 1–2; V. Cable, "The Asians of Kenya," *African Affairs* 68, vol. 272 (1969): 218–31, 220; Michael Adam, ed., *Indian Africa: Minorities of Indian-Pakistani Origin in Eastern Africa* (Dar es Salaam, Tanzania: Mkuki Na Nyota Publishers, 2015), 1.

India and Pakistan, by the British.² In East Africa and particularly Kenya, the term *muhindi* (plural, *wahindi*) in the Kiswahili language is often used generically to identify South Asian people from the Indian subcontinent as one collective group.³ The terms South Asian, Asian, and Indian are used here interchangeably.

Background of Asian Indian Immigration in Kenya

Even before the twentieth century, Indians had a marked presence through trade in the coastal islands of Lamu, Mombasa, and Zanzibar. Substantial migration from the Indian subcontinent into East Africa took place during the building of the Kenya-Uganda Railway between 1896 and 1901. As was common practice under the British indentured labour system, Indians were recruited to work on African plantations. However, indenture in East Africa took on a distinct form where about thirty-two thousand Indian workers were brought to Kenya alone for the sole purpose of railway construction.⁴ Most of these indentured laborers returned to British India after the railway was built.

Another prominent wave of mass migration followed the indentured laborers. This form of migration was led by independent, self-financed initiatives by Indians mainly from the states of Gujarat, Punjab, and Goa. It comprised primarily of the search for better economic prospects given the demand for their skills and labour. These Indian migrants not only set up business and trade in wholesale, retail and manufacturing, but also made entry into skilled, clerical, and professional fields including medicine, teaching, and banking.⁵ The pre- and post-independence influential role of the Asians to

---

2. C. Salvadori, *Through Open Doors: A View of Asian Cultures in Kenya* (Nairobi, Kenya: East African Educational Publishers Ltd, 1989), 5; Pascale Herzig, "Communal Networks and Gender: Placing Identities Among South Asians in Kenya," *South Asian Diaspora* 2, vol. 2 (2010): 165–84, 165; Dharam P. Ghai and Yash P. Ghai, eds., *Portrait of a Minority: Asians in East Africa.* (Nairobi, Kenya: Oxford University Press, 1970), ix.

3. Salvadori, *Through Open Doors*, 7; Ghai and Ghai, *Portrait of a Minority*, 1; Herzig, "Communal Networks and Gender," 165.

4. D. Gupta, "South Asians in East Africa: Achievement and Discrimination," *South Asia: Journal of South Asian Studies* 21 sup. 1 (1998): 103–36, 103; Michael Adam, "From Trading-Post Indians to the Indian Africans," edited by Michael Adam; *Indian Africa: Minorities of Indian-Pakistani Origin in Eastern Africa* (Nairobi: Kenya, Mkuki na Nyota, 2015), 7.

5. S. Rao, *Indian Dukawallas: Their Contribution to Political and Economic Development of Kenya* (Nairobi, Kenya: Free Press Publishers, 20160, 253–64; Herzig, "Communal Networks and Gender," 166; Dharam Ghai, "Economic Survey," Editors, Dharam P. Ghai and Yash P. Ghai, *Portrait of a Minority: Asians in East Africa* (Nairobi, Kenya: Oxford University Press, 1970), 95–96; Gupta, "South Asians in East Africa," 127–30.

Kenya's economy especially given their relatively minority immigrant status in a majority host African society, has been identified as remarkable and indispensable.⁶

Following Kenyan independence in 1963, government policies understandably focused on Africanization and Kenyanization which promoted the socio-economic and political welfare of Kenyan Africans. Many Asians unsure of their roles and future prospects consequently left the country.⁷ Herzig describes this exodus as follows: "The Asian minority population demonstrated an enormous growth from 11,800 in 1911 to 176,000 in 1962, followed by the exodus after independence when almost 40,000 Asians left Kenya within seven years."⁸ After the 1969 Trade Licensing Act which favoured promoting African business and trade, many Asian trader licenses were revoked. Coupled with restrictions from Britain toward Asian immigration, another eighteen thousand Asians left Kenya in a single year.⁹ An estimated one hundred thousand Asians live in Kenya, with more than half residing in the capital city of Nairobi. The remainder live in other major urban areas, perpetuating the urbanized pattern of Asian settlement in East Africa.¹⁰

Migratory movement from the Indian subcontinent into Kenya and East Africa continues to this day, although the demographics vary substantially. Asian migrants in Kenya can be traced down to five generations yielding interesting intercommunal (Asian-African) and intracommunal (Asian-Asian) sociocultural community dynamics. As Salvadori states, "The 'Asian Question' is a continuous source of discussion, often heated debate, in private, in parliament and in the press."¹¹ A particular social dynamic of interest to scholars is the issue of Asian-African integration.¹²

The Problem of Indian-Asian Integration in Kenya

In 2017, the Kenyan government officially declared that Kenyan Asians be recognized as the nation's forty-fourth tribe. This indigenous tribal affiliation,

---

6. Gupta, "South Asians in East Africa," 103.
7. Gupta, "South Asians in East Africa," 131–33.
8. Herzig, "Communal Networks and Gender," 166.
9. Salvadori, *Through Open Doors*, 11; Rao, *Indian Dukawallas*, 130.
10. Adam, *Indian Africa*, 17; and author's estimate.
11. Salvadori, *Through Open Doors*, 12.
12. S. Aiyer, *Indians in Kenya: The Politics of Diaspora* (Cambridge: Harvard University Press, 2015), 1–8; Salvadori, *Through Open Doors*, 10–12.

according to Fred Matiang'i, the then acting Interior Minister of Internal Security, meant that the Kenyan Asians would be included as part of the nation's diverse peoples.[13] Consequently, the Asians would no longer be regarded as outsiders or perceived as different, but on par with other Kenyan nationals. They will not be classified with the label "other" as was the case in the last National Census.

This tribal affiliation provoked mixed reactions across the Kenyan society. Inevitably, given the rich mix of diversity present across and within the Asian communities, some found it problematic to classify all the Asians as one homogenous group, notwithstanding the often socio-politically charged associations surrounding tribal discrimination and rivalry. On the other hand, there were positive reactions by many who saw the move as one of embrace and inclusion, adding to the rich tribal tapestry of Kenya, and of being finally accepted into mainstream Kenyan society as "first-class citizens."[14]

The government's attempt at inclusivity and a sense of shared identity to grant Asian diaspora in Kenya a tribal status was noble. However, the portrait of a united, homogenous integrated community of Kenyan Asians as a cultural whole perceived by the host nation, does not capture the vast diversity of these Asian communities. Salvadori's social anthropological work on Asian cultures in Kenya, for example, illustrates this rich diversity. Far from a homogenous community, the Asians can be classified in various ways: their place of origin (e.g., Gujarat, Punjab, Tamilnadu or Goa); language; occupations; or religion (e.g., Hindu, Jain, Sikh, Muslim, Zoroastrians, and Christian). These religious groups are further sub-divided into smaller sects where they associate themselves by distinctive community centers and places of worship.[15] As Herzig confirms, "South Asians in Kenya are not a monolithic ethnic group, but they are differentiated by religion and region of origin."[16] Religion is a "primary frame of reference" for the Asians in Kenya with their culture embedded within it.[17] Defined in terms of religion, the majority of the Asians in Kenya and East Africa are identified as Hindu.[18] The heterogenous character and contributions

---

13. R. Ombuor, "Kenyans of Asian Descent Become Nation's 44th Tribe," *VOA* (28 July 2017).

14. Z. Verjee, "Kenya's 44th tribe: Why I'm Finally a First-Class Citizen of My Country," *CNN* (2017).

15. Salvadori, *Through Open Doors*, 7.

16. Herzig, "Communal Networks and Gender," 172.

17. Salvadori, *Through Open Doors*, 7.

18. C. Peach, "South Asian Migration and Settlement in Great Britain 1951–2001," *Contemporary South Asia* 15, no. 2 (2006): 133–46.

of the Asian communities in Kenya has been comprehensively profiled by a Kenyan Asian, Sharad Rao.[19]

A unique social feature that permeates Asian cultures is their communalistic orientation. Among the dominant group of Hindu Asian immigrants, this value is often expressed in terms of caste and is thus exclusivist. The conception of caste can serve as a community identity marker of belonging and differentiation within or across communities. For the Indian diaspora in Africa, Yengde observes, "caste changed forms and adopted an evolved identity through hybridization within a new social and geographical context. Although the rigid caste practices in India are not duplicated in Africa, the essence and spirit of caste persists."[20] Further empirical research is needed to comprehend such caste hybridization in East Africa. Negatively, caste can degenerate into what may be called casteism. For non-Asians especially, this notion of caste is perceived as separatist, segregationist or racist if it becomes conceptualized as a major barrier to Asian integration into mainstream African society.[21] Misunderstandings among Africans concerning the Asian cultural value of communal endogamy can also be interpreted as a racial insult.[22]

The problem of integration was further complicated under British rule. As Yash Ghai astutely observes, colonial rule's "compartmentalization of society into three or so racial groups" promoted "economic, social and political discrimination and segregation."[23] This compartmentalization, it can be argued, served to preserve the Asian communal mindset and culture, their caste differences, and their practice of endogamy. It also yielded and maintained a separatist mindset represented in distinct residential, educational, medical, and recreational localities for the different communities, not to mention discriminatory economic differentials between Africans, Europeans, and Asians.

The development of Kenya as a nation state with a national identity has been an ongoing process since gaining independence in 1963. The complexity of forging a national identity is exemplified when the "dominant" group of African Kenyans is itself composed of various ethnic groups or tribes which are

---

19. S. Rao, *Indian Dukawallas: Their Contribution to Political and Economic Development of Kenya*. Nairobi, Kenya: Free Press Publishers, 2016.

20. S. Yengde, "Caste among the Indian Diaspora in Africa," *Economic and Political Weekly* 50, no. 37 (2015): 65–68.

21. R. Warah, "Hurdles to Meaningful Integration of Asians in Kenya," *Wajibu* 7, no. 3 (1992): 12–14; Cable, "Asians of Kenya," 219.

22. Salvadori, *Through Open Doors*, 11.

23. Ghai, "Future Prospects," 131.

themselves in the process of culture change. In this sense, Warah, for example, questions the very notion of whether a dominant Kenyan culture even exists.[24] As Githiora identifies, Kenya's ethno-linguistic groups have "retained strongly grounded, localized identities which primarily are defined in terms of language, but also through claims to specific physical spaces, external community linkages, economic roles and practices – all within new boundaries and altered ways of life."[25] Ethnic-based divisions continue to be a major factor, especially in Kenyan politics.[26] However, it can be argued that a common perception of Kenyan national identity does exist and integrates to some extent the nation's diverse groups. One critical factor in forging a sense of solidarity, unity, and intimacy among the various peoples is the functional role of Kiswahili that is widely acknowledged as the national language along with English.[27] In my experience, more established Asians in Kenya have varying levels of proficiency in Kiswahili, which they often speak with an Asian dialect. This is an indicator of their integration into Kenyan society.

The above-mentioned social concerns are critical in determining the measure of Asian-African integration, not only in the sociocultural realm, but also in the political sphere where Asians have largely been aloof given their main concentration in business and trade. The social realities and diversities of Asian migrants in Kenya call for more social scientific empirical research to gauge their nature of integration into Kenyan society, in terms of both cultural assimilation and adaptation. For example, over recent decades, many Asians with their own religio-cultural backgrounds have embraced the Christian faith, the dominant religion of Kenya. This faith transformation phenomenon calls for empirical study on how their new changing social identities are negotiated at the personal, extended family, and community levels in terms of integration. Interspersed with this phenomenon of faith affiliation change are issues of integration surrounding exogamy (still rare) in terms of interracial marriages and changing perceptions of caste and communal dynamics between Asians and Africans.[28]

---

24. Warah, "Meaningful Integration," 222.

25. C. Githiora, "Kenya: Language and the search for a Coherent National Identity," in *Language and National Identity in Africa*, ed. Andrew Simpson (Oxford: Oxford University Press, 2008), 235–51, 235.

26. E. Musambi, "Kenya Election Result: William Ruto Defies the Odds for Victory." BBC News (15 August 2022), https://www.bbc.com/news/world-africa-62485332.

27. Githiora, "Kenya," 236.

28. Adam, *Indian Africa*, 177–204.

Diaspora Mission among Asian Indians in Kenya

The experiences of Asian immigrants in Kenya and their integration into mainstream Kenyan society are complex and varied. The strife and solidarity between the Asians and Africans are often commonly witnessed in tension. These are coupled with identity issues of what it means for Asians to be Kenyan or Indian, for example. Such realities are often brought to the fore. Two examples, both of which were witnessed by this author, will help illustrate this tension.

The first example is the unfortunate Westgate Shopping Mall terrorist attack in 2013, which resulted in the death of over sixty people, the majority of whom were of Asian descent. During and after the incident, there was an impressive solidarity of Africans and Asians in the rescue and recovery efforts. Despite their diverse Asian backgrounds, there people collectively identified themselves as Kenyans, demonstrating a spirit of unity and patriotism. There was a visible display of unity and of what being a Kenyan, Asian-Indian, and African meant to ordinary citizens.[29] Second, another sad chapter in Kenya's history was the failed 1982 coup d'état attempt to overthrow the former President Moi and his government. This event and its aftermath culminated in the loss of life of over one hundred soldiers and over two hundred civilians including non-Kenyans.[30] There followed consequent looting and ransacking of mostly Asian shops and homes that were taken advantage of and targeted by Africans. This incident reflected African resentment of the Asians and many families expressed intentions of leaving the country, albeit few actually did.[31]

The above picture of Asian migration into Kenya has been presented mainly from a historical and sociological perspective. However, the theological implications must also be mentioned and explored further in future studies. From a missional diasporic perspective, we can safely maintain that over and above human traditions and motivations for Asians immigrating into Kenya and other parts of Africa, God ultimately "decided their boundaries" as "his purpose was for the nations to seek after God and perhaps feel their way toward him and find him though he is not far from any one of us" (Acts 17:26–27). Some Kenyan churches have realized this divinely appointed opportunity and incorporated in their ministry mandate a vision to reach out to the Asians with the message of tribal and racial reconciliation made possible through the good

---

29. Aiyer, *Indians in Kenya*, 1–2.

30. Charles Mitchell, "Kenya President says 129 Killed in Coup Attempt," *UPI* (5 August 1982); K. Mutunga, "Moment of Bravado that Changed Kenya," *Daily Nation* (31 July 2012).

31. Salvadori, *Through Open Doors*, 11.

news of salvation in Christ. When this message applied, it opens the door for Africans, Asians, and others to embrace their unity in Christ amid their cultural diversity as equal image-bearers of God (Eph 4:1–4; Gal 3:26–28; Rev 7:9).

As a second-generation person of Asian descent resident in Kenya and a first-generation follower of Christ, I (Harshit) believe biblically-based contextual approaches are key to bridging the reconciliatory message of Christianity. The former UK Home Secretary Roy Jenkins viewed integration "not as flattening process of assimilation, but as equal opportunity, accompanied by cultural diversity, in an atmosphere of mutual tolerance."[32] Such an approach appreciates human unity and celebrates cultural and ethnic diversity in God's image, thus paving the way for meaningful biblical integration of Asians with Africans in Kenya.

Africans In India: A Case for Diaspora Missions

African migration to India has a long history dating back to AD 1100 with the Siddis from East Africa settling down in the states of Gujarat, Karnataka, and Andhra Pradesh. Historical records seem to indicate that the Portuguese brought the Siddis to India.[33] The Siddis are considered tribals and they are among the landless poor of the country. Their social condition continues to be marginalized and a small percentage of Siddis are Christians.[34] With the challenge of a large number of communities and people groups remaining unreached, the Siddis seem to be an invisible community.

Contemporary migration to India from Africa falls into three main categories: students, medical tourists, and drug traffickers. A fresh wave of migration began in the early twenty-first century, mostly from the English-speaking countries in East Africa (especially Tanzania and Uganda), Sudan, and Nigeria. African migrants strive to build spaces of security and social networks, but they face an uphill task in a land with rising Afrophobia.[35]

Churches, as vibrant communities, have historically been at the front line of responding to calamities, disasters, and needs around them. The responses of the churches have also helped a great deal in building trust among vulnerable

---

32. John Stott, *Issues Facing Christians Today* (Grand Rapids: Zondervan, 2006), 270.

33. Anish M. Shah et al., "Indian Siddis: African Descendants with Indian Admixture," *American Journal of Human Genetics* 89, no. 1 (July 15, 2011): 154–61.

34. Ashraf Shaikh, "A Community Forgotten and Marginalised: The Siddis of Gujarat," *Youth Ki Awaaz* (July 15, 2020).

35. Shambhavi Bhushan, "Africans in India: When will Racism, Violence, and Discrimination End?" *The Quint* (August 11, 2021).

communities. However, this does not seem to be the case always since there are communities whose needs are apparently unknown for various reasons. India has not been an immigrant-friendly nation due to stringent policies and immigration laws in place. Nevertheless, there are countless illegal immigrants in India posing challenges to law enforcement agencies.[36] The push and pull factors inducing migration are complex. Therefore, detailed empirical research is required for understanding and presenting these facts, and to make a case for the diaspora mission among Africans in India.

Student Migration

India is a preferred destination for African students for higher education with most of the students hailing from Nigeria and Sudan. This preference is mostly due to affordability and attractive marketing.[37] Geographical proximity is another pull factor for African student migration to India.[38] There are about sixty thousand Africans living in India overall. According to the Association of African Students in India, there are about twenty-five thousand African students studying in various Indian universities.[39]

University students hailing from Africa are able to access scholarships under the Indian Council of Cultural Relations (ICCR) initiatives. Another forum that African students benefit from is the Indian Technical and Economic Cooperation (ITEC). However, many of these scholarships are offered within bilateral agreements and are not available to all African students. India is pushing its new National Education Policy and it remains to be seen how well the interests of African students are addressed.[40]

In spite of government policies appearing to be favourable to African students, the reality is not so promising. In the absence of a forum for dialogue between Africans and Indians, stereotypes have made lives difficult for African students. They are generally seen as criminals and drug peddlers. Cultural

---

36. Press Trust of India, "Two Crore Illegal Bangladeshi Living in India: Govt," *Business Standard India* (November 16, 2016).

37. Shamshir Malik, "African Students in India: The Conflicting Narratives of Capitalism and Nationalism," *Synergy: The Journal of Contemporary Asian Studies* blog (February 17, 2020).

38. Chetan Singai, "African Students in India 'Internationalization at Home,'" *Diplomatist* (December 29, 2019).

39. Karuna Madan, "The Dark Face of Indian Racism," *Gulf News* (January 20, 2019).

40. Singai, "African Students in India 'Internationalization at Home.'"

clashes are common and perceptions are not going to change overnight.[41] Forums like the African Studies Association of India exist to promote opportunity and harmony in the interest of African students in India.[42]

It is generally believed that international students are much more open and responsive to the gospel while living abroad. However, love and care are what students need the most in a context where they do not feel welcomed.[43] Currently, both in India and Africa, the churches seem to overlook the African students, rendering them virtually invisible. Regrettably, meaningful initiatives to connect with them and address their needs remain distant aspirations. However, when viewed through the lens of the diaspora, it becomes evident that students are not merely a mission field, but a mission force.

Consider, for instance, the diverse backgrounds of students from Nigeria and Sudan, encompassing both Christian and Muslim faiths. It is a remarkable prospect for local churches in India to realize the enriching potential of ministering to African students within their communities. These students hail from some of the most challenging countries to reach worldwide. Undoubtedly, a distinctive and unparalleled opportunity presents itself, wherein the advancement of the gospel can be achieved through the malleable intellects of these gifted and influential youth. It is imperative that this prospect not be disregarded or underestimated. By engaging with both Christian and non-Christian students, long-term and enduring outcomes that will have a lasting impact can be anticipated.

Medical Tourism

Medical tourism refers to "an emerging class of voyagers who are crossing international borders to obtain a range of medical services from dental care to liposuction."[44] In February 2017, the world's heaviest woman from Egypt flew to India for a sleeve gastrectomy surgery in Mumbai. India has been successful in attracting medical tourists and there has been a surging demand

---

41. Nagen Singh, "African Student's Cultural Survival in India – India News," *WION* (July 12, 2019).

42. African Studies Association of India, https://www.africanstudies.in/.

43. Leiton E. Chinn, "International Students: A Strategic Component of Diaspora Missions & the Great Commission," *Asia Missions Association* (June 22, 2016).

44. Anjana. "Medical Tourism Business – A Guide for Travel & Health Industry Enthusiasts!" *ColorWhistle* (October 21, 2019).

for Indian health care and hospitals.[45] India has turned out to be a favourite destination for medical tourism to African patients looking for quality yet affordable treatment.

The health care sector is a major concern throughout Africa even though it has shown remarkable signs of improvement in the recent past. Governments struggle to manage the enormous financial challenges and poor infrastructure. Many of the Sub-Saharan African nations remain the worst in the world in the health care sector as they are not able to spend the guideline of thirty-four dollars to forty dollars per person, set by the World Health Organization.[46] Also, Africans, whether wealthy or not, travel outside the continent in search of better health care.

The hospitals in India are not limited to a few cities but they are spread all over the country and patients have plenty of options to choose from. The hospitals also have experienced doctors and surgeons in addition to state-of-the-art equipment.[47] Moreover, India produces generic drugs for a fraction of the price in the developed world. The English language is also a vital link for most Africans as English is spoken widely in India. India is also home to alternative medicines like Siddha and Ayurveda.[48]

While it appears that medical tourism to India is an easy option, it is not without its downsides. The patients will still be spending large sums for travel, boarding, and lodging.[49] Hospitals also charge differential pricing for the treatments and services provided and the basis of such differentiation is sometimes arbitrary. The visa fee for medical tourists is twice that of a tourist visa. The insensitivity of the immigration officers is also a great concern and registration with the Foreigners' Regional Registration Office (FRRO) is a cumbersome procedure. It is mandatory that, "... every patient on a medical

---

45. Charlie Mitchell, "Indian Healthcare Taps the African Market," *African Business* (May 29, 2017).

46. Ludi Joseph, "Health Care in Africa: IFC Report Sees Demand for Investment," https://www.ifc.org/wps/wcm/connect/NEWS_EXT_CONTENT/IFC_External_Corporate_Site/News+and+Events/HealthAfricaFeature.

47. Guneet Bhatia, "Medical Tourism to India from Africa: Complete Medical Solution at an Affordable Cost," *MediGence* blog (October 8, 2017).

48. Pavithra Rao, "India's Medical Tourism Gets Africans' Attention," *Africa Renewal* (November 25, 2016).

49. Manjula Chaudhary, "A Study of Problems and Challenges Faced by Medical Tourists Visiting India," Gwalior: Indian Institute of Tourism and Travel Management (2011), https://tourism.gov.in/sites/default/files/2020-04/Med.pdf, 31.

visa must register with FRRO. At times critically ill patients find it difficult to 'go to' the FRRO office in person. Things are reportedly 'managed.'"[50]

The National Health Authority of India has plans to create an institutional mechanism for providing better services to medical tourists by networking with several Indian hospitals. If such a plan comes into force the medical tourists will be able to acquire relevant and reliable information concerning hospitals, facilities, specialist doctors, surgeries, etc., within a short span of time. As of now, India ranks tenth in the list of forty-six countries that are destinations for medical tourism in the world.[51]

For the church in India, the fact of the matter is that there are vulnerable people in the backyard. People with health challenges go through several traumatic experiences both before and after the treatment phase. Several psychological, emotional, and physical struggles are to be anticipated. Caring for the needy, especially the sick, is not an option for the local church. It would be amazing to see the Indian church ministering to the needs of medical tourists from Africa.

Drug Trafficking

Interpol says drug trafficking is an issue faced by all parts of the world with nations being either source, transit, or destination, and international borders are becoming increasingly porous as criminals and traffickers become more creative in their operations.[52] India happens to be one of the favourite destinations for drug trafficking with vulnerability on several fronts. Also, the demand for drugs has increased exponentially in recent years and the drug menace is affecting Indian society in many ways.[53]

Drug trafficking is as much a menace in Africa as in India with the emergence of several drug networks. West Africa seems to be playing the role of a transition point between South America and Asia. The problem is much larger than what it appears to be with political and economic implications.[54]

---

50. Chaudhary, "A Study of Problems and Challenges Faced by Medical Tourists Visiting India," 71.

51. Priyanka Sharma, "NHA Plans an Information Portal for Medical Tourists," *Mint* (May 6, 2022).

52. Interpol. "Drug Trafficking," https://www.interpol.int/en/Crimes/Drug-trafficking.

53. Ketan Patil and Astha Pandey, "Drug Trafficking: A Growing Problem for India" (February 1, 2022): 34–41.

54. Emmanuel Akyeampong, "Diaspora and Drug Trafficking in West Africa: A Case Study of Ghana," *African Affairs* 104, no. 416 (2005): 429–47.

Asia has been at the receiving end since the 1970s and India is no exception. However, in recent years drug trafficking by Africans is becoming a greater challenge to the Indian law enforcement agencies since the traffickers are no longer organized and professional criminals but tourists.[55]

The seizure of large quantities of drugs from African travellers arriving at Indian airports seems to indicate that traffickers now prefer the air route. This preference may have been induced by the restrictions imposed due to the pandemic.[56] There is a high demand for heroin in the north-Indian cities and the traffickers have chosen the southern cities as distribution hubs for the rest of India.[57] Instant statistics for the number of Africans arrested for drug trafficking are not available but newspaper reports confirm that Africans are arrested time and again.

The number of imprisoned African nationals in Indian prisons may not be staggering, but the dent the issue creates and narratives created around it are worrying. Among multiple reasons for growing Afrophobia, drug trafficking seems to be the prominent one. The criminal behaviour of a small number of Africans is detrimental to the safety and peace of a large number of Africans living in India.[58] While no simple solutions seem to be available, intervention of some kind is the cry of the Africans in India.

The Indian and the African church have nothing much to offer as a solution to the drug menace even as the debate on decriminalizing drug use is still on. With little or no intervention by the church, its position appears to be more inconsequential.[59] "What can change the *status quo*?" remains a distressing question even as attempts are made at the micro level to reach out to the prisoners.[60] It remains to be seen what popular perceptions about African involvement in drug trafficking will look like in the future, and what responses the Indian or African church would come up with.

---

55. Mpho Mashaba, "Drug Trafficking in India and African Connection," https://www.sspconline.org/opinion/DrugTraffickinginIndiaandAfricanConnection_MphoMashaba_050706.

56. Mahesh Buddi, "To India via Africa: Drug Cartels Chart New Route," *Times of India Hyderabad* (June 8, 2021).

57. Pinto Deepak, "African Smugglers Turn to Cities in South to Dodge DRI," *The New Indian Express* (July 21, 2021).

58. Jideofor Adibe, "Impact of Xenophobic Attacks against Africans in India on Afro-India Relations," *Journal of African Foreign Affairs* 4, no. 1/2 (2017): 85–98, 86.

59. David Agren and Bronwen Dachs, "Church Urges World to Face Drug Abuse and Related Problems," *Catholic Philly* (April 4, 2016).

60. Rohan Swamy, "Reel-Time Stories," *Indian Express* (April 26, 2012).

Regardless of how heinous a crime might be, the worth of a human soul never diminishes. The teachings of Jesus in Matthew 25 about the prison visits and divine perspectives are not something that could be brushed aside easily. With a myriad of needs surrounding the Indian church, the voice of the African prisoners may go unheeded. Nevertheless, the cries for help would continue until help arrives.

Missional Responses

The number of Africans residing in India is but an obscure fraction of the number of Christians in India, leave alone the population of India. However, the responses from below to reach out to the African community are worth mentioning. Although empirical data is unavailable, worshipping communities of Africans is a noteworthy feature in the cities like New Delhi, Mumbai, Pune, Hyderabad, and Bangalore. There are churches that reach out to these minorities, and there are others that have allowed the African community to have their own services in their premises. Diaspora mission of this kind is just "a drop in the ocean" but a move in the right direction. As envisaged by Wan, these initiatives might very well move into the next phases of diaspora missions.[61] Missional responses are not significant, but not absent.

Conclusion

Human migration is a contemporary global reality that has made the world borderless and this will continue to surge in the coming decades. The movement of people between Africa and India will continue to increase in both directions. The church in Africa and India needs to be concerned about diaspora missions and respond proactively to the diaspora communities. Diaspora mission to the Africans in India and Indians in Africa is indeed a pressing need! The African and Indian church cannot afford to overlook such an opportunity to be witnesses of Christ. They must harness their missional potential to reach these diaspora communities with the gospel. Such global South-South partnership can provide models of accelerating missions.

---

61. Enoch Wan, *Diaspora Missiology*, 2011.

References

Adam, Michael, ed. *Indian Africa: Minorities of Indian-Pakistani origin in Eastern Africa*. Dar es Salaam, Tanzania: Mkuki Na Nyota Publishers, 2015.

Adibe, Jideofor. "Impact of Xenophobic Attacks against Africans in India on Afro-India Relations." *Journal of African Foreign Affairs* 4.1/2 (2017): 85–98.

African Studies Association of India. https://www.africanstudies.in/.

Agren, David, and Bronwen Dachs. "Church Urges World to Face Drug Abuse and Related Problems." *Catholic Philly* (April 4, 2016). https://catholicphilly.com/2016/04/news/world-news/church-urges-nations-society-to-address-ongoing-issues-related-to-drugs/.

Aiyar, S. *Indians in Kenya: The Politics of Diaspora*. Cambridge: Harvard University Press, 2015.

Akyeampong, Emmanuel. "Diaspora and Drug Trafficking in West Africa: A Case Study of Ghana." *African Affairs* 104.416 (2005): 429–47.

Anjana. "Medical Tourism Business – A Guide for Travel & Health Industry Enthusiasts!" *ColorWhistle* (October 21, 2019).

Bharati, A. "A Social Survey." Pages 13–62 in *Portrait of a Minority: Asians in East Africa*. Edited by Dharam Ghai. Nairobi, Kenya: Oxford University Press, 1965.

Bhatia, Guneet. "Medical Tourism to India from Africa: Complete Medical Solution at an Affordable Cost." *MediGence* blog (October 8, 2017).

Bhushan, Shambhavi. "Africans in India: When will Racism, Violence, and Discrimination End?" *The Quint* (August 11, 2021). https://www.thequint.com/opinion/africans-in-india-when-will-racism-violence-and-discrimination-end-opinion.

Brown, J. *Global South Asians: Introducing the Modern Diaspora*. New Approaches to Asian History. New York: Cambridge University Press, 2006.

Buddi, Mahesh. "To India via Africa: Drug Cartels Chart New Route." *Times of India Hyderabad* (June 8, 2021). https://timesofindia.indiatimes.com/city/hyderabad/to-india-via-africa-drug-cartels-chart-new-route/articleshow/83325600.cms.

Cable, V. "The Asians of Kenya." *African Affairs* 68.272 (1969): 218–31.

Chaudhary, Manjula. "A Study of Problems and Challenges Faced by Medical Tourists Visiting India." Gwalior: Indian Institute of Tourism and Travel Management, 2011. https://tourism.gov.in/sites/default/files/2020-04/Med.pdf.

Chinn, Leiton E. "International Students: A Strategic Component of Diaspora Missions & the Great Commission." Asia Missions Association, June 22, 2016. http://www.asiamissions.net/international-students-a-strategic-component-of-diaspora-missions-the-great-commission/.

Deepak, Pinto. "African Smugglers Turn to Cities in South to Dodge DRI." *The New Indian Express* (July 21, 2021). https://www.newindianexpress.com/cities/hyderabad/2021/Jul/21/african-smugglers-turn-to-cities-in-south-to-dodge-dri-2333002.html.

Ghai Dharam P., and Yash P. Ghai, eds. *Portrait of a Minority: Asians in East Africa*, Nairobi, Kenya: Oxford University Press, 1970.

Githiora, C. "Kenya: Language and the search for a Coherent National Identity." Pages 235–51 in *Language and National Identity in Africa*. Edited by Andrew Simpson. Oxford: Oxford University Press, 2008.

Gupta, D. "South Asians in East Africa: Achievement and Discrimination." *South Asia: Journal of South Asian Studies* 21.s1 (1998): 103–36.

Herzig, Pascale. "Communal Networks and Gender: Placing Identities Among South Asians in Kenya." *South Asian Diaspora* 2.2 (2010): 165–84.

Interpol. "Drug Trafficking." https://www.interpol.int/en/Crimes/Drug-trafficking.

Joseph, Ludi. "Health Care in Africa: IFC Report Sees Demand for Investment." https://www.ifc.org/wps/wcm/connect/NEWS_EXT_CONTENT/IFC_External_Corporate_Site/News+and+Events/HealthAfricaFeature.

Madan, Karuna. "The Dark Face of Indian Racism." *Gulf News* (January 20, 2019).

Malik, Shamshir. "African Students in India: The Conflicting Narratives of Capitalism and Nationalism." *Synergy: The Journal of Contemporary Asian Studies* blog (February 17, 2020).

Mashaba, Mpho. "Drug Trafficking in India and African Connection." https://www.sspconline.org/opinion/DrugTraffickinginIndiaandAfricanConnection_MphoMashaba_050706.

Mitchell, Charles. "Kenya President says 129 Killed in Coup Attempt." *UPI* (August 5, 1982).

Mitchell, Charlie. "Indian Healthcare Taps the African Market." *African Business* (May 29, 2017).

Musambi, E. "Kenya Election Result: William Ruto Defies the Odds for Victory." BBC News (August 15, 2022).

Mutunga, K. "Moment of Bravado that Changed Kenya." *Daily Nation* (July 31, 2012).

Ombuor, R. "Kenyans of Asian Descent Become Nation's 44th Tribe." *VOA* (July 28, 2017).

Patil, Ketan, and Astha Pandey. "Drug Trafficking: A Growing Problem for India" *Asian Journal of Forensic Sciences* 1, no. 1 (2022): 34–41.

Peach, C. "South Asian Migration and Settlement in Great Britain 1951–2001." *Contemporary South Asia* 15, no. 2 (2006): 133–46.

Press Trust of India. "Two Crore Illegal Bangladeshi Living in India: Govt." *Business Standard India* (November 16, 2016).

Rao, Pavithra. "India's Medical Tourism Gets Africans' Attention." *Africa Renewal* (November 25, 2016).

Rao, S. *Indian Dukawallas: Their Contribution to Political and Economic Development of Kenya*. Nairobi, Kenya: Free Press Publishers, 2016.

Salvadori, C. *Through Open Doors: A View of Asian Cultures in Kenya*. Second Edition. Nairobi, Kenya: East African Educational Publishers Ltd, 1989.

Shah, Anish M. et al. "Indian Siddis: African Descendants with Indian Admixture." *American Journal of Human Genetics* 89.1 (July 15, 2011): 154–61.

Shaikh, Ashraf. "A Community Forgotten and Marginalised: The Siddis of Gujarat." *Youth Ki Awaaz* (July 15, 2020).

Sharma, Priyanka. "NHA Plans an Information Portal for Medical Tourists." *Mint* (May 6, 2022).

Singai, Chetan. "African Students in India 'Internationalization at Home.'" *Diplomatist* (December 29, 2019).

Singh, Nagen. "African Student's Cultural Survival in India – India News." WION (July 12, 2019).

Stott, John. *Issues Facing Christians Today*. Fourth Edition. Grand Rapids: Zondervan, 2006.

Swamy, Rohan. "Reel-Time Stories." *Indian Express* (April 26, 2012).

Verjee, Z. "Kenya's 44th tribe: Why I'm Finally a First-Class Citizen of My Country." *CNN* (2017).

Wan, Enoch. *Diaspora Missiology Theory, Methodology, and Practice*. Portland: Institute of Diaspora Studies, 2011.

Wanjohi, G. J., and G.W. Wanjohi, eds. *Social and Religious Concerns of East Africa: A Wajibu Anthology*. Washington, DC: Paulines, 2005.

Warah, R. "Hurdles to Meaningful Integration of Asians in Kenya," *Wajibu* 7, no. 3 (1992): 12–14.

Yengde, S. "Caste among the Indian Diaspora in Africa." *Economic and Political Weekly* 50.37 (2015): 65–68.

8

Chinese Diaspora Missions in Africa

Wenhui Gong

In October 2007 my missiology professor at Moody Bible Institute, Dr. Marvin Newell, mentioned the 95 percent and 5 percent reversal phenomenon of mission, based on the fact that 95 percent of North American seminary graduates stay in North America, to serve self-identified Christians who make up only 5 percent of the world's population. The other 5 percent of seminary graduates go on missions to serve 95 percent of the world's population, most of whom have never heard the gospel. God used this fact to call me into missions and used Rev. Douglas Wu, a missionary from South Africa, to confirm the mission field. In his mission blog, he shared about his gangster lifestyle, drug addiction, and jail record.[1] He bought a gun to kill an enemy who had caused him to lose one hundred thousand dollars. On his way, he met a missionary and was saved by the gospel through him. Shortly thereafter the missionary had a heart attack and died, moving the converted gangster to serve the Lord for the rest of his life.

A few days after I read his testimony, I received a call from Chinese International Mission (CIM), the organization with which Douglas worked, asking me to host him and his wife during their visit to the USA. I readily accepted the request. As they shared their ministry stories about Chinese diaspora in Africa with local churches, I knew that God was calling my family to Africa.

---

1. http://douglaswufamily.blogspot.tw/.

At the first annual Diaspora Ministries conference hosted by OMF International in London, UK, my wife Jane and I learned about the rapidly growing business relationship between China and Africa, and the influx of Chinese into Africa. By 2014 there were two million Chinese in Africa. Despite this influx of Chinese immigrants, local African churches and Western missionaries were finding it difficult to reach the Chinese with the gospel, let alone raising Chinese missionaries among them. Chinese churches were called to respond to this growing need. I made several trips to South Africa, East Africa, and West Africa to locate a place for our ministry. Finally, my family moved to Kenya as long-term missionaries with OMF International in July 2014. Later in July 2016, I founded Chinese Diaspora Mission as an international mission agency to help Chinese churches mobilize, equip, and send missionaries to make disciples among the Chinese diaspora and beyond, with Africa as our first mission field. In 2020, I completed my PhD dissertation titled *Mission Beyond: The Diaspora Chinese Diaspora in Africa*[2] and in 2022, I authored a Chinese book, 超越的使命:华人散聚宣教 (*Missions Beyond: Chinese Diaspora Missions*), based on my experience and research on Chinese diaspora missions in Africa. In this chapter, I share two diaspora mission strategies: mission focused on the diaspora and mission focused beyond the diaspora.

Missions Focusing on Diaspora

When diasporic people are in transition from their original comfortable and secure homeland, they prepare for sociocultural change and often become more open to receiving the gospel in foreign lands.[3] Many of the diaspora people need hospitality and charity, and if local Christians can receive some training about Chinese culture, show the love of God to them and share the gospel with them at the same time, "combining the practice of the Great Commandment with the Great Commission"[4] in a Chinese cultural context, this will result in effective "missions to the diaspora."[5]

---

2. Wenhui Gong, "Missions Beyond: The Diaspora Chinese in Africa." PhD diss., Biola University, 2020.

3. Enoch Wan, ed., *Diaspora missiology: Reflections on Reaching the Scattered Peoples of the World* (Pasadena: William Carey Library, 2015), 35.

4. Global Diaspora Network, *Scattered to Gather: Embracing the Global Trend of Diaspora* (Manila: LifeChange, 2010), 28.

5. Wan, *Diaspora Missiology*, 217.

Chinese and Africans have certain common cultural similarities. For instance, they both value spending time to visit friends, setting high priority on visitors, sharing resources with others, and supporting family members, which reflect their invisible values of people orientation, hospitality, friendship, and community respectively.[6] It is great for African churches to welcome people who are living in diaspora. However, welcoming the diaspora means much more than saying the Chinese greeting 你好 *ni how* (hello) and handing them a bulletin.[7] For the Chinese diaspora in Africa, the largest needs are practical help, information, and advice, in addition to Bible teaching. The diaspora will experience the church's welcome most personally in their work, home, children's schooling, accessing medical services, and dealing with the local government. This is especially true because most of the Chinese diaspora do not have a good enough command of the English language to function well in African society and because the Chinese value their children's education. For the diaspora Chinese to be welcomed by the African community and become trusted persons, rather than being viewed simply as "the rich one" who is taking advantage of them, time and effort must be spent on their physical and emotional needs as well as their spiritual needs.

Douglas Wu, the missionary working with the diasporic Chinese in South Africa that I met in Chicago, has won many Chinese to Christ and established three churches with more than ten cell groups in the past ten years. Douglas told me that he spent most of his time visiting the immigration jails (new immigrants being placed under arrest frequently happens in Africa), acting as an interpreter at times for driving license applications, helping to fill out legal documents, providing physical support for the diaspora, and locating schools for their children without any expectations.

Visiting is an important ministry for initial missions work to the diaspora. The most effective approach to build 关系 *guanxi* (relationship) is to go out visiting people. When recent immigrants come to a new place, many of them have a sense of fear and loss. Their highest priority is to survive in the new environment, which creates tremendous pressure on them. Some have to work at hard labour jobs that do not match their education background or experiences. Some suffer from loneliness. Like the Good Samaritan, we need to help them in their need. Through visiting and caring, we provide them with

---

6. Connecting 2 Culture, *Chinese Ministry Training, Level 1, Trainer's Guide* (London, United Kingdom: Connecting 2 Culture, 2014), 8.

7. Lih-Chenh Chen, "The Chinese Diaspora in Africa: A Pre-evangelistic Ethnography of the Chinese Diaspora in 21st Century Africa" (DMis diss. Western Seminary, 2012), 223.

information, encouragement, and understanding. Sometimes, a person may have personal needs beyond his resources and abilities. A church can mobilize corporate human power and financial resources to reach out and help them in such a time.

The different types of visits and the focus of each is an important consideration in implementing a care ministry.[8] Some visits are to newcomers who have recently moved into the area or begun attending church gatherings, while other visits are to regular attendees to express care and provide spiritual encouragement, and yet others to people with special needs who are sick, backslidden, have newborn babies or marital problems, or challenge with children's education. The purpose of the visits is to close the gap between people and the church by expressing care, to build up faith, to resolve misunderstandings, to address issues related to faith, to provide financial support, and to help people overcome other challenges.

The caring ministry gives attention to every newcomer. Each newcomer feels welcomed into the church and small group fellowship and feels connected with others. Beside newcomers, Chinese who have special needs such as work permit applications, family conflicts, accidents, and job changes may need care and visitation. Therefore, it is also important for the care and visitation team members to have open hearts and be ready at any time to welcome visits from the Chinese diaspora who are in need. Chinese people raised under Communism are more likely to be in a spiritual vacuum and more open to the gospel. If they receive help that demands no return at their time of need, they will come back to seek the love of Christ demonstrated by others.

This Chinese value of close family ties can be leveraged to reach the Fuqing Chinese people who often work or live in clans of ten, twenty, or even thirty in some African cities. When one of them is reached, the entire clan is often reached and they will all profess faith in Christ, go to church together, and build genuine community in God's household.

The findings of my research show that all diasporic Chinese Christian participants had a heart for pursuing success and cared about the honour of success. Their conversion of faith from Atheism, Buddhism, Daoism, or the Jehovah's Witnesses is also regarded as success of life.

---

8. Wenhui Gong, "Case Studies of Diaspora Missiology: Ethnographic Studies of Mission Ministries of Diaspora Chinese Churches in North America" (DMin diss. Logos Evangelical Seminary, 2015), 238–41.

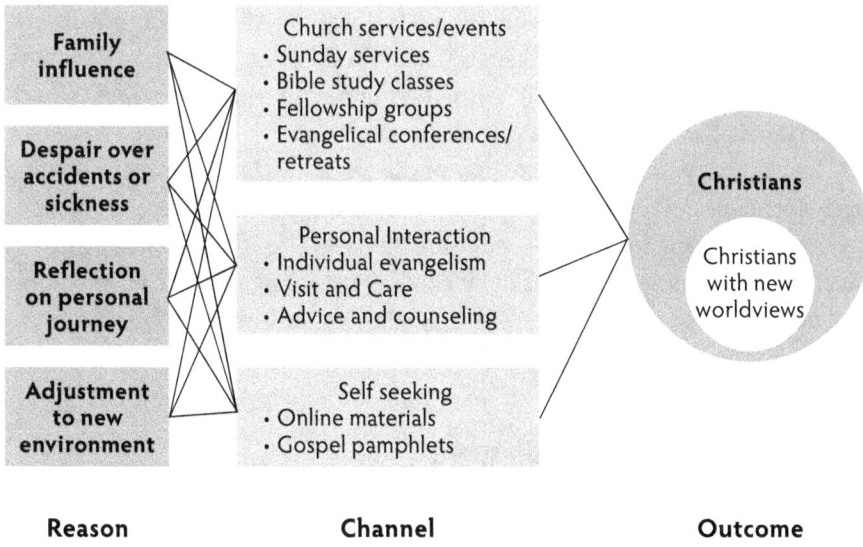

Figure 1. Process of conversion

They became Christians mainly through family influence, despair over accidents or sickness, reflection and personal pursuit journey, and feelings of loneliness or the need to fit into a new culture. After feeling the need, the reason for conversion, the participants came to Christ through three channels: church service/event, personal interaction, and self-seeking. Visiting and care with advising/counseling and individual evangelism resulted in the largest number of conversions. As a result, some of them really changed their worldview and they now live a new Christian life (Figure 1). However, as "true conversion in any society always involves a worldview change,"[9] not all of them had experienced true conversion, though a few of them did. Many lacked solid discipleship and church life due to lack of qualified life examples or discipleship leaders and a solid discipleship methodology.

One important thing that cannot be ignored is to utilize Chinese partnerships and mediators.[10] Chinese Christians and missionaries serve as the best bridge over language and cultural barriers to reach the Chinese diaspora, because most of them tend to isolate themselves from the African community.

---

9. Richard E. Elkins, "Blood Sacrifice and the Dynamics of Supernatural Power among the Manobo of Mindanao: Some Missiological Implications," *Missiology: An International Review* 21.3 (1993): 321–31, https://doi.org/10.1177/009182969302100304, 7.

10. Wenhui Gong and Kenneth Nehrbass, "Reaching Out to Diaspora Chinese in East Africa: Barriers and Bridges," *Missiology: An International Review* 45, vol. 3 (June 2017): 236–51, https://doi.org/10.1177/0091829617706981, 248.

The mediators can also serve as excellent trainers for African evangelists who wish to cross this cultural bridge and lead a solid discipleship program with iTIM (Institute for Training in Ministry) curriculum in the house church context, which will be discussed in the next section.

In summary, missions focusing on diaspora need to have the following basic principles: working among the Chinese diaspora in Africa requires a) cross-cultural and socio-economic sensitivity; b) building relationships; c) meeting the Chinese diaspora's daily needs; d) utilizing Chinese partnerships and mediators; e) ensuring solid discipleship and biblical worldview to transform the Chinese identity.

Missions Focusing Beyond Diaspora

Given that the diasporic people have cross-cultural and cross-regional mission capabilities, diasporic Chinese Christians should be missionaries in foreign lands. Partnership is an important path for missions by Chinese diaspora. The diasporic Chinese have abundant personal and financial resources, enabling them to access different cultures and participate in world missions.

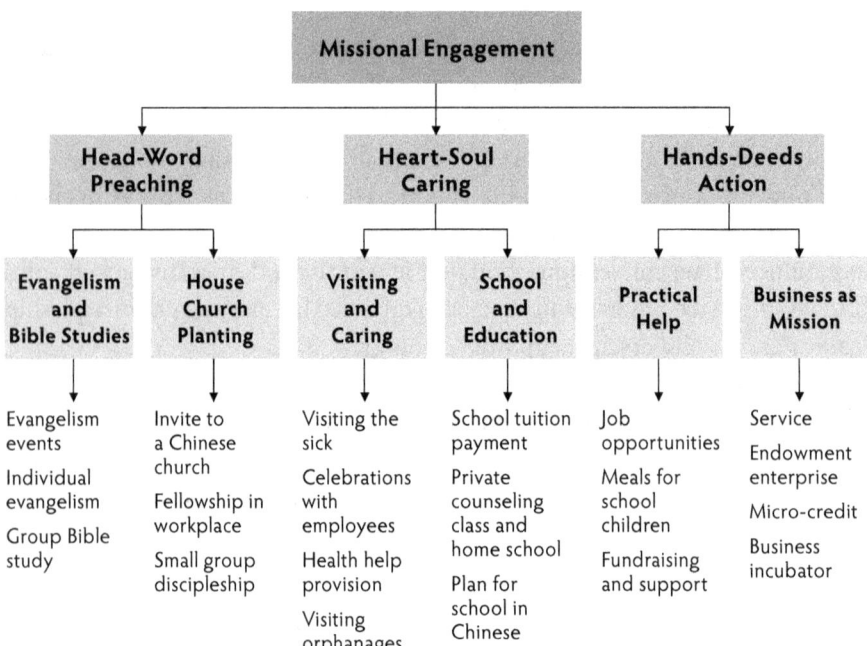

Figure 2. Missional engagement of the diaspora Chinese Christians in Africa

Chinese diaspora Christians have involvement in some missional engagement among the indigenous African population, which can be divided into three categories (Figure 2): a) Head-word preaching, b) Heart-soul caring, and c) Hands-deeds action. Each category has subcategories. **Head-word** preaching involves 1) evangelism and Bible studies and 2) house church planting. **Heart-soul** caring is demonstrated by 1) visiting and caring, and 2) school and education. **Hands-deeds** action consists of 1) practical help and 2) business as mission. Each subcategory can be broken down further into ministry items.

From the study, there were three areas of concern: 1) breadth which requires more people to be involved and they do more, 2) depth through laying solid foundations and operations systems, and 3) sustainability with a long-term plan for propagating or passing on the work to the future. As a result, a Chinese Diaspora Mission model is proposed.

Chinese Diaspora Mission in Africa has established a missional model (Figure 3). The model will mobilize Chinese churches worldwide to send short-term and long-term missionaries and raise up diaspora Chinese missionaries from their workplaces in Africa.

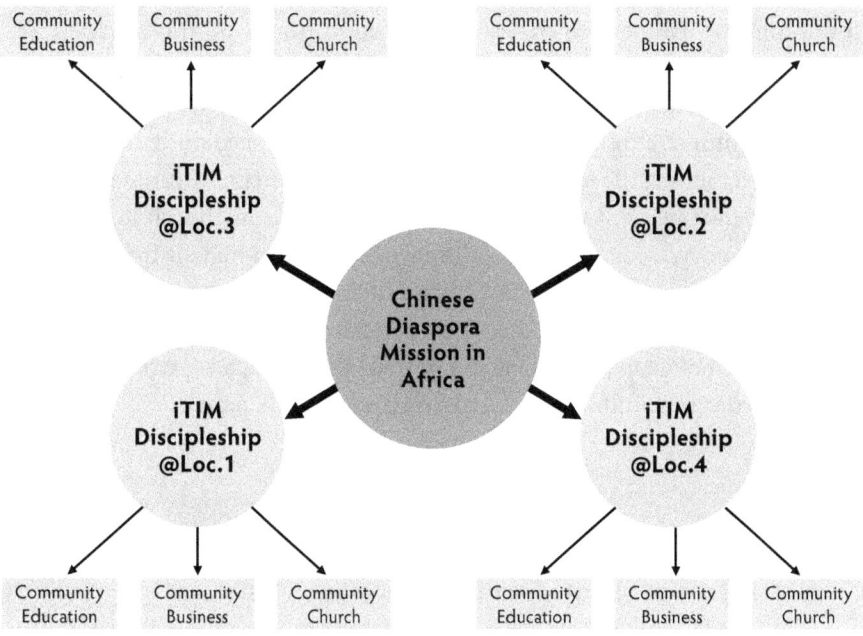

Figure 3. Chinese Diaspora Mission in Africa

There are two main parts of the model. The first part is discipleship – iTIM Discipleship. The goal of the iTIM Center is to provide systematic theological training and discipleship using the iTIM curriculum, designed for local African church pastors and leaders.[11] We use a 3-H methodology: Head, Heart, and Hands, representing Bible knowledge and theology, spirituality, and ministry applications, respectively. The learning process consists of group study with our unique workbooks and administrative system through the websites itim-online.org (in Chinese for the Chinese church) and itim-online.net (in English for the African church). The certified trainers are mainly short-term missionaries from Chinese churches who have been discipled through iTIM discipleship. They come to conduct four-day iTIM Seminars for the local Bible school principals and church pastor trainers, with twelve topics related to why iTIM, what iTIM is, and how iTIM works. Trainees are certified after completing the assignments and internship in six months. These certified trainers then use the iTIM curriculum to train local pastors and study leaders. Our online system keeps their ministry accountable.

The second part of the model concerns three areas of empowerment: a) church planting in local communities where trained African pastors use iTIM methods for church planting and discipleship. Chinese missionaries work alongside to grow their indigenous churches. b) Education in the communities – Chinese churches invest in education to promote literacy and equip people to work by giving them knowledge that can lead to independence. Local church leaders receive professional training in computer technology and business administration, and Chinese culture and language study can be added to the curriculum of the schools. c) Business development – Chinese Christian businessmen start joint ventures with certified African church leaders. The indigenous people can find jobs in the workplace and benefit from business profits. In five to seven years, the Chinese missionaries exit the business to let local Africans operate the business independently. This innovative model can empower the indigenous population and transform culture in Africa. It is God's mission and can be fulfilled in partnership with God's people.[12]

---

11. More information can be found at https://traininginministry.com/.

12. For additional discussion of the model and personal experiences with a CDM short-term mission trip, see David Fu and Joey Zhou, "Short-Term Missions in Africa with Chinese Diaspora Mission," *ChinaSource Quarterly* (Winter 2020), https://www.chinasource.org/resource-library/articles/short-term-missions-in-africa-with-chinese-diaspora-mission/.

Conclusion

Chinese Diaspora Mission in Africa was a new undertaking. We really did not know how to walk this way in Africa in the beginning. We prayed for special wisdom and ability and for extra grace to develop the Chinese Diaspora Missions in Africa. "Dear Lord, Show me your way." This prayer was always in my heart.

Chinese is the largest diaspora population in the world but currently there is less than one long-term Chinese missionary for every thirty thousand believers. While more than thirty thousand Chinese have responded to the missionary call, very few have become cross-cultural missionaries. Developing a mission platform to effectively mobilize Chinese churches must be a top priority. By means of the global mission platform that partners in Chinese churches have, with their financial, personnel, and other resources, the numerous diaspora Chinese can be reached and mobilized. Therefore, a Chinese mission agency serves multiple functions as a platform for the Chinese church to join in missions work: a platform for mission training, including cross-cultural training and language training; a platform for short-term mission, including internship, teaching, advising, medical, and counseling; a platform for providing personnel resources for missions, including full-time missionaries with an exit system, short-term missionaries to rotate the leadership training, and workplace missionaries as tentmakers to serve as a bridge between the field and sending church. The agency model must be user-friendly, be flexible to enroll in, have a flat administrative structure, have low administrative costs, and be accountable for its ministry. The administrative policies, procedures, partner development system, member-care system, and accountability system need to be worked out for the mission agency.

Chinese churches have recognized that partnering with mission agencies is the most practical and vital path for effective world mission. When Chinese churches partner with newly developed mission agencies, specifically with the iTIM discipleship program in Africa, it is expected that diaspora missional engagement will improve in breadth (more Chinese Christians involvement and more evangelism and discipleship involvement), depth (building up mature foundation and operations systems), and sustainability (enduring indigenous mission). An African proverb expresses this well: "If you want to go fast, go alone; if you want to go far, go together."

References

Chen, Lih-Chenh. "The Chinese Diaspora in Africa: A Pre-evangelistic Ethnography of the Chinese Diaspora in 21st Century Africa." DMis diss. Western Seminary, 2012.

Connecting 2 Culture, *Chinese Ministry Training, Level 1, Trainer's Guide*. London, United Kingdom: Connecting 2 Culture, 2014.

Elkins, Richard. E. "Blood Sacrifice and the Dynamics of Supernatural Power among the Manobo of Mindanao: Some Missiological Implications." *Missiology: An International Review* 21, no. 3 (1993): 321–31. https://doi.org/10.1177/009182969302100304.

Fu, David, and Joey Zhou. "Short-Term Missions in Africa with Chinese Diaspora Mission." *ChinaSource Quarterly* (Winter 2020). https://www.chinasource.org/resource-library/articles/short-term-missions-in-africa-with-chinese-diaspora-mission/.

Global Diaspora Network, *Scattered to Gather: Embracing the Global Trend of Diaspora*, 2017. Also, in Mandarin.

Gong, Wenhui. "Missions Beyond, The Diaspora Chinese in Africa." PhD diss. Biola University, 2020.

———. "Case Studies of Diaspora Missiology: Ethnographic Studies of Mission Ministries of Diaspora Chinese Churches in North America." DMin diss. Logos Evangelical Seminary, 2015.

Gong, Wenhui, and Kenneth Nehrbass. "Reaching Out to Diaspora Chinese in East Africa: Barriers and Bridges." *Missiology: An International Review* 45, no. 3 (June 2017): 236–51. https://doi.org/10.1177/0091829617706981.

Wan, Enoch, ed. *Diaspora Missiology: Reflections on Reaching the Scattered Peoples of the World*. Pasadena: William Carey Library, 2015.

———. "Mission among the Chinese Diaspora – A Case Study of Migrant and Mission," *Missiology* 31, no. 1 (2003): 35–43. https://doi.org/10.1177/009182960303100106.

9

African Diaspora and New Horizons in Theological Education in Africa

Bulus Galadima and Elizabeth Mburu

Introduction

Theological education is central to Christianity. One of the key titles of Jesus is rabbi, which means teacher. His ministry on earth revolved around teaching. Early in his ministry, he chose disciples whom he taught in public and in private. His last and central command to his disciples was to teach all the nations everything he had taught them (Matt 28:18–20). The apostle Paul echoes this when he said to Timothy, "And the things you have heard me say in the presence of many witnesses entrust to reliable men who will also be qualified to teach others" (2 Tim 2:2 NIV). Theological education overlaps with general education and they mutually enhance each other. Christianity has always been associated with education and influencing cultures. The formation of Europe cannot be comprehended without the educational mission of Christianity. Paying careful attention to this relationship is critical for the impact of the gospel in the society. Christianity shaped Western European culture as it is known today. Christianity played a large role in the flowering of arts, music, literature, technology and economy of the West.

In this chapter, theological education is the training or formation or equipping of the leaders of the church in how to live godly lives in the church and society and teach the members of the church to do the same. Theological education is not what one does only for oneself but also for others.

Landscape of Theological Education in Africa

Globally, theological education is facing numerous challenges internally and externally on the issues of faculty, enrolment, curriculum, pedagogy, resources, and relevance leading to the call by some for an abandonment of the enterprise. In spite of all of these challenges, we cannot abandon or give up on theological education. We must seek ways to redeem it and to restore its relevance. The "loss of any suitable framework for a community of scholars would be disastrous for the church."[1] In a similar vein, David Tarus, the Executive Director of ACTEA (Association of Christian Theological Education in Africa), states that "Theological education is a key player in the quality of the African church as well as the health and wellbeing of the African society."[2]

Leaders are key to the shape, growth and strength of the church. Gornik says, "Pastors are central to the story" of a church. In fact, "their vocational identities, spiritual journeys, and leadership styles set the course for the congregations . . . In many respects, churches are mirrors of their pastors. Each church expresses the concerns, approaches, and commitments of their pastor."[3] Thus, if we are to fully understand the nature of the church and indeed the Christian movement, we must understand how the leaders are formed through their theological education.

In light of the phenomenal growth of the church in Africa, there is a paucity of adequately trained leaders for the church. Furthermore, Africans and non-African scholars unanimously accede to the need for new and alternative framework for theological education in Africa and formation to "produce church leaders that are competent to meet the contextual challenges of this continent."[4] Over the centuries, several models of theological education have emerged in the church. Willem Wahl lists seven models of theological education: the classical model, vocational model, dialectical model, neo-traditional model, missional model, and ecumenical-diversified model. He identified the challenges facing theological education in Africa as "access; the lack of resources; sociopolitical and social-economic illness; an Africanized

---

1. Linda Cannell, *Theological Education Matters: Leadership Education for the Church* (Newburgh: EDCOT Press, 2006), 40.

2. Johannes J. Knoetze and Alfred R. Brunsdon, eds., *A Critical Engagement with Theological Education in Africa: A South African Perspective* (Cape Town: AOSIS Publishing, 2021), 54.

3. Mark Gornik, *Word Made Global: Stories of African Christianity in New York City* (Grand Rapids: Eerdmans, 2011), 52.

4. Willem Wahl, *Towards Relevant Theological Education in Africa: Comparing the International Discourse with Contextual Challenges* 33, no. 1, *Acta Theologica* (Bloemfontein, Jan 2013), 267.

scholarship and curricula; economic injustice and ecological destruction."[5] These issues paint an accurate picture of the state of theological education in Africa. The one important issue missing from this list is diaspora. African diasporas have and continue to be a force to be reckoned with in theological education in Africa.

African diasporas have been an integral part of Christianity right from the beginning. Christianity spread from Jerusalem into Antioch through the initiative of diaspora Christians and African diasporas (men from Cyrene, Acts 11:19–21). These African Christians on the move were at the centre of the birth of Christian missions in Antioch: Simon called Niger and Lucius of Cyrene (Acts 13:1–3). Barnabas and Saul were diaspora Christians themselves. It was this Antioch church that sent Barnabas and Saul out on mission.

African church historians identify four waves of Christianity. The role of diasporas in theological education has not been sufficiently explored in each of these waves. During the first wave, the Coptic Church teaches that Christianity came to North Africa through Mark the Apostle. Thomas Oden argues that Mark was a Jewish-African man of the diaspora. In preaching the gospel in North Africa, Mark was bringing the gospel "home."[6] The city of Alexandria where he first preached was already a cosmopolitan and intellectual centre before the coming of Christianity. The theological education of this period resulted in the establishment of the catechetical Alexandrian School by St. Mark. This centre produced famous Christian leaders like Athenagoras, Clement of Alexandria, Origen, and Dionysius, to mention a few. The works and ideas of those associated with the Alexandrian School are still read widely by the church. These works formed the earliest Christian systematic theology corpus. Oden discusses the influence of the theology of this period on Christianity in his book *How Africa Shaped the Christian Mind: Rediscovering the African Seedbed of Western Christianity*.[7] During the first wave, the method of training was catechetical and involved mentoring in all areas of life, the curriculum was contextual and encyclopedic not merely theological, and it addressed all the issues the church was dealing with in church and society. The enrolment was not limited to only Christians but open to all. Several of the early leaders of

---

5. Wahl, *Towards Relevant Theological Education in Africa*, 268–69.

6. Thomas Oden, *The Ancient Memory of Mark: Reassessing Early Church Tradition* (Downers Grove: InterVarsity Press, 2011), 22 and 138–39.

7. Thomas Oden, *How Africa Shaped the Christian Mind* (Downers Grove: InterVarsity Press, 2010), 46–48.

the church belonged to diasporas. They were moving back and forth between Europe, Asia and Africa. St. Augustine was a prime example.

The second wave of Christianity during the colonization of the continent left very little legacy of theological education. There were Western and African priests but no clearly organized training of clergy on the continent was discernable. Isichei noted that the weakness of Christianity during this period "was its close association with the slave trade. There was a basic contradiction between converting Africans and purchasing them as slaves."[8] She adds that this Christianity did not have a strong impact on the society because of the strong influence of the culture, dearth of ministers and the injustice of colonization. This was true of both Roman Catholic and Protestant presence on the continent.[9] Most of the issues revolved around theological education.

The third wave of Christianity in Africa was birthed from the great revivals in Britain and America. Protestant missionaries arrived in Africa and penetrated the interior of Africa at great financial and human costs. They established theological institutions to train leaders for the church. The theological institutions during the colonial era were modelled after theological institutions in the West in instructors, curriculum, and pedagogy, except in enrolment which was African male for the most part with one of the earliest being Fourah Bay College established in 1827. Indigenous and diaspora Africans were instrumental in the success of Christianity during this period. Diaspora Christians like the Nova Scotia settlers were key to the establishment of Sierra Leone.[10] They came back to the continent to bring the gospel. One recaptive, Samuel Ajayi Crowther, a graduate of Fourah Bay, was a key leader of Church Missionary Society (CMS)'s Niger Mission.[11] He was instrumental in the translation of the New Testament and the *Book of Common Prayer* into Yoruba as well as other translations into Nupe and Igbo. His translation work became the standard for the translation of the Bible into other African

---

8. Elizabeth Isichei, *A History of Christianity in Africa* (Grand Rapids: Eerdmans, 1995), 71.

9. John Newton went on three slave trading trips after his conversion. After one of the trips, he wrote, "I never knew a sweeter or more frequent hours of divine communion than in my last two voyages to Guinea." Isichei, *A History of Christianity in Africa*, 71. There was no contradiction for him between being a devoted Christian and engaging in the slave trade.

10. Lamin Sanneh, *West African Christianity: Religious Impact* (Maryknoll: Orbis Books, 1983), 59.

11. Sanneh, *West African Christianity*, 75–76.

languages. Walls says, "his place in the history of translation and evangelization has often been undervalued."[12]

The fourth wave coincides with the African pre-independence period in the early 1900s reaching its zenith in the 1960s with the independence of seventeen countries. The primary source of acquiring theological education in Africa has been "from public universities, colleges and seminaries to Bible schools and Theological Education by Extension (TEE), theological education in Africa presents itself as a vibrant and dynamic undertaking." These institutions train leaders "to serve the church and society."[13] Africans took over leadership of the mission-led churches and established new churches. Theological education during this fourth wave is criticized for being modelled after western theological institutions with mostly African instructors, but Western curriculum, pedagogy, resources and maleness dominated enrolment.

There have been numerous attempts to address some of these criticisms. In order to be relevant, some theological institutions mostly in East Africa and a few in West Africa have become full-fledged universities. In West Africa, particularly Nigeria, several denominations have established Christian universities in addition to the seminaries. Christian faith-based universities make up 23 percent (thirty-nine) of the total number of universities (one hundred and seventy) in Nigeria.[14] In their bid to address contextual issues and become more relevant Nairobi Evangelical Graduate School of Theology, now Africa International University, established the Institute for the Study of African Realities. In a similar vein, Akrofi-Christaller Institute of Theology, Mission and Culture in Ghana was established to study theology and African Christianity. TEE and the South African Theological Seminary are examples of two initiatives seeking to make theological education accessible to all members of the church (male and female) by bringing the education to them. Many AICs (African Initiated Churches) and Pentecostal Churches shun formal education and have set up their own informal training of their leaders. They engage in discipling and mentoring leaders and depend exclusively on the messages and writings of their founders. Other innovative approaches have been adopted by groups like MMD (More Than a Mile Deep). They use African scholars to

---

12. Andrew Walls, "Samuel Ajayi Crowder," *Dictionary of African Christian Biography* (1998), https://dacb.org/stories/nigeria/crowther5-samuel/.

13. Johannes J. Knoetze and Alfred R. Brunsdon, eds., *A Critical Engagement with Theological Education in Africa: A South African Perspective* (Cape Town: AOSIS Publishing, 2021), 25.

14. https://sportafriq.com/christian-faith-based-universities-now-make-up-23-of-the-total-universities-in-nigeria/.

develop non-formal, competency-based, reflective practitioners, in a situation-controlled contexts model to train Christian leaders.

African diaspora participation in shaping theological education is steadily growing. Many African scholars in diaspora have been invited or of their own accord travel back to the continent regularly to teach in theological institutions and engage in various ministerial formation conferences and seminars as the Cape Town Diaspora Consultation 2022 of the Global Diasora Network demonstrates. One of the most notable is the role of Tite Tienou, a diaspora African in the establishment of the French graduate seminary FATEAC in Abidjan, Ivory Coast which is now a university, Université De L'Alliance Chrétienne D'Abidjan. The pandemic of the last few years compelled many schools to explore online education.

What Happens in Africa Does Not Stay in Africa

The growth of the church in Africa has not led to human flourishing. African predominantly Christian countries are ranked the poorest in the world. There are political conflicts on the continent. Theological education in Africa ought to position the church to be a part of the societal intellectual discourse. Pillay says that; "There is a need for Christian scholars . . . for church educational foundations to rediscover their confidence; and to help reframe intellectual pursuits in line with the broader quest for truth, purpose, and meaning, and the development of a humane society."[15]

African theological education can have global impact. African Christianity of the early church had global influence introducing monastic spirituality, scholarship through the clergy, refining the theology of the person of God, Christ and the Trinity to mention a few. The phenomenal growth of the church in Africa is no longer contested. Pew Center projects that by 2050, 38 percent of the world's Christians will come from Africa. One challenge occurring as a result of this growth is that the theological institutions are not able to train enough leaders for the church. Walls says that Christianity now has not one but many centres. This means that this "multi-centric Christian mission has the potential to revitalize theological activity and revolutionize theological

---

15. Gerald Pillay, "Education as Mission: Perspectives on New Opportunities," in *Mission in the 21st Century*, eds. Andrew Walls and Cathy Ross (Maryknoll: Orbis Book, 2008), 173.

education."[16] These various centres will contribute the agenda and solutions to these new issues because western categories do not have answers to these issues.

As Africans move, they move with their religion and culture. They are changing the religious demography of Christianity in the West, making this dying religion in the West more vibrant. In view of the phenomenal growth of the church in Africa and the diaspora and global mobility, how do we address the issues of quantity and quality in theological education? How do we produce leaders for the church who are locally adept and globally aware? It is to this concern that we now turn.

Table 1: Models of Theological Education in Africa

Types of Institution	Faculty	Curriculum	Pedagogy	Spiritual Formation	Access	Cost
ACTEA (Seminaries & Universities)	Mostly western	Western/ Classical	Academic	Less effective focus on academics	Least accessible to women	Too expensive
More than a Mile Deep	Indigenous & Western educated	Competency based	Academic/ mentoring (Action/ Reflection/ Action)	Effective competency based	Accessible to women	Affordable
(African Initiated Churches)	Indigenous	Ministry based	Mentoring/ less academic	Effective (custom to church tradition)	Most Accessible to women	Most Affordable

Biblical/Theological Principles for Engaging Diasporic Contexts

There is already a growing recognition that theological education in Africa needs to move forward and escape the stagnation that has characterized it, particularly pre-COVID. Brundson points out that "theological education in Africa is both a dynamic and vibrant endeavour growing purposefully towards the future" and that "even though Africa has a lot to be thankful for in terms of theological education, several challenges are endemic to the continent that will require innovative thinking and ongoing commitment of all stakeholders

---

16. Andrew Walls, "Afterword" in *Mission in the 21st Century*, eds. Andrew Walls and Cathy Ross (Maryknol: Orbis, 2008), 203.

in order to carry theological education into an uncertain future."[17] As we have alluded, we need a theological education that is both "appropriate for the African context"[18] *and* globally informed.

We must maneuver ourselves in a global context that requires us to be sensitive to issues beyond our own horizons. How can we position ourselves so that our theological education is glocal – both locally contextual as well as globally sensitive, without losing the African identity we are struggling so hard to understand and perhaps even find? Paul's Areopagus speech in Acts 17 provides us with a biblical and theological lens through which we can engage our new and emerging contexts – which is where theological institutions find themselves. The following section focuses on equipping our students in our context to be sensitive to diasporic contexts and issues, as there will be a natural flow beyond the continent. The principles and implications are relevant for both formal and non-formal theological education.

A Demonstration by the Apostle Paul

Paul was brought up in Jerusalem and influenced by Hellenistic ideas. He was a Pharisee and trained under Gamaliel of the school of Hillel. As a Hellenistic Jew he had a knowledge of Judaism, the Septuagint and Greek culture. He is the equivalent of our modern-day theologian and Bible teacher. He understood that God's salvific calling extends to all peoples. Being a diaspora person himself, Paul was able to bridge other cultures. Paul stepped into the framework of his opponents, without veering from his own Christ-centred worldview. He gave epistemological privilege to the gospel message while allowing the surrounding diasporic context room for the expression of key theological concepts.

Art in Athens reflected its worship and the numerous idols on display revealed the pride of the city. Ancient sources affirm that Athens had more idols and sacred feasts than the rest of Greece put together; they accepted any and all foreign gods, even providing a temple and an altar for them. It was a place where diasporas felt represented and even accepted. While this religious context was very different from Paul's monotheistic worldview, it was not an obstacle to him.

---

17. Alfred Brundson, "Current Perspectives on Theological Education in Southern Africa: Achievements and Challenges with Reference to Southern Africa," in *A Critical Engagement with Theological Education in Africa* (Cape Town, AOSIS Publishing, 2021), 17–18.

18. Brundson, "Current Perspectives on Theological Education in Southern Africa," 27.

Paul engaged his audience in a discussion which eventually turned into a debate with his primary antagonists, the Epicurean and Stoic philosophers. Athens had people from many different contexts and these philosophers reflected this. The agora (Athenian marketplace) was the place where philosophers debated and presented their views and was thus the perfect place for Paul to begin. However, his message was received with mixed feelings. Bruce notes that "Stoics and Epicureans alike . . . looked on him as a retailer of second-hand scraps of philosophy, . . . a type of itinerant peddler of religion not unknown in the Agora."[19] Though his views were disparaged, Paul was not deterred. While some regarded him as an "idle babbler," with nothing constructive to offer, others thought he was advocating strange deities, their interpretation of his preaching about Jesus and the resurrection (v. 18). His argument was so intriguing that they were curious to know more. The fact that Paul had the ability to hold his own in such "exalted" company reveals he was well versed in the philosophies and writings of the time and competent in argumentation. However, his strategy was to affirm what is accurate in their context and correct what was erroneous by revealing to them the truth of God.

This strategy gave Paul entrance to the Areopagus and an opportunity to share more about his God and the implications of Christ's resurrection. The Areopagus was not only the town house, or guildhall of their city, housing magistrates and space for conducting business and justice, it was also a meeting place for learned men and women, providing a forum for the exchange of ideas. No new gods could be admitted without the approval of this court.[20] Paul did not just confine himself to familiar spaces. He went into the strategic spaces of those whose contexts differ from his and he engaged in constructive dialogue.

This speech provides us with a sound rationale and methodology for how to engage and navigate other cultures and worldviews when interpreting and presenting the biblical message. This lies at the core of *glocal* theological education in new and emerging contexts and is relevant for both formal and non-formal theological education. Here are four principles from the above passage.

First, we must find points of contact between African and diasporic contexts. In this way, we can capitalize on a common knowledge base without necessarily agreeing on its nuances. Paul uses their prior knowledge of "an unknown god" as his bridge for introducing to them the true God. He fills their gap in knowledge regarding this deity and satisfies their curiosity for the

---

19. F. F. Bruce, *The Book of the Acts* (Grand Rapids: Eerdmans, 1988), 331.
20. Faber, *Clarion* 42, no. 13 (1993), http://spindleworks.com/library/rfaber/aratus.htm.

new and the strange. Paul spent his time in Athens observing the people and seeking to understand what they believed about God. Epicureans believed that while gods did indeed exist, they were apathetic towards human affairs.[21] Since religion was a source of fear, the banishing of gods was a means to attaining peace and a good life.[22] Stoics, on the other hand, believed that the world had been created by Zeus, a power, a being, but a force which permeates all things and unites them into one cosmos. This divine force, also known as reason or *logos*, was therefore viewed as extremely immanent, thus leading them to a pantheistic view of reality. It implies that humans were responsible for aligning themselves with this purpose, through tragedy and triumph. While they had a monotheistic view, they accommodated other gods, and regarded them as "metaphorical expressions of the God at work throughout nature."[23] God was also seen as material, being made out of a fine and subtle body known as pneuma (breath).[24] Paul's initial comment opened avenues of communication and set the tone for the rest of his speech, turning and moving the narrative forward in a new direction. His introduction also dispelled any notion that he was introducing a new deity. As Chrysostom points out, he shows "that they have anticipated what he proclaimed."[25]

Second, the knowledge of local and global backgrounds and contexts is crucial. Paul understood Epicurean and Stoic backgrounds, even going so far as to use their texts to his advantage. In verse 28, Paul states, "for in him we live and move and exist" (NASB), the fourth line from a poem by Epimenides, the Cretan (c. 600 BC).[26] When Paul uses this phrase, it is not strange to the hearers – both pagan and Christian. The Genesis account (Gen 1:27–28) records the very personalized creation of mankind by God. He adds "as even some of your own poets have said, 'For we also are His offspring,'" extracted from another poet, a Stoic named Aratus. The poem, *Phaenomena*, was well

---

21. Diogenes Laertius, *Lives of Eminent Philosophers. Volume II: Books 6–10*, trans R. D. Hicks, Loeb Classical Library 185 (Cambridge: Harvard University Press, 1925), 123–24.

22. Anthony Kenny, *An Illustrated Brief History of Western Philosophy* (Malden: Blackwell Publishing, 2006), 94.

23. J. C. Thom, "Stoicism," in *Dictionary of New Testament Background: A Compendium of Contemporary Biblical Scholarship*, eds. Craig Evans and Stanley Porter Jr. (Downers Grove: InterVarsity Press, 2000), 1140.

24. Kenny, *Illustrated Brief History*, 97.

25. Francis Martin, *Ancient Christian Commentary on Scripture New Testament*, vol. 5. (Downers Grove: InterVarsity, 2006), 216.

26. Bruce, *Acts*, 339.

known to his hearers.[27] It is a reference to the heathen god Zeus (Roman equivalent Jupiter), who was regarded, in this poem, as the supreme God.

For the followers of Christ in the crowd, and indeed, for a modern reader today, this might be jarring. Why would Paul defend God's sovereignty over mankind by quoting pagan poets? This displays Paul's genius. He knew that every human being possesses the innate knowledge of the divine being who is the creator. This belief is expressed in every society. Paul uses this as another bridge, taking his hearers back to their own poets, and their expression of human existence in relation to a divine being.

Third, expand the existing context with a new one. People cannot conceptualize new ideas in a vacuum. By going to the very heart of their worldview, their assumptions about and conception of deity, the nature of man and the nature of the world, Paul first establishes a common starting point. Having done so, he extends their prior knowledge, moving them from the known to the unknown.

Only after he has established a point of connection between his hearers and himself, does Paul go on to explain the implications of being God's offspring. If humanity stems from God, God cannot be like gold or silver or stone. The phrase "an image formed by the art and thought of man" (v. 29 NASB), states that man is himself the originator of these idols. Paul believes that it is ludicrous to suppose that God who "births" all humanity can possibly be a product of human imagination and sculpted into an image. Moreover, God's purpose in creating humankind is so that they would seek him. While God's creative act affirms his transcendence, this statement affirms his immanence. This is the difference between theology in context and contextualization. Paul does not just reframe his own biblical understanding but re-conceptualizes it from his current cultural context.

Fourth, learn to major on the majors and minor on the minors. We should not compromise gospel truth but allow creativity in how this is expressed in different contexts. Paul's assumption about the nature of knowledge ties his entire argument together and concludes it. He believed that God revealed in nature is general revelation and God revealed through his word and his Son, Jesus Christ, is special revelation. He regards all truth as coming from God. For Paul, faith and reason are complementary, together creating a cohesive worldview.

Paul knew the anti-gospel implications of the Epicurean and Stoic philosophies. Epicureans taught that knowledge was empirical, and perception

---

27. Bruce, *Acts*, 339.

was the basis of all reason. Epicurus affirmed the reliability of the senses to provide accurate information and held that if one was misled about reality, the fault lay with the individual, since genuine appearances had been used as a basis for false judgments.[28] Stoics believed that knowledge was gained empirically through cognitive impressions and that reason was a crucial tool in making decisions that would lead to a virtuous life. This is particularly seen in their perspectives regarding self-denial, a virtue that was viewed as contributing to the highest end in life. Stoics believed that all passions had to be suppressed (*apatheia*). Hence, "The will must be directed to live in accordance with human nature by obeying reason."[29]

What is the logical conclusion of Paul's argument? He declares that human beings were no longer ignorant because they have God's true revelation regarding himself (v. 30, 31 cf. Rom 3:25). This revelation must lead to action, namely repentance, since their ignorance is no longer excusable. Knowledge of God here does not mean mere mental assent but rather "it involves moral and religious responsibilities, and . . . the hearers are summoned to repentance."[30]

Paul concludes his speech with the gospel, which in itself demands knowledge beyond the cognitive. Paul links the resurrected Christ with the sovereign God, showing that what he has been talking about is not a new deity, but one approved by God. He thus gives epistemological privilege to the gospel message. Having heard that idolatry is not reasonable, Paul calls them to respond in a practical way, by worshipping the true God, one who is not made out of gold or silver or stone – a product of human imagination.

These principles have implications for every aspect of theological education in Africa, especially in this diasporic milieu. First, we must extend the curriculum beyond the current traditional models in many theological institutions. Institutions that offer programs that are meant only for the local context need to become relevant in a glocal context. We need to include missional theological education as well as content that relates to diasporic communities – refugees, migrants, and immigrants. In this way, they can address the diverse diasporic communities without compromising on the core truths of the gospel. Offering one example outside the African continent, Dallas International University in the US started an MA in Human Migration in the Fall of 2022. This program equips students to serve diaspora communities,

---

28. Kenny, *Illustrated Brief History*, 94.
29. Kenny, *Illustrated Brief History*, 97.
30. Bruce, *Acts*, 341.

teaching them how to engage migrants and refugees through understanding their cultural, language, and religious contexts.

However, a course or a program in diaspora is not enough. We must integrate this diaspora paradigm into theological education so that *glocal* thinking becomes second nature to our students. Take, for instance, an OT Bible survey course. When studying Israelites in diasporic contexts like the Egyptian bondage or the Babylonian exile, it should relate the texts to the contemporary diasporic contexts. The same goes for the NT, for example the book of James or 1 Peter. Valuable principles can be drawn from these texts to guide the church on how to engage these diasporic contexts today and answer questions like: What is the mandate of the church? Should we provide insight into immigration laws? What is our duty towards illegal immigrants in our midst?

Though it may seem impossible to expand the current curriculum, theological institutions cannot ignore the current diasporic nature of the world without becoming irrelevant. Pedagogically, we must become more creative in delivery, testing and evaluation of our students. We need to build on our existing base and incorporate new modes of content delivery. A hybrid model that includes face to face and virtual modes of teaching and learning will ensure that theological education is accessible to a greater number of students and to a broader range both within and outside the continent. This opens up opportunities for virtual migrants. The COVID-19 pandemic has already started us off on this path. Many theological institutions on the continent have some form of online teaching/learning presence that is now used in a hybrid fashion in conjunction with face-to-face modes of delivery.

Furthermore, our resources must go beyond the current holdings to include contextual resources that not only engage students in their own contexts, but also in contexts beyond their own. This will allow them to identify and expand points of contact with their diasporic communities, broadening their thinking and challenging them to integrate into as well as interrogate the contexts they find themselves in. The resource challenge is one that faculty need to take seriously. We need to partner with publishers sympathetic to these concerns. We must also learn how to use social media platforms to create awareness, disseminate content and engage individuals in relevant discussions around diaspora issues. Using diaspora guest speakers and visiting refugee camps are beneficial. All these are means of equipping students to be effective in these rapidly evolving ministry contexts.

The vision for faculty can be expanded through partnerships and dialogue across theological institutions in different parts of the world, as well as hiring diverse faculty to create a global context within our own institutions. We must also ensure that we are not caught up in uneven power dynamics that will compromise our vision for diaspora. In many cases, those with economic power tend to dictate what happens even if the partnership is meant to be on an equal footing. One way to forestall this is to focus on South-South partnerships and collaborations rather than resource driven South-North partnerships. This means that we must aim for self-sustainability in order to accommodate more diversity and embrace hybridity. This includes Africans living outside the continent in different parts of the world. They are an excellent resource as they form an effective bridge between local and global contexts and contribute from their lived diaspora experience.

Finally, our policies for students should stress inclusion. We need to encourage more international students, address their challenges, and create a space for them to be more engaged in the local communities in which they are studying, be it physical or virtual. This has multiple benefits for the students but even more, gives the local communities exposure to diaspora communities that have come to them.

Conclusion

This chapter has shown that the concept of diaspora is crucial for theological education. African diasporas have been critical actors in every wave of Christianity and aspect of theological education in Africa and beyond. Even as we reimagine theological education, the diaspora contexts must inform how theological education is reconstructed. The approach we have outlined above challenges the traditional *commitment* to silos in theological education. The diaspora realities demand that we look beyond our contexts and take seriously multiple contexts and more complex dynamics in our educational approaches. For instance, we must be aware that how we prepare pastors and missionaries for diasporic ministries in Morocco and Greece (as transit points) is going to be different from that of South Africa and Germany (as destinations). Diaspora phenomena is accelerating, and it must be taken into consideration in theological education and Christian witness.

References

Bruce, F. F. *The Book of the Acts*. The New International Commentary on the New Testament. Revised edition. Grand Rapids: Eerdmans, 1988.

Brundson, Alfred. "Current Perspectives on Theological Education in Southern Africa: Achievements and Challenges with Reference to Southern Africa," *A Critical Engagement with Theological Education in Africa: A South African Perspective*, eds. Johnanes J. Knoetze and Alfred Brundsdon. Cape Town: AOSIS Publishing, 2021, 17–36.

Cannell, Linda. *Theological Education Matters: Leadership Education for the Church.* Newburgh: EDCOT Press, 2006.

Dictionary of African Christian Biography. 1998. https://dacb.org/.

Evans, Craig A., and Stanley A. Porter, eds. *Dictionary of New Testament Background.* Downers Grove: InterVarsity Press, 2000.

Gornik, Mark. *Word Made Global: Stories of African Christianity in New York City.* Grand Rapids: Eerdmans, 2011.

Isichei, Elizabeth. *A History of Christianity in Africa.* Grand Rapids: Eerdmans, 1995.

Kenny, Anthony. *An Illustrated Brief History of Western Philosophy.* Malden: Blackwell Publishing, 2006.

Knoetze, Johannes J., and Alfred R. Brunsdon, eds. *A Critical Engagement with Theological Education in Africa: A South African Perspective.* Cape Town: AOSIS Publishing, 2021.

Laertius, Diogenes. *Lives of Eminent Philosophers. Volume II: Books 6–10.* Translated by R. D. Hicks. Loeb Classical Library 185. Cambridge: Harvard University Press, 1925.

Martin, Francis. *Ancient Christian Commentary on Scripture New Testament*, vol. 5. Downers Grove: InterVarsity Press, 2006.

Oden, Thomas. *The Ancient Memory of Mark: Reassessing Early Church Tradition.* Downers Grove: InterVarsity Press, 2011.

———. *How Africa Shaped the Christian Mind.* Downers Grove: InterVarsity Press, 2010.

Pillay, Gerald. "Education as Mission: Perspectives on New Opportunities." In *Mission in the 21st Century*. Edited by Andrew Walls and Cathy Ross. Maryknoll: Orbis Books, 2008, 165–74.

Sanneh, Lamin. *West African Christianity: Religious Impact.* Maryknoll: Orbis Books, 1983.

Thom, J.C. "Stoicism," in *Dictionary of New Testament Background: A Compendium of Contemporary Biblical Scholarship*, eds. Craig Evans and Stanley Porter Jr. Downers Grove: InterVarsity Press, 2000, 1139–42.

Wahl, Willem. "Towards relevant theological education in Africa: Comparing the International Discourse with Contextual Challenges," 33, no. 1, *Acta Theologica*. Bloemfontein, Jan 2013.

Walls, Andrew, and Cathy Ross, eds. *Mission in the 21st Century: Exploring the Five Marks of Global Mission.* Maryknoll: Orbis Book, 2008.

10

A Postcolonial Evangelical Approach to Theology: A Rerouting of Mission

Godfrey Harold[1]

Introduction

Swinton and Mowat argue that theological reflection is critical reflection "on the practice of the Church as they interact with the practices of the world, to ensuring and enabling faithful participation in God's redemptive practice in, to and for the world."[2] Browning contends that "theology must be more than methodological," theology must be done in such a way that it "illuminates Christian practice in the light of life's concrete problems and issues."[3]

Thus, theology has to read and understand the signs of the times to respond to current challenges with the conviction that the transforming power of the gospel is relevant and remains true in every context of human existence. If correctly promoted, understanding the *missio Dei* can contribute to building strong communities of faith and transforming communities and nations. To reach this end, theology should constantly strive to reinvent itself in light of the challenges it faces from within the church, society, other religions, and

---

1. Much of the substance of this chapter previously appeared in G. Harold, "An Evangelical Understanding on the *Missio Dei* as Inclusion of Justice: A Critical Theological Reflection," *Pharos Journal of Theology*, 100 (2019): 1–10.

2. J. Swinton and H. Mowat, *Practical Theology and Qualitative Research* (London: SCM Press, 2006), 7.

3. D. Browning, *A Fundamental Practical Theology* (Minneapolis: Fortress, 1991), 15.

its local context, more specifically in South Africa as the church becomes the agency through which compassion and the justice of God are revealed.

Postcolonial theory can be defined as a theoretical approach that attempts to disrupt the dominant discourse of colonial power. This chapter seeks to address how evangelicalism as a product of Western Christianity can be disrupted so that it takes the lived experience of Africans seriously. Postcolonial theory affects both the colonized and the colonizer. There are complicated power dynamics both during the colonial experience and in the aftermath. Edward Said argues that beyond the physical and economic aspects of colonialism, there was the defining of the "Other." The Other, Said contends, is the result of a binary worldview, in which the world was divided into an us-and-them structure. Said describes the process of "Othering" of the colonies by the Western metropole, the European colonizers' home nation.[4]

Theological Influence within Evangelicalism

This paper seeks to engage with the praxis of evangelicalism within South Africa as it relates to the *missio Dei* through acts of compassion (*passio actus*) within society. The understanding that the church's mission predominately within evangelicalism is evangelism with the focus on the "saving of a person's soul" can be traced to the theological influences of European missionaries working among South Africans, whose focus was to maintain white supremacy. Because of their antagonism towards liberalism they viewed social engagement as an activity that is inextricably linked to the loss of sound doctrine, spiritual dynamism, and a watering down of the gospel.[5] This anthropocentric theological perspective of mission is evidenced by what Guder observes, "Western missionary enterprises planted churches that reflected their national identity in a foreign country making their institutional expansion and survival priority."[6] A theological influence among many evangelicals is the premillennial understanding of the eschaton as American personnel entered her ranks. Such an eschatology stressed the imminent return of Christ and an urgency to proclaim the gospel to those who had not heard it. Thus, emphasis is placed on evangelization and individual conversion because missionaries have impacted

---

4. E. Said, *Orientalism* (New York: Vintage Books, 1978).

5. W. E. Hack, "A Relevant Praxis in Applied Ecclesiology for the Evangelical Church in South Africa" (DTh Thesis, University of Durban Westville, 1993).

6. D. L. Guder, ed., *Missional Church: A Vision for the Sending Church in North America* (Cambridge: Eerdmans, 1998), 5.

the churches' ethos, structure and theological conviction as they worked with an understanding of the *missio Dei* as the church's mission, namely: evangelism. This soterian-centred (evangelism) focus creates a dysfunctional understanding of the gospel as it relates to the *missio Dei*, thus creating a dualism between a person's spiritual and physical condition. Therefore, it is imperative to redress this faulty assumption in our teaching of mission. I believe that the correct theological understanding (*orthodoxy*) of the *missio Dei* will more likely lead to the right action (*orthopraxis*) in holistically forming a community that is consistent with our convictions and that the story of Christ is a truthful account of our existence (Docetic). Therefore, a Christian understanding of compassion is determined by the vicarious suffering of Christ. This understanding must move us into seeing that the *missio Dei* incorporates social action (James 2:14).

Padilla argues that the most critical question that should be asked concerning the life and the mission of the church today is not related to its relevance but the content of the gospel. Far more basic, however, is the consideration of the nature of the gospel that could meet human needs.[7] The "what" of the gospel determines how it should affect practical life. Teaching the inclusion of social justice enables one to develop a theology based on compassion and justice that sees active and practical compassion as an issue of faith in Christ (1 Cor 12:26; Heb 10:34) founded on the *missio Dei*.

Evangelicals and the *Misso Dei*

Evangelicals, while emphasizing mission, have paid very little attention to the *missio Dei* because Harold citing Wicker states that the evangelicals' "understanding of mission is quite different to the *missio Dei*."[8] The concept of *missio Dei* within evangelicalism is formulated as a strictly soterian perspective rather than seeing God's mission in all of the world. This view sees God as the centre (theo-centric) of mission, not a church or denomination.[9]

Evangelicals tend not to use the term *missio Dei* because it is sometimes tainted by liberalism. Evangelicals see mission purely in terms of salvation, therefore they do not take the *missio Dei* seriously, which impacts their social

---

7. R. Padilla, "My Theological Pilgrimage," in *Shaping a Global Theological Mind*, Darren C. Marks, ed. (Burlington: Ashgate, 2008), 127–38.

8. G. Harold, "An Evangelical Understanding on the *Missio Dei* as Inclusion of Justice: A Critical Theological Reflection," *Pharos Journal of Theology*, 100 (2019), 2.

9. T. Englesviken, "*Missio Dei*: The Understanding and Misunderstanding of a Theological Concept in European Churches and Missiology," *International Review of Mission* 92, no. 367 (2003), 481–97.

engagement in society. Chester and Timmis argue that divine activity in history was discerned through a framework of Enlightenment values rather than the testimony of the Bible.[10] Therefore, they call for God's mission to be defined in biblical terms. For most evangelicals the term *missio Dei* is often used, not to provide a broader context to the mission of the church, but as a contrast to the mission of the church. Some American evangelicals, therefore, see the *missio Dei* as a liberal formulation and shy away from using it, for fear of being labelled liberal or maybe even the fear of having overseas funding suspended. The understanding that the mission of the church is evangelism with the focus on the "saving of a person's soul" as the gospel, can be traced to the fundamentalist theological influence that viewed social engagement as an activity that is inextricably linked to the loss of sound doctrine, spiritual dynamism, and a watering down of the gospel.[11] This anthropocentric theological perspective on mission is evidenced by a singular focus or evangelism rather than a theocentric focus on God's mission. Evangelical theology therefore must seek an understanding of *missio Dei* in light of a missional hermeneutical reading of the Bible. Wright provides us with a precise definition of what a missional hermeneutic is:

> A missional hermeneutic is not content to call for obedience to the Great *Commission* (though it will assuredly include that as a matter of non-negotiable importance), nor even to reflect on the missional implications of the Great *Commandment*. Behind both, it will find the Great *Communication* – the revelation of God's identity, God's action in the world and God's saving purpose for all creation. Moreover, for the fullness of this communication, we need the Bible in all its parts and genres, for God has given us no less.[12]

Stålsett argues that "A theology from above, from God, is reflected and manifested in theology from below. A theology from below joins revelation and praxis. In this dialogue of the divine with the humane, theology takes shape, and Christ becomes incarnate to every new generation."[13] Harold therefore argues that mission primarily is God's mission and the church is invited to

---

10. Chester and Timmis, *Total Church* (Wheaton: Crossway, 2008), 103.

11. Hack, "A Relevant Praxis in Applied Ecclesiology." DTh Thesis, University of Durban, 1993.

12. C. H. J. Wright, *The Mission of God* (Downers Grove: IVP Academic, 2006), 60–61.

13. G. Stålsett, "Does Theology Need the Church?" *Ministerial Formation* (July 1999), 5.

participate with God on mission, establishing his reign.[14] Thus, the church is an instrument God uses to bring about wellbeing in the world. The bringing out of wellbeing calls for understanding the *missio Dei* that includes justice and compassion.

This understanding militates toward an understanding that compassion and justice are part of God's mission. Few themes are more central to any dialogue on social ethics than justice and compassion. Chester writes that the "*missio Dei* incorporates the proclamation and demonstration of the gospel."[15] It is not that evangelism and social involvement are to be taught/done alongside each other. They are to be integral parts of each other. However, our evangelism must lead one to social engagement and *vice versa*. For Chester, "Integral mission can be defined as bringing the whole of life under the lordship of Jesus Christ and includes the affirmation that there is no biblical dichotomy between evangelistic and social responsibility."[16] Because God shows concern for the poor and the foreigner, the church must do the same. Jesus Christ furthers this preferential option for the poor, the oppressed and the marginalised in his statements and his ministry. Compassion is, therefore, the process of self-dispossession, where one puts self at risk, in a free re-enactment of the dispossessed state of those who suffer.

The biblical word for justice in the Old Testament finds its meaning in two different words. The first is *sedaqah*, which is translated as righteousness in the English Bible, means to fix something as it should be, when applied to human actions and relationships it means to speak with conformity to what is right and expected (Lev 19:36; Deut 25:15). The second word is *sapat*, which refers to legal action over a wide range (judicial action), to act as a lawgiver, to act as a judge by arbitrating between parties in conflict thus passing judgment. In its broadest definition, it means "to put things right." Another word that speaks of justice but in a more personal sense is *mispat*. This word is frequently used about widows and children, and it means to act justly for those who might be exploited in an unfair world. Wright states that while there is considerable overlap between these words, *sedaqah* is something you aim to achieve, whereas *mispat* is something you do.[17] Metzger states "biblical justice involves making

---

14. G. Harold, "Compassionate Acts as Missional Theosis: A Call to the Evangelical Church of Southern Africa (ECSA)," *Pharos Journal of Theology*, 103 (2022).

15. T. Chester, ed., *Justice, Mercy and Humility: Integral Mission and the Poor* (London: Paternoster, 2002), 19.

16. Chester, *Justice, Mercy and Humility*, 19.

17. C. J. H. Wright, *The Mission of God's People* (Grand Rapids: Zondervan, 2010), 91.

individuals, communities, and the whole of the cosmos, by upholding both goodness and impartiality."[18] It stands at the centre of true religion, according to James, who says that the kind of "religion that God our father accepts as pure and faultless is this: to look after orphans and widows in their distress and to keep oneself from being polluted by the world" (James 1:27). Padilla states that simple liberation from human masters is not what the gospel speaks.[19] Freedom in Christian terms means subjection to Jesus Christ as Lord, deliverance from bondage to sin and Satan, the heart that has been made free with the freedom of Christ cannot be indifferent to the human longing for deliverance from economic, political, or social oppression.

The *missio Dei* and the Kingdom Of God

Bosch observes the theocentric perspective of mission:

> In the new image mission is not primarily an activity of the church but an attribute of God. God is a missionary God. It is not the church that has a mission of salvation to fulfill in the world; it is the mission of the Son and the Spirit through the Father that includes the church. Mission is seen as a movement from God to the world; the church is viewed as an instrument for that mission. There is a church because there is mission, not vice versa. To participate in mission is to participate in the movement of God's love toward people since God is a fountain of sending love.[20]

A missional church is therefore an authentic community of faith that primarily directs its ministry focus outward toward the context in which it is located and to the broader world beyond. The church thus is to be a light to the world, a testimony that Israel failed to be, the city on a hill promised by Isaiah. The church now manifests the kingdom to the nations. So "live such good lives among the pagans that, though they accuse you of doing wrong, they may see your good deeds and glorify God on the day he visits us" (1 Peter 2:12). Therefore, the church becomes the missional agent through the *missio Dei* the mission of God as engaged in the world.

---

18. P. L. Metzger, "What is Biblical Justice?" *Christianity Today* (2010), https://www.christianitytoday.com/pastors/2010/summer/biblicaljustice.html.

19. R. Padilla, "What is Integral Mission?" (2016), https://poetice.org/wp-content/uploads/2016/02/Rene-Padilla.pdf.

20. D. Bosch, *Transforming Missions: Paradigm Shifts in Theology of Mission* (New York: Orbis, 1991), 390.

Within evangelicalism, the kingdom of God and its significance to the mission of God were brought into focus over the years. Two differing opinions exist within evangelicalism first, that there is personal salvation now, but it is only limited to a conscious confession of Christ. The leading advocates of this position were John Stott, the architect of the Lausanne Covenant and Ron Sider. Both Sider and Stott insist that "the Kingdom of God in the New Testament is fundamentally a Christological concept, and such may exist only where Jesus Christ is consciously acknowledged as Lord."[21] Sider and Stott further state that this righteous kingdom influences and impacts the society it engages in.[22] Therefore, political liberation is not salvation. With this focus upon the kingdom of God, speaking of salvation means a new life, community, and world.

The new community is the church, and the new world only concerns the future. Sider and Parker argue that the salvation language as such cannot be used to refer to the imperfect emergence of justice and peace in society at large before the return of Christ. Similarly, Sider agrees that no New Testament claim speaks of the kingdom of God apart from the conscious confession of Christ.[23] Therefore, salvation is personal and only refers to a personal confession of Jesus Christ to receive the salvation that Christ offers, thus enabling a person to live out the radical demand of this new kingdom. This understanding equates God's kingdom with the church. This understanding is the most pervasive within evangelicalism; prominence is given to belief rather than praxis.

The alternative view is that corporate salvation is not limited to the conscious confession of Christ is held by Vinay Samuel and Chris Sugden. They argue that salvation is not only experienced individually, but also that experience of the kingdom goes far beyond the church, through which the promise and grace are brought into society.[24] They maintain that God's kingdom is seen not only in the church but also "in God's activity in the world beyond the church as just relationships that belong to the kingdom are established in society."[25] The argument is made that one does not have to personally confess

---

21. R. Sider and J. Stott, *Evangelism, Salvation and Social Justice* (Nottingham: Grove Books, 1977), 23.

22. Sider and Stott, *Evangelism, Salvation and Social Justice*, 23.

23. R. Sider and J. Parker, "How Broad is Salvation in Scripture?" in *Word and Deed*, ed. B. Nicholas (Exeter: Paternoster, 1985), 85–108, 104, 105.

24. V. Samuel and C. Sugden, "Evangelism and Social Responsibility," in *Word and Deed*, ed. B. Nicholas (Exeter: Paternoster, 1985), 189–214, 211.

25. V. Samuel and C. Sugden, "God's Intention for the World," in *The Church in Response to Human Need*, eds. V. Samuel and C. Sugden (Oxford: Regnum, 1987), 52.

Christ to experience the benefits of the kingdom of God. The kingdom as it exists now, Samuel and Sugden posit "it is not an individual spiritual entity. It is corporate and permeates with its influence all life."[26] Although transformation is not salvation, in the sense of regeneration and justification, people who do not confess Christ will also benefit from the transformation that the kingdom brings to society. In responding to the Lausanne Covenant, they state that "the term redemption is appropriate for God's activity outside the church, when we see it not simply as the experience of regeneration, forgiveness and new life, but in wider terms as God's activity in fulfilling his intention for the world."[27] The church's mission then is seen as a subset of a larger mission that is part of God's mission to the world and not the entirety of God's work in the world.[28] The shift to a theocentric understanding of missions began to gain attention through the work of Karl Barth. In 1932 Barth used the term God's *missio*. He broke from tradition by grounding mission first in God and not in the human endeavour of the church. Hartenstein used the same theology but changing the term to "*missio Dei*" which suggests that from eternity past the Triune God has been on a mission.[29] The next step in the crystallisation of the concept came in 1952 during the meeting of the International Missionary Council in Willingen, Germany. Vicedom claims that the significance of the *missio Dei* indicates that mission is not the "mission of the church or our mission, but a work that belongs to God."[30] Wright states this quite aptly "mission flows from the inner movement of God in personal relationships."[31] In the aftermath of these thoughts, a shift in the church's thinking started to occur and the theology of mission moved from believing that the church owns a mission, to God being a missionary father, and the church participating in his mission. It is not that Jesus gave the church a mission, but rather Jesus invites the church to join the Father's pre-existing outreach. Bosch claims that when one focuses on church

---

26. Samuel and Sugden, "God's Intention for the World," 141.

27. Samuel and Sugden, "God's Intention for the World," 153.

28. E. Arthur, "*Missio Dei* and the Mission of The Church" (2013), https://www.wycliffe.net/more-about-what-we-do/papers-and-articles/missio-dei-and-the-mission-of-the-church/.

29. S. B. Bevan and R. P. Schroeder, *Constants in Conflict: A Theology of Mission for Today* (New York: Orbis Books, 2004), 291.

30. G. F. Vicedom, *The Mission of God: An Introduction to a Theology of Mission* (St. Louis: Concordia, 1965), 5.

31. C. J. H. Wright, "Mission as a Matrix for Hermeneutics and Biblical Theology," in *Out of Egypt: Biblical Theology and Biblical Hermeneutics*, eds. C. Bartholomew, M. Moller, and R. Parry (Grand Rapids: Zondervan, 2004), 133.

planting as a primary means of mission, the church ceases to point to "God or to the future, it points to itself."[32]

An Evangelical Construct of the *missio Dei*

While plenty of resources deal with the *missio Dei* from an ecumenical perspective many believe it has run its course because it has lost its biblical grounding. However, many evangelical theologians embrace the *missio Dei* by re-conceptualising aspects of it within evangelical theology.[33]

The theoretical model (Figure 1) of Wright will be used to give clarity and build a framework for understanding what "holistic mission" looks like.[34] The *missio Dei* in Wright's model encompasses three overarching themes: Building the church (using evangelism and teaching), serving society (using justice and compassion) and caring for creation. The unique aspect of Wright's model is its christological emphasis in the *missio Dei* which is consistent with evangelical teaching.

The transactional nature of the gospel is critically brought into focus by asking "What is the gospel?" Stearns rightfully observes that "in our evangelistic efforts to make the gospel accessible and simple, we seem to have boiled it down to a kind of fire insurance that one can buy."[35] McKnight argues that evangelicals have developed a "salvation culture" not a "gospel culture," thus reducing the gospel to a message of personal salvation that is not consistent with Scripture.[36] He states that the soterian-centred gospel of the plan of salvation and method of persuasion is given so much weight that they crush the story of Jesus. Therefore, for him, salvation is the intended result of the gospel story of Jesus. McKnight defines the gospel "as the work of God to restore humans to union with God and communion with others, in the context of community, for the good of others in the world."[37] Newbigin argues that the very God-centred nature of

---

32. Bosch, *Transforming Missions*, 332.

33. Wright, *The Mission of God* (Downers Grove: InterVarsity Press, 2006); Chester, *Justice, Mercy and Humility*; S. McKnight, *The King Jesus Gospel* (Grand Rapids: Zondervan, 2011); J. G. Flett, "Missio Dei: A Trinitarian Envisioning of a Non-Trinitarian Theme," *Missiology* 37, no. 1 (2009): 5–18; P. Pikkert, *The Essence and Implication of Missio Dei* (Ontario: ALEV Books, 2017).

34. Wright, "The Church and Global Mission" (2012), https://www.wycliffe.net/more-about-what-we-do/papers-and-articles/the-church-and-global-mission/.

35. R. Stearns, *Hole in the Gospel* (Nashville: Thomas Nelson, 2009), 17.

36. McKnight, *The King Jesus Gospel*, 28–33.

37. S. McKnight, *Embracing Grace: A Gospel for All of Us* (Massachusetts: Paraclete Press, 2005), xiii.

mission implies that the church is an essential role player.[38] Thus, the purpose of the church is to support the *missio Dei*, and the church on mission exists to serve the community through the Lordship of Christ, acknowledging the *imago Dei* in all of God's children.

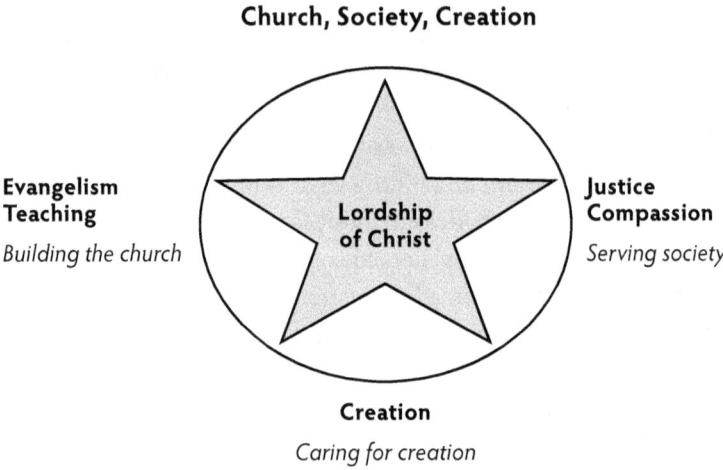

Figure 1. Model for Holistic Mission[39]

Conclusion

This *missio Dei* is praxis-orientated, taking into consideration the context of the lived social realities of the people. Thus, a post-colonial understanding of evangelicalism calls for an integrated approach to mission. The *missio Dei* is therefore liberation from spiritual and social oppression. To teach God's mission only with a soterian focus is to negate the function of the whole gospel, which is to transform the people and the world in which we live. For evangelicals to become relevant, we must redress our colonial assumption concerning the mission of God.

---

38. Newbigin, *The Open Secret*, 76.

39. Wright, "Holistic Mission" (2012), https://www.wycliffe.net/more-about-what-we-do/papers-and-articles/holistic-mission/.

References

Arthur, E. "*missio Dei* and the Mission of the Church." https://www.wycliffe.net/more-about-what-we-do/papers-and-articles/missio-dei-and-the-mission-of-the-church/. 2013.
Bevan, S. B., and R. P. Schroeder. *Constants in Conflict: A Theology of Mission for Today*. New York: Orbis Books, 2004.
Bosch, D. *Transforming Missions: Paradigm Shifts in Theology of Mission*. New York: Orbis, 1991.
Browning, D. *A Fundamental Practical Theology*. Minneapolis: Fortress, 1991.
Chester, T., ed. *Justice, Mercy and Humility: Integral Mission and the Poor*. London: Paternoster, 2002.
Chester, Tim, and Steve Timmis. *Total Church: A Radical Reshaping around Gospel and Community*. Wheaton: Crossway, 2008.
Englesviken, T. "*Missio Dei*: The Understanding and Misunderstanding of a Theological Concept in European Churches and Missiology." *International Review of Mission* 92, no. 367 (2003): 481–97.
Flett, J. G. "Missio Dei: A Trinitarian Envisioning of a Non-Trinitarian Theme." *Missiology* 37, no. 1 (2009): 5–18.
Guder, D. L., ed. *Missional Church: A Vision for the Sending Church in North America*. Cambridge: Eerdmans, 1998.
Hack, W. E. "A Relevant Praxis in Applied Ecclesiology for the Evangelical Church in South Africa." D'Th Thesis, University of Durban Westville, 1993.
Harold, G. "An Evangelical Understanding on the *Missio Dei* as Inclusion of Justice: A Critical Theological Reflection." *Pharos Journal of Theology*, 100 (2019): 1–10.
_____. "Compassionate Acts as Missional Theosis: A Call to the Evangelical Church of Southern Africa (ECSA)." *Pharos Journal of Theology*, 103 (2022): 1–11.
McKnight, S. *Embracing Grace: A Gospel for All of Us*. Massachusetts: Paraclete Press, 2005.
_____. *The King Jesus Gospel*. Grand Rapids: Zondervan, 2011.
Metzger, P. L. "What is Biblical Justice?" *Christianity Today* (2010). https://www.christianitytoday.com/pastors/2010/summer/biblicaljustice.html.
Newbigin, L. *The Open Secret: An Introduction to the Theology of Mission*. London: SPCK, 1995.
Padilla, R. "My Theological Pilgrimage," in *Shaping a Global Theological Mind*, Darren C. Marks, ed. Burlington: Ashgate, 2008, 127–38.
_____. "What is Integral Mission?" (2016). https://poetice.org/wp-content/uploads/2016/02/Rene-Padilla.pdf.
Pikkert, P. *The Essence and Implication of Missio Dei*. Ontario: ALEV Books, 2017.
Said, E. *Orientalism*. New York: Vintage Books, 1978.
Samuel, V., and C. Sugden. "Evangelism and Social Responsibility." In *Word and Deed*. Edited by Bruce Nicholas. Exeter: Paternoster, 1985, 189–214.

_____. "God's Intention for the World." In *The Church in Response to Human Need*. Edited by V. Samuel and C. Sugden. Oxford: Regnum, 1987, 128–60.

Sider, R., and J. Parker. "How Broad is Salvation in Scripture?" In *Word and Deed*. Edited by B. Nicholas. Exeter: Paternoster, 1985, 85–108.

Sider, R., and J. Stott. *Evangelism, Salvation and Social Justice*. Nottingham: Grove Books, 1977.

Stålsett, G. "Does Theology Need the Church?" *Ministerial Formation* (July 1999), 5.

Stearns, R. *Hole in the Gospel*. Nashville: Thomas Nelson, 2009.

Swinton, J., and H. Mowat. *Practical Theology and Qualitative Research*. London: SCM Press, 2006.

Vicedom, G. F. *The Mission of God: An Introduction to a Theology of Mission*. St. Louis: Concordia, 1965.

Wright, C. J. H. "Mission as a Matrix for Hermeneutics and Biblical Theology." In *Out of Egypt: Biblical Theology and Biblical Hermeneutics*. Edited by C. Bartholomew, M. Moller, and R. Parry. Grand Rapids: Zondervan, 2004, 102–43.

_____. *The Mission of God*. Downers Grove: InterVarsity Press, 2006.

_____. *The Mission of God's People*. Grand Rapids: Zondervan, 2010.

_____. "The Church and Global Missions" (2012). https://www.wycliffe.net/more-about-what-we-do/papers-and-articles/the-church-and-global-mission/.

_____. "Holistic Mission" (2012). https://www.wycliffe.net/more-about-what-we-do/papers-and-articles/holistic-mission/.

11

Sub-Saharan Migration Transit Patterns from Africa and into Europe

Mitch Hamilton

Enter through the narrow gate; for the gate is wide and the way is broad that leads to destruction, and there are many who enter through it. For the gate is small and the way is narrow that leads to life, and there are few who find it. Matthew 7:13–14 NASB

Introduction

Movement is a human condition, and each of us is on a road of transition, both physically and spiritually. In an African context, the depths of one's pockets often direct those transitional pathways. The rich can fly anywhere they can afford to secure a visa. Over 90 percent of Africa's nineteen million intercontinental migrants are of this economic class.[1] They depart at a staggering rate of nearly five hundred thousand per year.[2] Due to their wealth, they have the luxury of

---

1. M. McAuliffe and A. Triandafyllidou, "World Migration Report 2022," Geneva: International Organization for Migration (2021), https://publications.iom.int/books/world-migration-report-2022, 61. See also Maureen Achieng, "African Migration Report: Challenging the Narrative," Addis Abba: International Organization for Migration (2020), https://publications.iom.int/system/files/pdf/africa-migration-report.pdf, 2, 5. Nearly 85 percent of intercontinental and 93 percent of all African transcontinental migration is regular, meaning that these migrants were able to secure the necessary papers to live and work in their chosen country. This implies a level of wealth that is only found in the top tier of the African economy.

2. McAuliffe and Triandafyllidou, 60.

following legal, comfortable, and often profitable pathways. Many will make their way to the European Union, where at least five million fellow Africans hold residence permits.[3] The poor, on the other hand, can only go where their feet will carry them. Generally, that is not very far.

This chapter is neither about the mobility of the very rich nor the immobility of the very poor. Each could be its own study and certainly deserves additional treatment. Instead, this chapter focuses on those in the middle, who tend to make decisions out of desperation, and who often land in desperate situations. Gravity has a way of taking water from the mountains to the coast, typically following the path of least resistance. African migration is not that different. Until now, the places of origin have been the domain of anthropologists, places of destination the challenge for politicians, and transitional zones the focus of journalists. But it is the church, in each of those zones, that has been tasked to globally engage those on the move, care for their needs, and to share the hope of the gospel.

Indeed, there is a way that leads to life, and its gate is often found on these broad migratory pathways. It is at these intersections where unreached peoples, often from unreachable places, encounter Christianity for the first time. Our goal as Christian leaders is to help the people of God to love their migratory neighbours in such a way that they can find that narrow gate and lead them to the life-giving waters of Christ. That begins with understanding.

Motivation for Movement

Migration has been a part of the African landscape for centuries and continues today. The circular routes of shepherds and traders are now followed by students, laborers, and those pursuing a better life. Their numbers are incalculable due to the context, and their movement patterns are nearly impossible to trace. Their motivations, however, are often based on harsh geopolitical and economic realities.

---

3. It is hard to know the total number of Africans legally present in the European Union. Estimates range from 5–7 million. See D. Tarchi, et al., "Atlas of Migration – 2021," Luxembourg: Publications Office of the European Union (2021), https://knowledge4policy.ec.europa.eu/atlas-migration_en#citation and "Statistics on Migration to Europe: Overall Figures of Immigrants in European Society," Brussels: European Commission (2022), https://ec.europa.eu/info/strategy/priorities-2019-2024/promoting-our-european-way-life/statistics-migration-europe_en. See also Fabrizio Natale, Silvia Migali, and Ranier Munz, "Many More to Come? Migration From and Within Africa," Luxemburg: Publications Office of the European Union (2018), https://op.europa.eu/en/publication-detail/-/publication/547c4391-41eb-11e8-b5fe-01aa75ed71a1/language-en.

Africa is a continent of fifty-four countries and is continually in turmoil. In 2017 alone, half the world's violent conflicts were in Africa.[4] These conflicts have, to date, created over twenty-four million internally displaced persons.[5] Making the situation more complicated, poverty plagues sub-Saharan Africa. Nine out of ten people live on less than US$5.50 per day, and four on less than US$1.90.[6] Twenty-eight of the world's twenty-nine poorest countries are found in sub-Saharan Africa.[7] One should, therefore, not be surprised to find localized movements as people seek physical and economic security in nearby urban centres. Unfortunately, life in the city offers little comfort. Nearly 60 percent of African city dwellers live in slum conditions.[8] Those who arrive with backgrounds of displacement are often pressed into those spaces, greatly accentuating the problem.[9]

Nevertheless, some are positioned to escape the above realities. Across Africa, over twenty-one million residents have moved to a neighbouring country to find employment.[10] Another nineteen million have left the continent. For much of the twentieth century, Europe has been a destination of choice for her colonial citizens. Migrants from West and North Africa played a vital role in her post-war reconstruction and economic development.[11] Many chose

---

4. Tsion Tadesse Abebe, "Breaking Africa's Cycle of Forced Displacement," Institute for Security Studies (26 February 2019), https://issafrica.org/iss-today/breaking-africas-cycle-of-forced-displacement.

5. UNHCR, "Global Trends: Forced Displacement in 2021," Copenhagen: UNHCR Statistics and Demographics Section (2022), https://reliefweb.int/attachments/66a09358-2cf3-448c-846a-d29f9f8f768c/62a9d1494.pdf14.

6. Samuel Freije-Rodriguez and Michael Woolcock, "Poverty and Shared Prosperity 2020: Reversals of Fortune," Washington, DC: The World Bank (2020), https://www.worldbank.org/en/publication/poverty-and-shared-prosperity, 3, 40.

7. Nirav Patel, "Figure of the Week: Understanding Poverty in Africa," Washington, DC: Brookings Institute (21 November 2018), https://www.brookings.edu/blog/africa-in-focus/2018/11/21/figure-of-the-week-understanding-poverty-in-africa/.

8. Somik Vinay Lall, J. Vernon Henderson, and Anthony J. Venables, "African Cities: Opening Doors to the World," Washington, DC: World Bank Group (2017), https://documents.worldbank.org/en/publication/documents-reports/documentdetail/854221490781543956/africas-cities-opening-doors-to-the-world, 38.

9. Marie McAuliffe and Martin Ruhs, "World Migration Report 2018," Geneva: International Organization for Migration (2018), https://worldmigrationreport.iom.int/world-migration-report-2018, 230.

10. McAuliffe and Triandafyllidou, "World Migration Report 2022," 60. See also Christina Udelsmann Rodrigues, "Intra-African Migration," Belgium: Directorate-General for External Policies (2020), https://www.europarl.europa.eu/cmsdata/226385/Study_Intra-Africa_Migration.pdf, 2, 23.

11. John Salt and Hugh D. Clout, *Migration in Post-War Europe: Geographical Essays* (London: Oxford University Press, 1976), 88, 98, 155.

to settle, build their lives, and give birth to subsequent generations. They, in turn, would contribute richly to a diverse European citizenship. Contemporary Europe is a reflection of these immigrants, and her economy would quickly collapse if those movements were to end.

Undoubtedly, migration to Europe has become a financial boom for sub-Saharan Africa. In 2021, the African diaspora remitted an estimated US$45 billion to their home communities.[12] For many families, these remittances are a lifeline that guarantees their survival and often fund future movements. In some countries, such as The Gambia, those remittances exceed a third of their national GDP.[13] The resources often supplement governmental programs and help provide vital infrastructure projects such as roads, sanitation, schools, and hospitals. These benefits are tangible and, as such, become a powerful motivator to sponsor the next generation of migrants.

Means of Movement

It is crucial for missional strategists to understand that while the first step of migration may be voluntary, subsequent steps are often beyond the control of the typical migrant. One may think of migration in terms of the currents found in a river. Multiple factors can contribute to the rate of flow and the degree of turbulence encountered along the way.[14] Initially, the waters can move very fast as they descend through the foothills, but they can slow dramatically when they reach coastal zones. Perhaps it may be helpful to visualize the facilitation of migration along three parameters.

- **Direct Migration:** This migratory pathway is legal and almost entirely under the control of the migrant. It often involves little more than purchasing a bus or plane ticket and a willing relative to offer a place to live. This is the typical route for regional movements and the preferred route of the African upper class for international

---

12. Achieng, "African Migration Report," 118.

13. Dilip Ratha et al., "Recovery: Covid-19 Crisis Through a Migration Lens," Washington, DC: KNOMAD-World Bank (2021), https://www.knomad.org/sites/default/files/2021-11/Migration_Brief%2035_1.pdf, 58–59.

14. Nikos Papastergiadis, *The Turbulence of Migration: Globalization, Deterritorialization, and Hybridity* (Cambridge: Polity Press, 2000), 5–6.

travel. As noted above, as much as 90 percent of all Africa to Europe migration is along regular pathways.[15]
- **Smuggling Networks:** These networks, in essence, facilitate the illegal entry of people into countries different from their own for material benefit.[16] Those without legal and financial options will pay smugglers to create irregular pathways to arrive at their desired destination. Although these migrants may not be in control for much of the voyage, their movements are generally considered voluntary.[17] The route selected and the rate of success often depend upon the resources available for the journey.
- **Human Trafficking:** Criminal networks often work with smugglers to exploit migrant populations, particularly along the Western and Central routes. This exploitation often involves coercion or force, ending with their involuntary participation in the drug, sex, and labour markets.[18] These networks can be local, whereby victims are immediately pressed into service, or they can be international, transporting individuals across the Mediterranean.

It is not uncommon for an African migrant to begin their journey as a direct migrant, to then encounter a circumstance that dictates the use of a smuggler, and in the end, become the victim of a trafficker. Once again, things can change quickly along these migration routes.

---

15. Africa Europe Foundation Debate, "Africa and Europe: Facts and Figures on African Migrations," London: Mo Ibrahim Foundation (2022), https://mo.ibrahim.foundation/sites/default/files/2022-02/aef_summit_african-migrations.pdf, 3.

16. Phillipe Fargues and Marzia Rango, "Migration in West and North Africa and Across the Mediterranean," Geneva: International Organization for Migration (2020), https://publications.iom.int/books/migration-west-and-north-africa-and-across-mediterranean, 231.

17. Antoine Meyer, "People on the Move: Handbook of Selected Terms and Concepts," Paris: UNESCO (2008), https://unesdoc.unesco.org/ark:/48223/pf0000163621, 44.

18. "Overview of Serious and Organized Crime in North Africa," Lyon: INTERPOL (2018), https://www.interpol.int/content/download/12852/file/Overview%20of%20Serious%20and%20Organized%20Crime%20in%20North%20Africa-EN.pdf, 21–23.

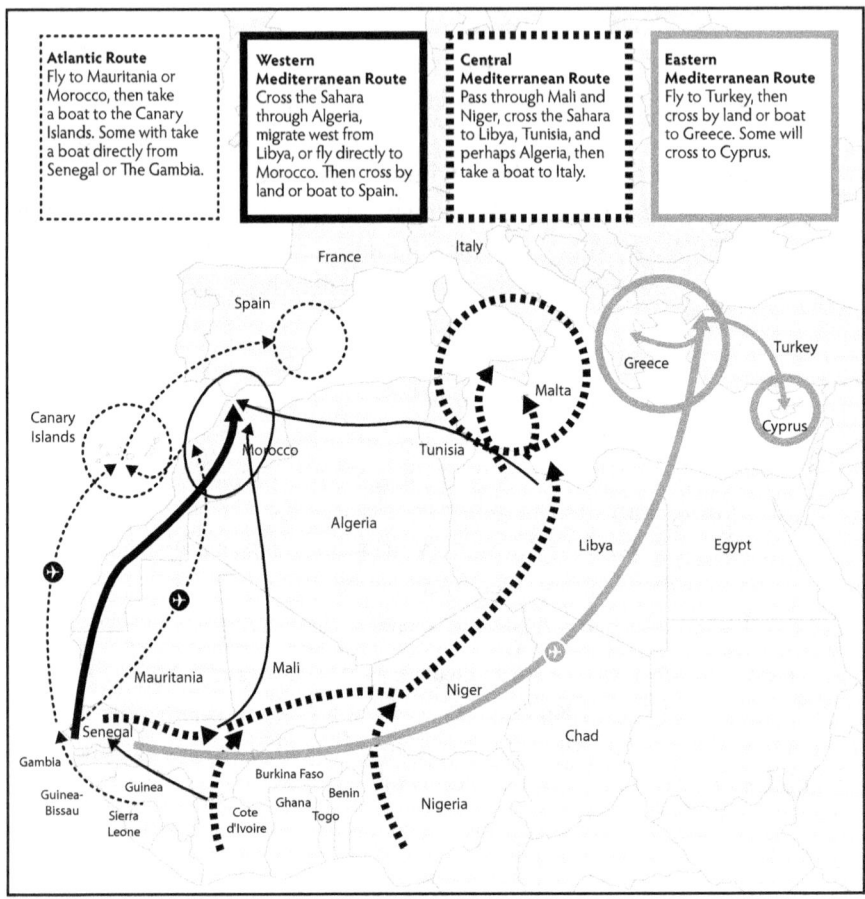

Figure 1. Migration Routes

Routes

There are four distinct irregular migration routes departing the African continent. Each of these four routes originates from a different circumstantial and financial context. All require smuggling networks, although perhaps at various points along the way. For example, on the Eastern Route, migrants can legally fly to Turkey before securing assistance to cross into Greece or Cyprus illegally. On the Atlantic Route, migrants can fly directly to Morocco before paying a smuggler to transport them to the Canary Islands. On the Central and Western routes, those with fewer resources must engage smugglers earlier, incurring greater risks as they cross the Sahara Desert and the Mediterranean Sea.

Smuggling networks typically use two financial schemes. The first is a "pay in advance" approach. This can be expensive, with some charging over US$20,000.[19] Migrants testify that with enough money, one can secure a visa to almost anywhere in the world. At these elevated costs, the success rate is high, and the time from departure to arrival can be as short as a few weeks.[20] This is the predominant scheme for the Eastern Mediterranean Route and for those who fly to Morocco and then take the boats to the Canaries.

The second is a "pay as you go" approach. In this scheme, migrants progressively pay for each leg of the journey. Those with adequate resources have an assistant, family or friend, who will deposit money with the smuggler at each stage of the trip. Others anticipate that they will have to work along the way to complete the journey. Obviously, the latter scheme draws upon migrants with many fewer resources than the former and places them at greater risk of falling into the hands of traffickers. Their journey can take years, and many will become stranded or die along the way.

Risks

The risks sub-Saharans face along migratory pathways can be significant, particularly for those who utilize the "pay as you go" model. The primary service smugglers can offer is assistance with transit through dangerous territories. Without an organized system, one could not safely pass the bandits, jihadists, militias, traffickers, and government-controlled borders. The smugglers will also provide the logistics for the journey across the Sahara and the Mediterranean. Even with this level of assistance, the routes can be arduous and very dangerous. Thus, the first and most obvious risk is loss of life.

The journey across the Sahara Desert is perilous. As many as twenty-five migrants are packed into a pickup truck, travelling in caravans for the four-day journey. If a truck breaks down or anyone falls out, they are mercilessly left

---

19. The Migrant Project "Irregular Migration to Europe: What is the Cost for Nigerians?" Durban: The Migration Project (2022), https://www.themigrantproject.org/?s=cost+for+nigerians&post_type=page#:~:text=what%20is%20the-,cost,-for%20Nigerians%3F.

20. The price smugglers pay for falsified visas and European passports can be exorbitant. See Alarm Phone, "Border Business – How the E.U.'s Militarization Fuels Smuggling Networks Between North Africa and Spain," Berlin: Watch the Med (2022), https://alarmphone.org/en/2022/03/31/border-business/?post_type_release_type=post.

behind. It is unknown how many perish in the desert, but the numbers are estimated to be one in five.[21] The challenge is in knowing how many make the attempt. One three-month period in early 2022 saw fifteen thousand migrants pass through a single checkpoint in Northern Chad.[22] If one were to consider the annual flows through all the checkpoints, the numbers would become staggering.

One can draw the same conclusions for the voyage across the Mediterranean, where one in thirteen boats is lost, or the Atlantic passage to the Canary Islands, where an estimated one in three boats is lost.[23] The International Organisation Migration (IOM) Missing Migrants project attempts to count the deaths, but their numbers are statistically developed from anecdotal reports.[24] How many leave African beaches cannot be measured. Ultimately, the total number of lives lost will likely never be known.

A second risk is to expend all of one's resources and consequently become stranded along the way. Currently, there are an estimated one million Sub-Saharan African migrants in the Maghreb with no way home.[25] They cannot move forward due to a lack of finance and cannot return home out of shame. Many have exhausted their family's resources. From their perspective, silently suffering in their transit country is better than openly facing their

---

21. The numbers who die in the desert are notoriously difficult to estimate. Relevant reports and migrant testimonials lead this author to believe that the number is at least one in five. See Tom Miles and Stephanie Nebehay, "Migrant Deaths in the Sahara Likely Twice Mediterranean Toll: UN," London: Reuters (12 October 2017), https://www.reuters.com/article/us-europe-migrants-sahara/migrant-deaths-in-the-sahara-likely-twice-mediterranean-toll-un-idUSKBN1CH21Y. See also Fargues and Rango, "Migration," 152.

22. Safa Msehli, "IOM Deplores Deaths at Chad-Libya Border and Calls for Stronger Action for Migrant Protection," Geneva: International Organization for Migration (1 July 2022), https://www.iom.int/news/iom-deplores-deaths-chad-libya-border-and-calls-stronger-action-migrant-protection.

23. As with desert crossings, the loss of life in the Mediterranean is challenging to assess. One in thirteen does not factor the bodies not found. Migrants testify that the losses in the Atlantic are over 30 percent. See Kate Dearden et al., "Calculating Death Rates in the Context of Migration Journeys: Focus on the Central Mediterranean," Berlin: International Organization for Migration – Global Migration Data Analysis Center (2021), https://publications.iom.int/system/files/pdf/mortality-rates.pdf, 7.

24. Achieng, "African Migration Report," 32.

25. Morocco has an estimated seven hundred thousand sub-Saharans and another four hundred to nine hundred thousand in Libya. The numbers in Tunisia and Algeria are not known. See Driss El Ghazouani, "A Growing Destination for Sub-Saharan Africans, Morocco Wrestles with Immigrant Integration," Washington, DC: Migration Policy Institute (2 July 2019), https://www.migrationpolicy.org/article/growing-destination-sub-saharan-africans-morocco. See also "IOM Libya Migrant Report Round 41," Geneva: International Organization for Migration (February–April 2022), https://displacement.iom.int/sites/default/files/public/reports/DTM_Libya_R41_Migrant_Report_FINAL.pdf.

home community in failure. By this point, their poverty is extreme, and the disillusionment among many migrants is very high. Acts of desperation, such as storming the fences at the Spanish enclaves of Melia or Ceuta, become an effort of last resort.[26]

A third risk is to arrive in Europe and then face the reality that their dream may have been empty. Between one and two million sub-Saharan migrants are living in Southern Europe, many working for abhorrently substandard wages.[27] Traffickers have coerced others by paying for their passage across the water, only to be then forced to labour in the fields of Spain or Italy.[28] Many women began their journey trusting that their contact offered a respectable job at a decent wage, only to find later that they had been sold as sex workers in European brothels.[29] Many of the above migrants testify that after having made the journey, they now regret having ever left home.[30]

Rewards

It is evident, however, that the perceived rewards can also be alluring. One cannot discount the fact that many sub-Saharans successfully arrive in Europe. Smugglers are like travel agents, selling package deals to willing customers. They operate by word of mouth and gain new clients through the success and satisfaction of previous customers. Creative marketing can mediate known risks. There is a scheme along the Western and Atlantic Routes where migrants are offered a guaranteed trip. In other words, if their boat fails or is intercepted by the Moroccan Coast guard, they can have a seat in the next boat for free.

---

26. Phone, "Border Business."

27. As with most other statistics, one must try to make an informed estimate of the number of migrants in any one place. Non-official migration reports and agricultural labour needs lend to this figure. See Marie Granier, "Migrant Seasonal Workers in the European Agricultural Sector," Brussels: European Parliamentary Research Service (2021), https://www.europarl.europa.eu/RegData/etudes/BRIE/2021/689347/EPRS_BRI(2021)689347_EN.pdf, 6.

28. Waly, "Global Report on Trafficking in Persons 2020," 110. See also Aryn Baker, "It Was as If We Weren't Human: Inside the Modern Slave Trade Trapping African Migrants," *Time* (14 March 2019), https://time.com/longform/african-slave-trade/.

29. "Nigeria Trafficking in Human Beings: Country of Origin Information Report," Geneva: European Asylum Support Office (April 2021), https://euaa.europa.eu/sites/default/files/publications/2021_04_EASO_Nigeria_Trafficking_in_Human_Beings.pdf, 32.

30. The author has spoken with hundreds of migrants around the Mediterranean Rim who testify that the reality of migration is far different from what they perceived when they left home. If given a chance, many would have made very different decisions.

They can do this as many times as they need to be successful. According to one source, the cost of the deal was around six thousand euros.[31]

There is a premise that suggests that if the migrants were only better informed, it would curb illegal movements. Unfortunately, there is a long history of success in the oral traditions of sub-Saharan Africa. Every community testifies to those who gained a measure of wealth due to some form of migration. Like a lottery, the news of a single winner overpowers the realities of the thousands who lose. In an honour/shame culture, few make their losses known. Complicating the matter, Africans have a high tolerance for risk. Suffering, sickness, and death are common. They are a communal people, and the individual's responsibility to contribute to the family's well-being is paramount, even if the risks are high.

This author spoke with a migrant who had twice attempted to take a boat from Senegal to the Canary Islands along the Atlantic Route. They were intercepted by the coast guard and forced to return the first time. The second time their motor failed, and they were shipwrecked on a beach in Mauritania. The loss of life was high. He nodded when asked if he would try a third time. To explain, he imagined a scenario whereby a commander requested his soldiers to volunteer for what would likely be a suicide mission. They would save their people and come home as heroes if they were successful. If they died while fighting, they would die with honour. The only shame would be in refusing to volunteer. In his culture, that level of shame would be too much to bear.

Conclusion

Matthew, the Gospel writer, may have been drawing from migratory realities as he described the pathway to spiritual life. Every road leads somewhere, even if one does not understand the true destination when the choice is made. Paul reminded the Athenians in Acts 17:26–27 that God walks among the migrants and can be found on every route:

> He made from one man every nation of mankind to live on all the face of the earth, having determined their appointed times and the boundaries of their habitation, that they would seek God if perhaps they might grope for him and find him, though he is not far from each one of us. (NASB)

---

31. Phone, "Border Business."

From a missional perspective, focusing on the migrants and the churches that lie in the transitional zones can be strategic. Places of origin and places of destination are undoubtedly important, but receptivity to the gospel becomes either clouded by the intense desire to "go" or diminished by the energy required to assimilate into their new home. Transitional spaces, however, tend to be places where hopelessness abounds, and hearts are hungry for a message that brings life. And while it is possible to locate such zones geographically, we must remember that almost every urban context is a place of transition for someone. This reality compels the modern church in every location to seek to engage those who pass by her doors daily.

By his Spirit, we can be assured that our Lord guides each migrant along the places of transition for a purpose. At each step of the way, God brings an increased awareness of their need for him and an increased opportunity to engage those who can share the good news of redemption. May the light of the church, both in Africa and Europe, shine brightly on their pathways and guide them to Christ.

References

Abebe, Tsion Tadesse. "Breaking Africa's Cycle of Forced Displacement." Institute for Security Studies (26 February 2019). https://issafrica.org/iss-today/breaking-africas-cycle-of-forced-displacement.

Achieng, Maureen. "African Migration Report: Challenging the Narrative." Addis Abba: International Organization for Migration (2020). https://publications.iom.int/system/files/pdf/africa-migration-report.pdf.

Africa Europe Foundation Debate, "Africa and Europe: Facts and Figures on African Migrations." London: Mo Ibrahim Foundation (2022). https://mo.ibrahim.foundation/sites/default/files/2022-02/aef_summit_african-migrations.pdf.

Alarm Phone. "Border Business – How the E.U.'s Militarization Fuels Smuggling Networks Between North Africa and Spain." Berlin: Watch the Med (2022). https://alarmphone.org/en/2022/03/31/border-business/?post_type_release_type=post.

Baker, Aryn. "It Was as If We Weren't Human: Inside the Modern Slave Trade Trapping African Migrants." *Time* (14 March 2019). https://time.com/longform/african-slave-trade/.

Dearden, Kate, Dionis Sanchez, Julia Black, and Frank Laczko. "Calculating Death Rates in the Context of Migration Journeys: Focus on the Central Mediterranean." Berlin: International Organization for Migration – Global Migration Data Analysis Center (2021). https://publications.iom.int/system/files/pdf/mortality-rates.pdf.

El Ghazouani, Driss. "A Growing Destination for Sub-Saharan Africans, Morocco Wrestles with Immigrant Integration." Washington, DC: Migration Policy Institute

(2 July 2019). https://www.migrationpolicy.org/article/growing-destination-sub-saharan-africans-morocco.

Fargues, Phillipe, and Marzia Rango. "Migration in West and North Africa and Across the Mediterranean." Geneva: International Organization for Migration (2020). https://publications.iom.int/books/migration-west-and-north-africa-and-across-mediterranean.

Freije-Rodriguez, Samuel, and Michael Woolcock. "Poverty and Shared Prosperity 2020: Reversals of Fortune." Washington, DC: The World Bank (2020). https://www.worldbank.org/en/publication/poverty-and-shared-prosperity.

Granier, Marie. "Migrant Seasonal Workers in the European Agricultural Sector." Brussels: European Parliamentary Research Service (2021). https://www.europarl.europa.eu/RegData/etudes/BRIE/2021/689347/EPRS_BRI(2021)689347_EN.pdf.

"IOM Libya Migrant Report Round 41." Geneva: International Organization for Migration (February–April 2022). https://displacement.iom.int/sites/default/files/public/reports/DTM_Libya_R41_Migrant_Report_FINAL.pdf.

Lall, Somik Vinay, J. Vernon Henderson, and Anthony J. Venables. "African Cities: Opening Doors to the World." Washington, DC: World Bank Group (2017). https://documents.worldbank.org/en/publication/documents-reports/documentdetail/854221490781543956/africas-cities-opening-doors-to-the-world.

McAuliffe, Marie, and Martin Ruhs. "World Migration Report 2018." Geneva: International Organization for Migration (2018). https://worldmigrationreport.iom.int/world-migration-report-2018.

McAuliffe, M., and A. Triandafyllidou, "World Migration Report 2022." Geneva: International Organization for Migration (2021). https://publications.iom.int/books/world-migration-report-2022.

Meyer, Antoine. "People on the Move: Handbook of Selected Terms and Concepts." Paris: UNESCO (2008). https://unesdoc.unesco.org/ark:/48223/pf0000163621.

Miles, Tom, and Stephanie Nebehay. "Migrant Deaths in the Sahara Likely Twice Mediterranean Toll: UN." London: Reuters (12 October 2017). https://www.reuters.com/article/us-europe-migrants-sahara/migrant-deaths-in-the-sahara-likely-twice-mediterranean-toll-u-n-idUSKBN1CH21Y.

Msehli, Safa. "IOM Deplores Deaths at Chad-Libya Border and Calls for Stronger Action for Migrant Protection." Geneva: International Organization for Migration (1 July 2022). https://www.iom.int/news/iom-deplores-deaths-chad-libya-border-and-calls-stronger-action-migrant-protection.

Natale, Fabrizio, Silvia Migali, and Ranier Munz. "Many More to Come? Migration From and Within Africa." Luxemburg: Publications Office of the European Union (2018). https://op.europa.eu/en/publication-detail/-/publication/547c4391-41eb-11e8-b5fe-01aa75ed71a1/language-en.

"Nigeria Trafficking in Human Beings: Country of Origin Information Report." Geneva: European Asylum Support Office (April 2021). https://euaa.europa.eu/

sites/default/files/publications/2021_04_EASO_Nigeria_Trafficking_in_Human_Beings.pdf.

"Overview of Serious and Organized Crime in North Africa." Lyon: INTERPOL (2018). https://www.interpol.int/content/download/12852/file/Overview%20of%20Serious%20and%20Organized%20Crime%20in%20North%20Africa-EN.pdf.

Papastergiadis, Nikos. *The Turbulence of Migration: Globalization, Deterritorialization, and Hybridity*. Cambridge: Polity Press, 2000.

Patel, Nirav. "Figure of the Week: Understanding Poverty in Africa." Washington, DC: Brookings Institute (21 November 2018). https://www.brookings.edu/blog/africa-in-focus/2018/11/21/figure-of-the-week-understanding-poverty-in-africa/.

Ratha, Dilip, Eung Ju Kim, Sonia Plaza, Ganesh Seshan, Elliot Riordan, and Vandana Chandra. "Recovery: Covid-19 Crisis Through a Migration Lens." Washington, DC: KNOMAD-World Bank (2021). https://www.knomad.org/sites/default/files/2021-11/Migration_Brief%2035_1.pdf.

Rodrigues, Christina Udelsmann. "Intra-African Migration." Belgium: Directorate-General for External Policies (2020). https://www.europarl.europa.eu/cmsdata/226385/Study_Intra-Africa_Migration.pdf.

Salt, John, and Hugh D. Clout. *Migration in Post-War Europe: Geographical Essays*. London: Oxford University Press, 1976.

"Statistics on Migration to Europe: Overall Figures of Immigrants in European Society." Brussels: European Commission (2022). https://ec.europa.eu/info/strategy/priorities-2019-2024/promoting-our-european-way-life/statistics-migration-europe_en.

Tarchi, D., F. Sermi, S. Kalantaryan, P. Saslama, M. Avlvaraz, and M. Belmonte. "Atlas of Migration – 2021." Luxembourg: Publications Office of the European Union (2021). https://knowledge4policy.ec.europa.eu/atlas-migration_en#citation.

The Migrant Project "Irregular Migration to Europe: What is the Cost for Nigerians?" Durban: The Migration Project (2022). https://www.themigrantproject.org/?s=cost+for+nigerians&post_type=page#:~:text=what for Refuees%20is%20the-,cost,-for%20Nigerians%3F.

United Nations High Commision for Refugees (UNHCR), "Global Trends: Forced Displacement in 2021." Copenhagen: UNHCR Statistics and Demographics Section (2022). https://reliefweb.int/attachments/66a09358-2cf3-448c-846a-d29f9f8f768c/62a9d1494.pdf.

Waly, Ghada. "Global Report on Trafficking in Persons 2020." Vienna: United Nations Office on Drugs and Crime (2020). https://www.unodc.org/unodc/en/data-and-analysis/glotip.html.

12

Human Trafficking in Africa and Beyond

Anne Abok

The notion of the rights of every human person is significant to any engagement that touches on dignity, flourishing, and freedom. Sometimes this flourishing depends on the ability to move freely from one geographical location to the other. In other instances, such movement can lead to abuse of human rights in the form of irregular migration, human smuggling or human trafficking. Every person has the right to freedom, movement, and a life that is free from exploitation and violence as stated in the Universal Declaration of Human Rights, articles 1, 2, 3, 4, and 5.[1]

The right to freedom of movement is when people can lawfully move freely within a country and have the right to leave any country. It also includes the right to enter a country of which they are citizens. Such movements when undertaken unlawfully frequently end up in egregious crimes where fundamental human rights are abused. Hence, migration in itself is not a problem, but when it is done unlawfully it may result in cases of irregular migration, human smuggling, or human trafficking. Migration happens everywhere in the world and Africa is not left out. As a matter of fact, a finding by The Africa Europe Facts and Figures of African Migration estimates that in 2020, the total number of African migrants was 40.6 million.[2]

---

1. Universal Declaration of Human Rights, https://www.un.org/en/udhrbook/pdf/udhr_booklet_en_web.pdf.

2. Africa and Europe Facts and Figures on African Migrations, https://www.friendsofeurope.org/wp/wp-content/uploads/2022/01/AEF_Summit_African-Migrations.pdf.

Irregular Migration, Human Smuggling, and Human Trafficking

It is necessary for us in this chapter to look at these three concepts that are often interchanged. According to the Glossary on Migration of the International Organization on Migration (IOM), irregular migration is "the movement of persons that takes place outside the laws, regulations, or international agreements governing the entry into or exit from the State of origin, transit or destination." IOM further points that "categories of migrants who may not have any other choice but to use irregular migration channels can include refugees, victims of trafficking, or unaccompanied migrant children."[3] Human smuggling refers to "the procurement, in order to obtain, directly or indirectly, a financial or other material benefit, of the irregular entry of a person into a State Party of which the person is not a national or a permanent resident."[4]

According to the Palermo Protocol, human trafficking is defined as

> The recruitment, transportation, transfer, harbouring or receipt of persons, by the means of threat or use of force or other forms of coercion, of abduction, of fraud, of deception, of the abuse of power or of a position of vulnerability or of the giving or receiving of payments or benefits to achieve the consent of a person having control over another person, for the purpose of exploitation.[5]

It further clarifies that "exploitation shall include, at a minimum, the exploitation of the prostitution of others or other forms of sexual exploitation, forced labour or services, slavery or practices similar to slavery, servitude or the removal of organs."[6] Human trafficking involves exploitation of people's vulnerability. It is therefore a form of modern slavery. Modern slavery is the severe exploitation of other people for personal or commercial gain and it is happening all around us. We do not see it because we are not looking. It occurs when people are subjected to forced labour of any sort with little or no wages. Such people can be enslaved in businesses that we all benefit from, as domestic servitude in our houses or even on our farms.

---

3. International Organization for Migration (IOM), "Glossary on Migration," https://publications.iom.int/system/files/pdf/iml_34_glossary.pdf.

4. UN Report, "Protocol against the Smuggling of Migrants by Land, Sea and Air, supplementing the United Nations Convention against Transnational Organized Crime," UNTS vol. 2241, New York (15 November 2000).

5. UN Report, "Protocol to Prevent, Suppress and Punish Trafficking in Persons, Especially Women and Children, Supplementing the United Nations Convention against Transnational Organized Crime," UNTS 2237, New York (15 November 2000).

6. UN Report, "Protocol to Prevent, Suppress and Punish Trafficking in Persons."

The 2022 report from International Labour Organization (ILO), Walk Free, and International Organization for Migration (IOM) reveals that almost fifty million people are estimated to be trapped in modern slavery worldwide. 49.6 million people are living in modern slavery (forced labour and forced marriage) on any given day. This is an increase of ten million since the last global estimates in 2017. Out of them one in four are children and 54 percent are female.[7] Africa is facing an alarming growth in human trafficking and modern slavery due to the myriad of conflicts that plague the continent.

Forms of Modern Slavery

Modern slavery takes many forms and most common is human trafficking.[8] Traffickers use violence, threats or coercion to recruit or lure their vulnerable victims with promises of a better life. The victims are then recruited with false promises of things like jobs, education and in some cases romance, where the traffickers play the "lover boy" and promise marriage. The victims are then transported, or harboured from a source community through a transit community to their destination for the purpose of exploitation through forced prostitution, labour, criminality, forced marriage or organ removal. The exploitation and harbouring can start happening from the source, transit and finally in the destination communities if the victims are at all able to survive the rigorous conditions. It is important to note that transporting or moving the victim does not define trafficking as it can take place within a single country, or even within a single community. What trafficking really means on a day-to-day basis is that girls are groomed and forced into sexual exploitation or tricked into accepting risky jobs or sports offers and trapped in forced labour at building sites, farms or factories, selling drugs and women.

Work is good and there is dignity in labour but not when people are forced to offer services against their will under threat and exploitative conditions. Then it becomes modern slavery in the form of forced labour. Debt Bondage or Bonded Labour is when the desperate poor borrow money and are forced to work or offer some sort of services to pay back. The conditions are usually exploitative. In some African countries like Nigeria, juju, a form of witchcraft,

---

7. Walkfree Report, "Global Estimate of Modern Slavery: Forced Labor and Forced Marriage," Geneva (September 2022), https://cdn.walkfree.org/content/uploads/2022/09/12142341/GEMS-2022_Report_EN_V8.pdf.

8. Anti-Slavery International, "What is modern slavery?" https://www.antislavery.org/slaverytoday/modernslavery/.

is used to keep the victims in this bondage. They are made to swear oaths in the shrine of the juju priest that they will work and pay up their debt to the madam, they will maintain the secrecy of the agreement and that they will never escape. Victims have paid up to sixty thousand Euros for their freedom. This form of slavery is the most common in all parts of the world.[9]

Descent-based slavery is mostly cultural and occurs where people are treated as property, and their "slave" status is passed down the maternal line, making it challenging for them to break free because they were born into this slavery. An example of their exploitation is when they are made to work without pay, herding animals, working in the fields or in their masters' homes, often in very isolated places. They can be inherited, sold, or given away as gifts or wedding presents. Children can be taken away from their mothers at an early age and put to work without ever attending school. Women and girls in this form of slavery often face sexual abuse and rape, and often have to bear their masters' children. In turn, their children will also be owned by their masters. Those who managed to leave their masters are stigmatized as belonging to the "slave-class" and discriminated against, even a long time after they left.[10] Children are also vulnerable globally to modern day slavery. Children make up one in four of the global modern slavery figures as seen in the above statistics. This includes child trafficking, child soldiers, child marriages and child domestic servitude. Another form is child begging, which in some parts of West Africa is the abuse of the religious notion of *Almajiri*. The word *Almajiri* is derived from the Arabic word *Almuhajirun* meaning an emigrant for the purpose of empowering children with Islamic knowledge. Some religious tutors, *mallams*, take more pupils than they can care for and then the children are made to beg for survival.[11] These children are seen begging on the streets, hawking, and engaging in acts that are injurious to their health as children. The *Almajiris* are thus exploited, resulting in a form of trafficking. Forced or early marriage is another form of trafficking, when a person is forced into marriage

---

9. UN Report, "Debt bondage remains the most prevalent form of forced labour worldwide" (15 September, 2016), https://www.ohchr.org/en/press-releases/2016/09/debt-bondage-remains-most-prevalent-form-forced-labour-worldwide-new-un.

10. Anti-Slavery International, "Descent-based slavery," https://www.antislavery.org/slavery-today/descent-based-slavery/.

11. Maryam M. Jungudo and Johnmary Ani Kelechi, "Justice and human rights violations: A study on Almajirici in northern Nigeria," in *Justice and Human Dignity in Africa: Collection of essays in honour of Professor Austin Chukwu*, eds. G. M. T. Emezue, Inge Kosch and Kangel Maurice (USA: IRCHSSA and HPC Books, 2014), 40–55.

against their will. Often victims of such early or forced marriages are children who are sold to older men. Most child marriages can be considered slavery.[12]

The figures of human trafficking are staggering. A United Nations report in 2016 found that globally 51 percent of identified victims of trafficking are women, 28 percent children and 21 percent men. 72 percent of people exploited in the sex industry are women and 63 percent of identified traffickers were men and 37 percent women. 43 percent of victims are trafficked domestically within national borders.[13] According to the Infographic on Human Trafficking Trends in Sub-Saharan Africa, an estimated 9.24 million individuals are enslaved in all of Africa, making up 23 percent of the total global enslaved population. Africa accounts for 8 percent of child sex trafficking in the world. The countries with the highest rates of modern slavery in sub-Saharan Africa are Eritrea (.93 percent of population), Burundi (.40 percent), Central African Republic (.22 percent), Mauritania (.21 percent), and South Sudan (.21 percent).[14]

Out of the 49.6 million modern slavery in the world as of 2021, 6.3 million are in forced commercial sexual exploitation.[15] Countries in West Africa tend to detect more victims than other countries in Sub-Saharan Africa, mainly children and for the purpose of forced labour. Out of 4799 victims detected in 26 Sub-Saharan Africa countries, 3336 were in West Africa including 2553 children.[16] This is because of the influence of economic and cultural practices in perpetuating trafficking and creating a market for traffickers in the region. Transnational organised crime is also deeply entrenched across West Africa, making trafficking in human beings a dominant variant.[17]

Sex trafficking occurs when victims are recruited, trapped, transported and exploited sexually. Sexual exploitation is any actual or attempted abuse of a position of vulnerability, differential power, or trust, for sexual purposes,

---

12. Aye Olatunde, Eleanor Taylor-Nicholson, and Victoria Nwogu, eds. *Access to Justice for Trafficked Persons in Nigeria: A Handbook for Legal Actors and Assistance Providers* (Abuja, Nigeria: NAPTIP, 2009), https://gaatw.org/publications/AtJHandbook_Final.pdf.

13. UNODC Report, "Global Report on Trafficking in Persons" (2020).

14. UN Office for Drugs and Crime (UNODC), "Human Trafficking Trends in Sub-Saharan Africa Infographic," http://asec-sldi.org/news/current/human-trafficking-sub-saharan-africa/.

15. Walkfree Report, 2.

16. UN Office for Drugs and Crime, "Global Report on Trafficking in Persons" (2020), https://www.unodc.org/documents/data-and-analysis/tip/2021/GLOTiP_2020_15jan_web.pdf.

17. Daniel Ogunniyi and Oladimeji Idowu, "Human trafficking in West Africa: An implementation assessment of international and regional normative standards," *The Age of Human Rights Journal* 19 (2022): 165–85, https://revistaselectronicas.ujaen.es/index.php/TAHRJ/article/view/6851/7339#:~:text=The%20West%20African%20region%20has,level%20assessment%20in%20West%20Africa.

including, but not limited to, profiting monetarily, socially, or politically from the sexual exploitation of another.[18] A National Overview of Prostitution and Sex Trafficking Demand Reduction Efforts, Final Report, points out that the difference between sex trafficking and prostitution is consent. Prostitution is usually classified as willful, and the person is usually involved of their own accord. Sex trafficking happens when the victim is forced against their will into sexual servitude.[19]

Pull and Push Factors of Human Trafficking in Africa

In looking at the root causes of sex trafficking, there are certain concepts that illuminate the explanation. These are often referred to as the pull and push factors, determinants or drivers. IOM says these drivers are complex and interlinking, influencing "an individual, family or population group's decisions relating to migration and displacement."[20]

The main push factors of African sex trafficking victims are economic, violence, and environmental crises. Poor economic conditions and underdevelopment are seen as the root cause of sex trafficking from Africa. Other factors such as corruption, poor governance, food insecurity, lack of infrastructure, unemployment, inequality, and weak policies contribute to the wide divide between the haves and the have-nots. The expectation of most African families is that their children grow up to become providers. This pressure makes most girls see themselves as the "sacrificial lamb" expected to bring financial freedom to their families. However, in the fourteen years of my work in the anti-trafficking space, I have seen that it is more the "poverty of values," not just the poverty of resources, that is the main push factor. This has to do with mindsets and cultural beliefs that the grass is always greener on the other side.

Violence as a result of religious crises and persecutions, human rights violations, armed conflicts, insecurity, and territorial displacement caused by *Boko Haram, Al Shabaap*, or kidnappings have made the continent a hard place for the youth to birth their dreams and pursue their visions of a better

---

18. Kofi A. Annan, "United Nations Secretariat, Secretary-General's Bulletin Special Measures for Protection from Sexual Exploitation and Sexual Abuse," UN Doc ST/SGB/2003/13, https://documents-dds-ny.un.org/doc/UNDOC/GEN/N03/550/40/PDF/N0355040.pdf, 1.

19. Michael Shively et al., "A National Overview of Prostitution and Sex Trafficking Demand Reduction Efforts," A report submitted to US Dept of Justice (30 April, 2012), https://www.ojp.gov/pdffiles1/nij/grants/238796.pdf, 1.

20. IOM, "Glossary on Migration."

life. Environmental crises such as natural disasters, climate change, and environmental degradation when inadequately managed can result in climate migration, which puts victims at a higher risk of sex trafficking.

The pull factors on the other hand can be as a result of the response to demand for labour or skills. Africans who believe there is a greener pasture beyond their borders are constantly migrating in search of this "better life." This search often plunges them into grave dangers which can even cost their lives. One would think that the many stories of horror that accompany such migrations would deter other aspiring Africans from embarking on such voyages. But not so, for some reason, the resilience of the African spirit kicks in and a fresh determination rises. The intending migrant then emphatically proclaims that they believe their own journey would be different. "God will help me . . ." they often say or you hear phrases like "I have faith in God to see me through. My God will not abandon me . . ."

In asking whether they know what lies ahead of them when they get to Europe, most say they see themselves working and earning good money to look after their families. They are fixed on this singular vision for a better life and it comes at high cost. Some are aware that the job that awaits them is that of selling sex to pay their debt bondage to earn their freedom before they can pursue their dreams of a better life for their families. International Organization for Migration has estimated that 80 percent of all Nigerian women that make it across the Mediterranean to Italy are forced into the sex trade.[21] In 2008, the Federal German police told our team that 80 percent of the illegal African prostitutes in Europe come from Benin City, Nigeria. They are in debt bondage to "Madams" – women who were mostly sex slaves themselves.

Case Studies

The following two stories illustrate the human trafficking realities in Africa today. Shakira James is from Edo State in Nigeria. She is twenty-nine years old from a family of seven. Shakira dreamt of becoming an artist and a school graduate. She believed travelling outside Nigeria would bring her dreams to reality. She thought she could study abroad. Shakira met the shock of her life when she had to pass through the desert dressed as a Muslim in order to cross over from Nigeria to her destination, which her traffickers said was Malaysia.

---

21. IOM Report, "Arrivals of Sexually Exploited Migrants, Chiefly from Nigeria" (21 July, 2017), https://www.iom.int/news/un-migration-agency-issues-report-arrivals-sexually-exploited-migrants-chiefly-nigeria.

She prayed silently that God would help her return to her country and vowed to help other African youth when rescued. She soon learned that there is no such thing as a greener pasture anywhere. Trusting her traffickers was the biggest mistake she made. She was forced into sex trafficking in Libya, the transit country, jailed from one prison to other with the police always after her. She was trapped and exploited. She had to have sex with strange and violent men until her uterus prolapsed.

Tony on the other hand was a businessman in Nigeria who wanted to become a football professional so that he would provide for his family and especially his sick mother. His brother promised to connect him with a football club in Cape Town, South Africa so he sold his auto spare parts business and joined his brother in Cape Town. After a while, his brother introduced him to selling women and drugs as a way of income, still under the guise of buying time until the football club was ready to absorb Tony. Tony made all the money and gave it to his brother, only for him to realize later that his own younger brother was his trafficker, and he, Tony, was trafficked and used to traffic other young South African women.

Trafficking routes are perilous. Traffickers smuggle their victims from source countries in West Africa to North African countries, like Libya, Algeria, and Morocco as transit, with the intention to reach Europe. The COVID-19 pandemic did not halt irregular migration of victims by land and sea along West African, North African and central Mediterranean routes. Rather, two and a half times as many people arrived in 2020 as in 2019. The European Border and Coast Guard Agency, Frontex, detected over thirty-five thousand six hundred irregular border crossings in 2020 along the Central Mediterranean route, compared to fourteen thousand in 2019. More than eleven thousand nine hundred people were returned to Libya in 2020 after being intercepted by the Libyan Coast Guard and more than 983 drowned trying to reach European shores. The largest irregular border crossing in the EU in 2020 was detected among people arriving along the Central Mediterranean route, followed by the Atlantic route from the West African coast to the Canary Islands, Spain.[22]

---

22. UNODC, "Key Findings on Characteristics of Migrant Smuggling: West Africa, North Africa, and the Central Mediterranean" (20 May 2021), https://www.unodc.org/res/som/docs/Observatory_Storymap_1_Final_2021.05.19.pdf.

A Call to the Global Church

Migration has been occurring since biblical times. All through Scripture we see that God cares for the migrants, vulnerable, destitute, abused and oppressed people. The story of God's chosen people, Israel, is a story of wandering in many places starting with Abraham. Joseph was sold by his brothers and later by the Midianites (Gen 37:12–28). Sex trafficking is one of the egregious crimes and abuse of human rights, involving some form of migration, mostly illegal. It is in such situations that God expects the global church to reach out to those who are caught up in the web to help them as victims and not to treat them as criminals. In the Bible we find God's concern for the wellbeing of migrants. Repeatedly, the Israelites were instructed to remember the strangers among them and treat them with love, compassion, and justice. God commands the Israelites not to ill-treat them (Exod 22:21) and not to take advantage of them (Deut 24:14).

The issues of compassion, mercy, and justice should be an integral part of the mission of God through the church. Micah 6:8 shows God's requirement for his people to act justly, love mercy and walk humbly with the Lord. In Luke 4:17–19 we see Jesus reading about being anointed by the Spirit of the Lord to proclaim good news to the poor and freedom for the prisoners, setting the oppressed free. The victims of human trafficking have experienced deceit, exploitation, and betrayal from those they trusted. This makes it difficult for them to trust anyone and as a result, they believe there is no one who is genuinely willing to assist them. It is even more disheartening to note that some victims were even trafficked by their religious leaders. Yet we know that all through the Bible God's heart is always with the broken, abused, exploited, marginalized, and discriminated –r eferred to as "one of the least of these" in Matthew 25. Whatever assistance or services we grant them we are doing it for our Lord Jesus. Here are some ways the church should respond towards the freedom of these captives.

Awareness and Prevention: The church should be informed and equipped to expose all forms of trafficking and how to prevent it. The church should address the conditions of vulnerability to trafficking in persons so that it is prevented from taking place in the first instance. This can be done through sound biblical teachings on values, work and wealth. Job and skills acquisition as well as financial assistance should be part of the ministry of the church.

Use and Abuse of Technology: The COVID-19 pandemic has heightened the use of technology in the exploitation of victims. The United Nations Day against trafficking in persons 2022 stated that prevention and awareness-raising activities on the safe use of the internet and social media could help mitigate the risk of people falling victim to trafficking online.[23] The UNODC identifies two types of strategy used by traffickers online – hunting and fishing. Hunting involves a trafficker actively pursuing a victim, typically on social media, initially posturing as a friend and later becoming aggressive as the relationship develops. Fishing strategies involve posting advertisements and waiting for potential victims to respond, often using advertisements for high-paying or prestigious jobs. While high proportions of child-trafficking cases involve platforms with higher levels of anonymity such as social media, cases where the victim is an adult are more likely to involve the use of free-standing webpages and other platforms involving open advertisements.[24] The church can cooperate with the private sector to harness innovation and expertise for the development of sustainable, technology-based solutions to support the prevention and combatting of human trafficking.

Acceptance and Belonging: Human trafficking cuts people off from their families, communities and even their faith in God. The church of Christ should be positioned to welcome them in and give them a sense of belonging. They are part of the body and should be accepted when society stigmatizes them (Rom 15:7–9; Col 3:11). The church must provide a sense of community to victims of trafficking.

Build Networks with Anti-Trafficking Organizations: The church should establish partnerships with specialized credible anti-trafficking agencies with multidisciplinary expertise. Trafficking in persons is a multifaceted crime that calls for a multidisciplinary or multisectoral approach to curb it. These organizations often run professional homes for rehabilitation and restoration and they too need the ongoing support from the church. The church should also be prepared to provide financial and spiritual assistance to such organizations to support them in caring for the victims.

Hospitality: This speaks of crisis intervention, which is the first step in rehabilitation as we learn from Romans 12:13. The victims must receive immediate support from the church in the form of food, clothes, prayers, medicals and referral to a safehouse or shelter for professional and holistic trauma involved support. The church is told to welcome and offer hospitality to people in need (Heb 13:2).

Advocacy: The body of Christ must be equipped to both be the voice of the voiceless and also help amplify the voice of the voiceless (Prov 31:8–9).

---

23. UN Report, "World Day Against Trafficking in Person 30 July," https://www.un.org/en/observances/end-human-trafficking-day.

24. UNODC, "Human Trafficking Trends."

Through advocacy, the church can ensure that victims are not punished for acts they commit after being trafficked. Another form of advocacy is mediation. The church can partner with credible organizations to play a very active role in the mediation between victims and their families or communities in the event of their deportation and re-entry to society. Sometimes victim protection, compensation or assistance is required and in most cases the process of forgiveness, although it should not replace justice.

Strengthen Supply Chain Integrity: Churches should challenge their congregants on how those who run businesses in the private sector should take measures to prevent risky practices, through strengthening their standards and codes of conduct and implementing due diligence measures that specifically address trafficking in persons right from the recruitment phase.

Capacity Building: As the figures show, human migration is on the rise and so is human trafficking. The church's involvement with poor and inadequate information can cause more damage than good. It is therefore imperative for the church to train people in the area of human trafficking, psychosocial support, trauma counseling so that the body of Christ is well informed to better offer assistance. This is a call to churches in originating countries in Africa, and destination countries in Africa and overseas to pay attention to serve the people who are being trafficked.[25]

References

Adeniyi, Olusegun. *From Frying Pan to Fire: How African Migrants Risk Everything in their Futile Search for a Better Life in Europe.* Ibadan: Bookcraft Africa, 2019.

Adichie, Chimamanda N. *The Thing Around Your Neck.* New York: Anchor Books, 2009.

Africa and Europe Facts and Figures on African Migrations. https://www.friendsofeurope.org/wp/wp-content/uploads/2022/01/AEF_Summit_African-Migrations.pdf.

Annan, Kofi A. "United Nations Secretariat, Secretary-General's Bulletin Special Measures for Protection from Sexual Exploitation and Sexual Abuse." UN Doc ST/SGB/2003/13. https://documents-dds-ny.un.org/doc/UNDOC/GEN/N03/550/40/PDF/N0355040.pdf.

---

25. List of Christian agencies engaged in addressing Human Trafficking in Africa are: Polaris Project, MeCAHT, Love Justice, EXIST, Mozaik Institute, Azalea, Coalition to Abolish Slavery and Trafficking (CAST), Rapha House, Girls Educational & Mentoring Services, Zoe International, The A21 Campaign, Not For Sale, NFN, EFN, ICAP, DOAF, Wholistic Outreach, Love 146, Saving Innocence, Journey Out (formerly known as The Mary Magdalene Project), etc.

Anti-Slavery International. "What is modern slavery?" https://www.antislavery.org/slaverytoday/modernslavery/.
Anti-Slavery International. "Descent-based slavery." https://www.antislavery.org/slavery-today/descent-based-slavery/.
Bello, Paul O., and Adewale Olutola. "The Conundrum of Human Trafficking in Africa." In *Modern Slavery and Human Trafficking*. Edited by Jane Reeves. London: Intechopen, 2021. https://www.intechopen.com/chapters/70938.
Ebegbulem, Patricia. *Stop Trafficking in Women and Children: It is a Crime against Humanity*. Third Edition. Ibadan: Book Builders Editions Africa, 2018.
Hepburn, Stephanie, and Rita J. Simon. *Human Trafficking Around the World: Hidden in Plain Sight*. New York: Columbia University Press, 2013.
Hoffman, Alecia D., and Seballa O. Abidde, eds. *Human Trafficking in Africa: New Paradigms, New Perspectives*. New York: Springer, 2021.
International Organization for Migration (IOM) Report. "Arrivals of Sexually Exploited Migrants, Chiefly from Nigeria" (21 July, 2017). https://www.iom.int/news/un-migration-agency-issues-report-arrivals-sexually-exploited-migrants-chiefly-nigeria.
International Organization for Migration (IOM). "Glossary on Migration." https://publications.iom.int/system/files/pdf/iml_34_glossary.pdf.
Jungudo, Maryam M., and Johnmary Ani Kelechi. "Justice and human rights violations: A study on Almajirici in northern Nigeria." In *Justice and Human Dignity in Africa: Collection of essays in honour of Professor Austin Chukwu*. Edited by G. M. T. Emezue, Inge Kosch, and Kangel Maurice. USA: IRCHSSA and HPC Books, 2014, 73–90.
Ogunniyi, Daniel, and Oladimeji Idowu. "Human trafficking in West Africa: An implementation assessment of international and regional normative standards." *The Age of Human Rights Journal* 19 (2022): 165–85. https://revistaselectronicas.ujaen.es/index.php/TAHRJ/article/view/6851/7339#:~:text=The%20West%20African%20region%20has,level%20assessment%20in%20West%20Africa.
Ojediran, Bisi. *A Daughter for Sale*. Quince Books, 2006.
Olatunde, Aye, Eleanor Taylor-Nicholson, and Victoria Nwogu, eds. *Access to Justice for Trafficked Person in Nigeria: A Handbook for Legal Actors and Assistance Providers*. Abuja, Nigeria: NAPTIP, 2009. https://gaatw.org/publications/AtJHandbook_Final.pdf.
Shively, Michael, Kristina Kliorys, Kristin Wheeler, and Dana Hunt. "A National Overview of Prostitution and Sex Trafficking Demand Reduction Efforts." A report submitted to US Dept of Justice (30 April, 2012). https://www.ojp.gov/pdffiles1/nij/grants/238796.pdf.
UN Office for Drugs and Crime (UNODC). "Global Report on Trafficking in Persons." (2020). https://www.unodc.org/documents/data-and-analysis/tip/2021/GLOTiP_2020_15jan_web.pdf.

UN Office for Drugs and Crime (UNODC). "Human Trafficking Trends in Sub-Saharan Africa Infographic." http://asec-sldi.org/news/current/human-trafficking-sub-saharan-africa/.

UN Office for Drugs and Crime (UNODC). "Human Trafficking in West Africa: Three out of four victims are children." (Feb 2021). https://www.unodc.org/nigeria/en/human-trafficking-in-west-africa_-three-out-of-four-victims-are-children-says-unodc-report.html (accessed 24 May 2023).

UN Office for Drugs and Crime (UNODC). "Key Findings on Characteristics of Migrant Smuggling: West Africa, North Africa, and the Central Mediterranean." (20 May 2021). https://www.unodc.org/res/som/docs/Observatory_Storymap_1_Final_2021.05.19.pdf.

UN Report. "Debt bondage remains the most prevalent form of forced labour worldwide." (15 September, 2016). https://www.ohchr.org/en/press-releases/2016/09/debt-bondage-remains-most-prevalent-form-forced-labour-worldwide-new-un.

UN Report. "Protocol against the Smuggling of Migrants by Land, Sea and Air, supplementing the United Nations Convention against Transnational Organized Crime." UNTS vol. 2241, New York (15 November 2000).

UN Report. "Protocol to Prevent, Suppress and Punish Trafficking in Persons, Especially Women and Children, Supplementing the United Nations Convention against Transnational Organized Crime." UNTS 2237, New York (15 November 2000).

UN Report. "World Day Against Trafficking in Person 30 July." https://www.un.org/en/observances/end-human-trafficking-day.

Universal Declaration of Human Rights. https://www.un.org/en/udhrbook/pdf/udhr_booklet_en_web.pdf.

Walkfree Report. "Global Estimate of Modern Slavery: Forced Labor and Forced Marriage." Geneva (September 2022). https://cdn.walkfree.org/content/uploads/2022/09/12142341/GEMS-2022_Report_EN_V8.pdf.

13

Trauma Healing for Refugees: Building Resilience and Restoring Dignity

Clene Nyiramahoro

Introduction

When we hear the word "trauma," we immediately think of wars, natural disasters, or other terrifying events that disrupt people's lives. While that is true, especially based on what we see happening in the world, we also should not lose sight of trauma perpetrated in our homes, our schools, our churches, our communities and many other places where people meet and interact with each other.

Refugees, however, deal with the kind of trauma that Diane Langberg calls "complex trauma." Those victims have never known themselves apart from trauma.[1] They do not know a life without trauma; trauma is their "normal," and it has defined their ways of looking at life and developing relationships with others and with God. Apart from the events that led them to flee their homes, there is trauma that comes with the dehumanizing treatment they get in their host communities and countries, the rejection, the abuse, the absence of justice, the loss of identity, the hopelessness and the overwhelming feeling of constant fear, powerlessness, and loss of self-worth.

---

1. Diane Langberg, "Trauma-Informed care," part of C4SO's Safe Church Training, a mandatory training for clergy (November 4, 2021), https://www.youtube.com/watch?v=xrVJ660AVG8&t=10s.

For the last twenty-eight years, I have lived in Kenya. When I first arrived in Kenya, after being forced to leave my home in Rwanda, I remember feeling despised, rejected, depressed, unworthy, abandoned, angry, and hopeless. I remember going to the United Nations High Commissioner for Refugees (UNCHR), totally unable to explain my case; I relied on the interpreter. I never knew what the interviewer was told. After the interview I went home waiting for the decision. There were only two expected responses: "rejected" or "accepted." When I finally received the letter after the decision had been made, the subject of it was "REJECTED." I was devastated. My journey to where I am today was long, lonely, and painful, but the Lord was near. Just as we read in his word, "The LORD is close to the brokenhearted, he saves those who are crushed in spirit (Ps 34:18 NIV). I had two children then, now I have six. The questions we had then are still loud in our minds: "Who are we?" and "Where is home?"

This chapter is inspired by my personal experience and the experiences of the people we serve who have lived in the refugee camps for several decades, with no hope of being in a place they can call home. The main purpose of this chapter is to help the church in Africa be aware that refugees are our neighbours that the Lord calls us to love and to care for. They are normal people who have only been forced to live in circumstances that make them believe they are less than human. If the church does not care, who will?

Refugees and Forcibly Displaced People in Africa: An Overview

Refugees are a sub-category of migrants. They have been forced to live outside their home countries, totally unprepared. They are in search of places they can call home. They feel forgotten, unwanted, misunderstood. They are in a "static state," and they can feel as if their lives are wasted. Their economic, social, psychological and spiritual needs are enormous. They are always seen as a burden by the host communities. They have lost control of their lives, and their situation is worsened by conditions of living in the refugee camp, a situation of human misery.

According to UNHCR, at the end of 2022 there were over one hundred million around the world who are forced to flee their homes who are internally displaced persons (IDPs), refugees or asylum-seekers, and around thirty million of these are in Africa, in some of the poorest countries in the world.[2] Should we wonder why they are unwanted?

---

2. UNHCR Global Report Africa, https://www.unhcr.org/africa.html.

Understanding Trauma and its Effects

The Trauma Healing Institute (THI) curriculum was initially developed by Margaret Hill, Harriet Hill, Richard Bagge, and Pat Miersma.[3] They defined trauma as a "heart wound" or any "event that causes a person to be overwhelmed with intense fear, helplessness, or horror." They describe it as any life-altering emotional and psychological injury caused by a single event or prolonged or repeated events that overwhelm a person's normal ability to cope. The program was designed to help the church and Christian leaders by offering simple practical ways to support people dealing with trauma in their congregations. It incorporates the best practices of mental health and biblical principles that any trained facilitator can understand and use without prior training in mental health. It exists in more than two hundred languages and in different versions that meet specific needs of people around the world.

People with wounded hearts may display exaggerated startle response, intrusive memories and nightmares. They have a tendency to isolate, and some become violent and aggressive. They tend to relive the experiences by talking about the same thing over and over again, yet they try to avoid anything that brings back painful memories. Some indulge in abusing alcohol or drugs or other destructive behaviors. Having been in a static situation for years, refugees develop what Langberg calls "generational trauma or complex trauma" which is passed on to their children and to their children's children.[4] The lament written by one pastor during a trauma healing workshop in 2021, in a refugee camp in Malawi called Dzaleka, echoes the hearts of many:

> O God, my Lord! Why have you taken so long to come to my rescue? Why have you forgotten me all this time? Why have you abandoned me in this camp? How long will I be called a "refugee"? When are you coming? Lord, when are you coming? Why are you not getting closer to me? Why is my heart full of pain? I am grieving all the time. I can't eat. When I go to bed I can't sleep. Look at my life and my struggles. Where is my resting place? Look! It is now 33 years since I left my country. I have lost hope. Oh God, look at me! Look at my struggles. Come to my help. Take away my pain. I struggle day and night. Forgive me my sins. However,

---

3. Harriet Hill, Margaret Hill, Richard Baggé, and Pat Miersma, *Healing the Wounds of Trauma: How Can the Church Help* (Philadelphia: American Bible Society, 2016), 19.

4. Diane Langberg, "Complex Trauma," Forum of Christian Leaders (January 21, 2016), https://www.youtube.com/watch?v=w9N49JvP_Fw&t=683s. Trauma Healing Institute Community of Practice in Philadelphia, 2018.

even in my struggles I will still wait for you. I will still trust you because I know you are a God of compassion. And I will praise you forever! (Used with permission).

Children born and raised in the camp have no idea what normal life looks like. The only life-model they know is their traumatized mother or father whose lives have been characterized by struggles. Their lives are full of constant stressors. The effects of being trapped in the camp are too serious to ignore. So many young people are working hard to get an education in the hopes of living better lives than what the parents gave them, but the refugee status stops them from getting employment. Those in urban areas are unable to secure proper identification documents, for no government recognizes them. Youths, in their desperation, are ready for anything and they have become soft targets for radicalization, thus becoming serious security threats. We expect them to be normal but they have not experienced any normal beyond the refugee camp. As Langberg puts it, "you cannot do what you cannot imagine."[5] Can this situation be reversed?

Why Trauma Healing?

At the heart of the Trauma Healing Institute program are healing groups. Healing happens in community, where people feel loved, cared for, and safe enough to share their pain. People discover they are not alone and are able to experience God's love in a personal way. Healing is a journey that begins by helping people to start answering life's important questions, such as, "If God loves us, why do we suffer? How can the wounds of my heart be healed? How can I grieve well? What can take my pain away? How can I forgive?" When leading trauma healing sessions, we give each other permission to openly express our burdens, listen to each other, comfort each other, and start building a healing community.

It is in healing groups that new bonds are created, and trust is established. People start to feel safe again to share their hearts without fear of being judged. Gradually a sense of community begins to form. People begin to feel well again. Brokenness is part of life, but God is very close to us when we are hurting (Ps 34:18; Rom 8:19–22). Wounded people come to the place of feeling loved again and special in the eyes of God (Rom 8:35, 38–39). Healing groups are led by people who have had opportunities to process their own pain through

---

5. Langberg, "Trauma-Informed care."

training. It has been said that hurting people hurt people, it can be equally said that healed people heal people. We approach trauma healing not as a program, but a healing journey.

Impact of Trauma Healing in Africa

The trauma healing initiative among the refugees in East and southern Africa was undertaken by SIL International under the Global Diaspora Unit. It was launched in 2019 after realizing that many of the language communities we serve are now scattered due to intractable conflicts, resulting in millions living in refugee camps. In partnership with the International Association for Refugees (IAFR) and There Is Hope in Malawi,[6] we launched our first trauma healing workshop in the Dzaleka refugee camp. By November 2021, more than seventy people had been trained to lead healing groups, at least fifteen training facilitators were certified, and more than three hundred people had been part of healing groups. During our first training, one participant said this:

> I have lived with my pain for a long time. I could not share with anyone. Even though I am a leader in my church, I did not feel safe to share with anyone. I know there are many women who are suffering like me. I am going to bring them together. The same way I have been helped, I need to help others.

This person started hosting healing groups in her house. Women began experiencing healing. The word spread in the camp. Those who completed their sessions never stopped coming. They told her, "We came here and we found help. Where do you want us to go?" As the numbers kept on growing, they started dreaming together. When hearts are healed, hope is built, and life becomes worth living. Now these refugee women, deprived of any kind of support, have started a community-based organisation called Tazama Group.[7] *Tazama*, a Swahili word that means "Come and see," was inspired by Psalm 46:8. They were amazed at what God was doing in their midst and they wanted to be a testimony to the rest of the world. Tazama is a support group with more

---

6. "There is Hope" is a faith-based Malawian Non-Governmental Organization (NGO) founded by Innocent Magambi, providing refugees of Dzaleka Refugee Camp as well as their Dowa host community with access to education and income generating activities and strengthening their spiritual well-being, http://thereishopemalawi.org/about.

7. Tazama is an organization started by Grace Simon Tuli who attended the TH workshop in 2019 done by SIL. In addition to running the TH groups, Tazama started to teach sewing and making soap to help the refugees at camp to give valid skills for income and to occupy their time so that their idle time will be diverted from absorbing traumatic memories of the past.

than three hundred members who, in addition to holding ongoing healing groups, have small income-generating projects. As their dignity is slowly being restored, they feel valued again and useful. They say "now we are no longer stuck, we are slowly climbing the ladder."

The director of SIL's Global Diaspora Team, Sunny Hong, conducted interviews in Dzaleka in November 2021, to find out the impact of trauma healing. Out of forty-one individuals, thirty-five participated in the interview. She found out that people understood the Bible better in healing groups compared to just listening to sermons in church. During the healing group sessions, they have an opportunity to read verses and ponder them together. That way, they said, God's word penetrates their hearts. One interviewee said, "Before trauma healing, through reading the Bible, I could get peace. But, after some hours, the terrible memories came back. After trauma healing it was not the same, some memories are really gone."[8]

The interviewee also liked the "hands-on-approach learning style." Listening to stories similar to theirs, expressing their feeling in a safe environment, and participating in various activities (skits, lament and other art expressions) helped in the process. Another interviewee said:

> Before attending the healing group, I was like a refrigerator. I kept everything (within me). [In the healing group] I learned that I should not keep things in my heart, because it was overcharging. I learned how to cry. Crying made my heart heal. It helped us know how to share our stories, which touch people's hearts. I learned how to pray to God despite our difficulties.

Healing groups helped in "building a community of trust" where participants can share their stories and know their stories will be treated with care and confidentiality.

> When I shared my story (before), it added to my wounds. The person I told would go to another person and talk about it. When I heard from the other person about my story, it increased my pain. It rubbed salt into my wounds again. But now I can talk to a trusted person, and it helps me to release my pain.

Ann Plantinga Kapteyn, in her dissertation on the impact of trauma in Central Africa Republic says:

---

8. Sunny Hong, "Impact of the trauma healing workshop," February 2021.

The program was successful in bringing a measure of emotional healing to participants, but beyond that, it engendered a new understanding of God's love and it helped to restore broken relationships within families, church communities, villages, and even to some degree between people groups.[9]

Trauma disempowers, but healing empowers. Over time, community is built, and resilience is established.

What can the Church in Africa do?

In the midst of hopelessness, refugees in African countries feel abandoned, they feel their voices are not heard, and they feel cheated and taken advantage of. They are in "black spots" where no one sees. They are forced to numb their pain. They struggle with these questions: Where is God? Does he even hear? Is he really just? Even those who have been Christians for a long time question God deep down in their hearts. As my pastor friend put it:

> my experience of being a refugee made me ask several questions about my religious beliefs. Certain questions were almost changing my faith. I started questioning the power of God, his justice and his presence in the world and many other religious matters.

While the church can feel powerless and inadequate, no one is ever prepared for the kind of crisis and vulnerability we see around us. Taking care of the wounded requires a certain amount of vulnerability. However, being silent makes us complicit in the injustices. Refugees are human too! Jesus is asking us to feed his sheep, to gather those that are scattered, to be a true shepherd who feels what the sheep feel. Diane Langberg[10] reminds us that "Jesus used his power to protect, to expose, to restore dignity," and he has given his church power and authority to do the same.

Refugees in Africa need to hear the evangelical church speak like Bishop Allesandro of the Catholic Parish in Kayole, one of the Nairobi areas that hosts many refugees: "You have a special place in the heart of the church, and you help the church to enlarge her heart to manifest her motherhood towards

---

9. Ann Plantinga Kapteyn, "From Horror to Healing: The Impact of the Oral Story-based Trauma Healing Program in Central African Republic," DIS Dissertation, Fuller Seminary, 2022.

10. Diane Langberg, *Redeeming Power: Understanding Authority and Abuse in the Church* (Grand Rapids: Brazos Press, 2020), 173.

the entire human family."[11] John Ortberg once said: "If we have not thought carefully about the intersection of crisis and ministry, we may have neglected the most soul-formative moments that occur in the lives of our people."[12]

Refugees are people in crisis. It is not their fault that they are suffering. Should the church of Christ be concerned? Looking back at Jesus' ministry, he went looking for the rejected, the despised, the abandoned, the weak. Should we not do the same? "The Church needs the wounded, and wounded hearts need the Church."[13] Together we build a stronger healed and healing community.

References

AMCEA. "The Catholic Church stands with You: Bishop Consoles Refugees on World Refugee Day." (July 23, 2022). https://amecea.org/kenya-the-catholic-church-stands-with-you-bishop-consoles-refugees-on-world-refugee-day/.

Friesen, James G., E. James Wilder, Anne M. Bierling, Rick Koepcke, and Maribeth Poole. *Living from the Heart Jesus Gave You*. East Peoria: Shepherd's House, Inc. 2013. http://www.lifemodel.org/.

Hill, Harriet, Margaret Hill, Richard Baggé, and Pat Miersma. *Healing the Wounds of Trauma: How Can the Church Help*. Philadelphia: American Bible Society, 2016. TraumaHealingInstitute.org.

Hong, Sunny. "Impact of Trauma Healing Workshops." Interview, Dzaleka (November 2021).

Kapteyn, Ann Plantinga. "From Horror to Healing: The Impact of the Oral Story-based Trauma Healing Program in Central African Republic." DIS dissertation, Fuller Seminary, 2022.

Langberg, Diane. *Redeeming Power: Understanding Authority and Abuse in the Church*. Grand Rapids: Brazos Press, 2020.

———. "Trauma-Informed care." Part of C4SO's Safe Church Training, this mandatory training for clergy focuses on trauma-informed care (November 4, 2021). https://www.youtube.com/watch?v=xrVJ660AVG8&t=10s.

———. "Complex Trauma: Understanding Treatment. Forum of Christian Leaders (January 21, 2016). https://www.youtube.com/watch?v=w9N49JvP_Fw&t=34s.

---

11. AMCEA, "The Catholic Church stands with You: Bishop Consoles Refugees on World Refugee Day" (July 23, 2022), https://amecea.org/kenya-the-catholic-church-stands-with-you-bishop-consoles-refugees-on-world-refugee-day/.

12. John Ortberg, "Don't Waste a Crisis: Crises, while unwanted, are windows of opportunity for the Cure of Souls" (2011), https://www.christianitytoday.com/pastors/2011/winter/dontwastecrisis.html. (From Menlo Church in California.)

13. James G. Friesen et al., *Living from the Heart Jesus Gave You* (East Peoria: Shepherd's House, Inc. 2013), 1.

Ortberg, John. "Don't Waste a Crisis: Crises, while unwanted, are windows of opportunity for the Cure of Souls." (2011). https://www.christianitytoday.com/pastors/2011/winter/dontwastecrisis.html.

UNHCR. "Global Report Africa." (2022). https://www.unhcr.org/africa.html.

UNHCR. "Protracted Refugee Situations: the Search for Practical Solutions." The State of the World's Refugees (January 1, 2005). https://www.unhcr.org/4444afcb0.pdf.

14

Eucharistic Hospitality: A Brief Postcolonial and Missional Reading

Mabiala Justin-Robert Kenzo

There is no doubt that despite talks of globalization, we live in an increasingly fractured world, in walled-up communities.[1] Despite the booming hospitality industry and "the abundant literature on the topic, the practice of true hospitality is in decline everywhere."[2] The situation calls for a move beyond current commodified market-driven[3] and socio-cultural practices, which equate hospitality with friendliness, for as Elizabeth Newman says, "to equate hospitality with generic friendliness or private service is to domesticate it."[4] True hospitality is extraordinary in nature. It goes against the grain of natural inclinations, calling into question the grounds for practices of hospitality enshrined in immigration laws, civil rights, and ways churches and societies welcome the Other.

The hospitality crisis has caught philosophers' attention, some of them reminding us that hospitality *qua* hospitality is an *aporia*, that is, an

---

1. Wright, "The New Tribalism," *Los Angeles Times* (1992): 1–2; *Miroslav Volf, Exclusion and Embrace: A Theological Exploration of Identity, Otherness, and Reconciliation* (Nashville: Abingdon Press, 1996), 60.

2. Arthur Sutherland, *I Was a Stranger: A Christian Theology of Hospitality* (Nashville: Abingdon Press, 2010), Kindle edition, 114.

3. Sutherland, *I Was a Stranger: A Christian Theology of Hospitality*, 170.

4. Elizabeth Newman, *Untamed Hospitality: Welcoming God and Other Stranger* (Grand Rapids: Brazos Press, 2007), 10–13.

impossible possibility.⁵ Christian theology has had to concede this point.⁶ In a related context, Emmanuel Levinas concludes that totalitarianism, a form of inhospitality, is a "natural outcome of Western metaphysics," as it exalts the Self.⁷ He proposes instead an ethics rooted in the primordial experience of one's responsibility for the Other.⁸ His essential claim is that the Other is inseparable from the Self. In the face-to-face encounter with the Other, one discovers oneself bound not only to the Other but to Transcendence also.⁹ He argues that opening oneself in hospitality is an act of obedience to the timeless moral imperative: "Thou shall not kill."¹⁰ Failure to exercise hospitality amounts to a double homicide – homicide of difference (otherness) and homicide of transcendence (absolute otherness). In contrast, beyond being logical, hospitality is a religious act.¹¹

Jacques Derrida centres his thinking on the distinction between conditional hospitality, which is common and governed by laws [plural] of reciprocity, and absolute hospitality, governed by the law [singular] of unconditionality.¹² Conditional hospitality busies itself with rights, duties, and obligations. It is "regulated" as well as "judicialized" hospitality. It is "engaged in an economy of exchange."¹³ Instead, absolute hospitality involves no reciprocity, debt, or exchange. It is not even based on the rights of strangers. True hospitality lies in this final form, with this implication that it is impossible in practice.¹⁴

Paul Ricoeur's contribution comes into focus in his ontology of oneself as another. He, too, postulates an essential link between Self and Other. To

---

5. Jacques Derrida and Anne Dufourmantelle, *Of Hospitality* (Palo Alto: Stanford University Press, 2000 [1997]).

6. Hans Boersma, *Violence, Hospitality, and the Cross: Reappropriating the Atonement Tradition* (Grand Rapids: Baker Academic, 2004).

7. Emmanuel Levinas, *Totality and Infinity: An Essay on Exteriority*, trans. Alphonso Lingus (Pittsburgh: Duquesne University Press, 1969 [1961]); Boersma, *Violence, Hospitality, and the Cross*, 29.

8. Jean Greisch, "Lévinas Emmanuel (1905–1995)," *Encyclopædia Universalis* (2015), https://www.universalis.fr/encyclopedie/emmanuel-levinas/.

9. Levinas, *Totality and Infinity*, 152; David Gauthier, "Levinas and the Politics of Hospitality," *History of Political Thought* 28, no. 1 (2007): 158–80.

10. Levinas, *Totality and Infinity*, 171.

11. Fleurdeliz R. Altez-Albela, "The Body and Transcendence in Emmanuel Levinas' Phenomenological Ethics," *Kritike* 5.1 (2011): 36–50.

12. Derrida and Dufourmantelle, *Of Hospitality*, 25, 73, 77, 79.

13. Westmoreland, "Interruptions: Derrida and Hospitality," *Kritike* 2, no. 1 (2008): 1–10.

14. Derrida and Dufourmantelle, *Of Hospitality*, 83; Jennie Germann Molz, "Appropriation, Aspiration and the Aporia of Absolute Hospitality," *Hospitality & Society* 5, no. 2-3 (2015): 109–16.

traditional Western ontology of a self-positing subject, he opposes a "wounded" cogito, whose subjectivity he defines in terms of "oneself as another."[15] Unlike Levinas, he construes the Self as an active agent.[16] He also rejects the death of the subject. The wounded Self is still something and not nothing. However, "to say Self is not to say myself," for the Self always implies the Other. So, hospitality is inherent to the being of the Self. It is essential to the maintenance of the world that it helps enlarge, making it habitable for a greater number of individuals, following the ethical perspective of "aiming at the good life *with and for others* in just institutions."[17]

At the heart of the crisis of hospitality is the question of the grounds for its practice. Ancient Romans had reasons why they practiced hospitality, which they codified into law. Likewise, other societies, past and present, have also had their own reasons. For some, hospitality is a matter of honour, and for others a matter of culture, law, or economy. The situation is the same in religions, each one having its reasons for the practice of hospitality. The question then is, why ought Christians to practice hospitality?

Confronted with the *aporia* of radical hospitality, Christian theology has responded with claims of its own. It asserts, for instance, that (1) Christian hospitality is radical; (2) it is grounded in the being of the Triune God; and (3) it is on display in creation, the incarnation, and the life of the Spirit. However, the Eucharist, which is not only "the fullest expression of God's hospitality" but also the re-enactment of all that the church is meant to be,[18] is the site *par excellence* for this manifestation.

In its original setting, the Eucharist is a meal, drawing from Jewish traditions and traditions proper to the Greco-Roman context of the early church.[19] Over time, it developed into a ritual "involving token foodstuffs."[20]

---

15. Paul Ricoeur, *Oneself as Another*, trans. Kathleen Blamey (Chicago: University of Chicago Press, 1994 [1992]), 180.

16. Peter Kemp, "Ricoeur Between Heidegger and Levinas," *Philosophy & Social Criticism* 21, no. 5–6 (1995): 41–61.

17. Ricoeur, *Oneself as Another*, 180.

18. Sutherland, *I Was a Stranger*, 218.

19. Mary Douglas, "Deciphering a Meal," in *Food and Culture: A Reader*, eds. Carole Counihan, Penny Van Esterik, and Alice Julier (New York: Routledge, 2018), 29–47; Dennis E. Smith, *From Symposium to Eucharist: The Banquet in the Early Christian World* (Minneapolis: Fortress Press, 2002).

20. Andrew McGowan, "Changing Courses: Eucharistic Origins," *Westar Institute Seminar Papers* Fall (2017), 35–48.

The biblical model is not to "focus on worship first and then eating together later." Instead, "the meal itself [was] worship" for the early church.[21]

Numerous accounts of Jesus eating meals with others signal the significance of the practice. Its radical turn is seen in how Jesus welcomed outsiders and outcasts to his meals. This phenomenon invites both a postcolonial interpretation where the Eucharist would be best seen as a liminal space for both the manifestation and the intersection of several theological motives, which all have bearings on hospitality. Liminal space implies borderlines and in-betweenness. The Eucharist as a "border experience that lies at the edge of the known and the unknown" is a space of "interconnectedness with each other, with creation, and with God."[22] Such a perspective implies an understanding that goes against the grain of historical debates on the Eucharist, which are, more than not, attempts at the domestication of transcendence.[23] Fossilizing revelation into colonizing theological formulas, whereas Eucharist needs to remain where it belongs, "at the edge of the known and the unknown."[24] Whatever may be said about it, "[t]he presence of Christ in the Eucharist is not something to be seized and held on to but rather is a presence which in eluding our grasp, transforms us."[25]

The Eucharist is a site for the manifestation of the Triune God. Such an assertion is somewhat counterintuitive, for the biblical narratives on the Eucharist put the very name of God under erasure. Yet, as early church fathers like Cyril of Alexandria were acutely aware, one encounters the Triune God, whose meal it is, in these texts. There has been a renewed interest in this link between the Eucharist and the Triune God. While warnings to avoid hurried associations between the Trinity and the Eucharist must be heeded,[26] there is no doubt that some of these are legitimate.[27]

---

21. Kendall Vanderslice, *We Will Feast: Rethinking Dinner, Worship, and the Community of God* (Grand Rapids, Michigan: Eerdmans, 2019), 1.

22. Emma Pavey, "Hospitality as Mission," https://www.academia.edu/9626424/.

23. See William C. Placher, *The Domestication of Transcendence: How Modern Thinking About God Went Wrong* (Louisville: Westminster John Knox Press, 1996).

24. Pavey, "Hospitality as Mission," 1.

25. Andrew Shepherd, *The Gift of the Other: Levinas, Derrida, and a Theology of Hospitality* (Eugene: Pickwick Publications, 2014), Kindle edition, 5976.

26. Graham Ward, "Hosting the Stranger and the Pilgrim," in *Saintly Influence: Edith Wyschogrod and the Possibilities of Philosophy of Religion*, eds. Eric Boynton and Martin Kavka (New York: Fordham University Press, 2009), 63–8; Kevin J. Vanhoozer, *Remythologizing Theology: Divine Action, Passion, and Authorship* (Cambridge: Cambridge University Press, 2010).

27. Caroline Redick, "Making a Home for Refugees," *International Journal of Public Theology* 13, no. 1 (2019): 40–54.

John Zizioulas, for one, argues that the Trinity is the revelation of being as communion. God "has no ontological content, no true being, apart from communion."[28] Key to his interpretation is the notion of perichoresis, which means that each divine person is "coinherent with" or "interpenetrates the other two." Zizioulas does not limit himself to the being of God. He argues that created in the image of God, to be human is to be related in communion.[29] So, before being human praxis, hospitality is primarily a matter of being.

Jürgen Moltmann, for his part, interprets the Trinity as communion in spatial terms. "Through [the] reciprocal indwelling, each of the Persons is once again an inhabitable space for the others."[30] In fact, "[t]hey not only empty themselves out for each other but provide hospitable welcome for one another, hosting each other eternally."[31] For him, this non-hegemonic hospitality is the way of being of the Triune God, which is at work within the Godhead and extends beyond the intra-divine relations. He sees it on display in creation, the phenomena of Shekinah, and the incarnation.[32]

In the Eucharist, the worshiper is invited to the table by this Triune God, not once but again.[33] As sacramental theology has it, each eucharistic moment is not a duplication of a rote activity; rather "an individualized, historically discrete, temporally unrepeatable moment."[34] The command to repeat the action is a repeated invitation to participate in the life of Triune God, namely in God's "perichoretic dance"[35] of non-hegemonic hospitality. The account of the Last Supper narratively takes a radical turn the moment Jesus, the host, presents the bread as "his" body and the cup as the new covenant in "his" blood. The invitation to eat and to drink announces a new dispensation whereby "God's hospitality [indeed, God's life] is made available through the broken body and shed blood of the Son of Man."[36]

---

28. John Zizioulas, *Being as Communion: Studies in Personhood and the Church*. Contemporary Greek Theologians (Crestwood: St. Vladimir's Seminary Press, 1985), 17.

29. Zizioulas, *Being as Communion*, 105–107.

30. Moltmann, *The Trinity and the Kingdom: The Doctrine of God* (Minneapolis: Fortress Press, 1993), 118.

31. Redick, "Making a Home for Refugees," 42.

32. Jürgen Moltmann, *The Trinity and the Kingdom: The Doctrine of God*, 119.

33. Edward L. Smither, *Mission as Hospitality: Imitating the Hospitable God in Mission* (Eugene: Cascade Books, 2021), 51.

34. Kenan B. Osborne, *Christian Sacraments in a Postmodern World: A Theology for the Third Millennium* (Mahwah: Paulist Press, 1999), 58.

35. Stanley J. Grenz and John R. Franke, *Beyond Foundationalism: Shaping Theology in a Postmodern Context* (Louisville: Westminster John Knox Press, 2001), 24.

36. Joshua W. Jipp, *Saved by Faith and Hospitality* (Grand Rapids: Eerdmans, 2017), 86.

The invitation sets worshipers apart as unique participants in the divine life. Amos Yong observes, "There is a sacredness, privacy, and intimacy around the Eucharist that clearly demarcates" insiders from outsiders.[37] Yet, just as the Eucharist closes the circle around the few, it also opens the same circle for the many. The Eucharist invites a radically missional interpretation.

In "Remembering Those for Whom No Table Has Yet Been Set," Arnold Cook tells the story of missionary Einar Mickelson who "prayed an unvarying prayer" during the celebration of the Eucharist: "Lord, today we remember those for whom no table has yet been set."[38] A eucharistic event is a missional event. Matthew and Mark are explicit about it: the blood of the covenant was poured out *for many* (Matt 26:28; Mark 14:24). Paul, likewise, asserts that the entire reenactment, in acts and words, is meant to be a proclamation (1 Cor 11:26). It is no wonder the Eucharist anticipates the eschatological "marriage supper of the Lamb" (Rev 19:9).

In summary, why then hospitality? Christians are called to exercise hospitality for more fundamental reasons than charity, friendliness, and legal or cultural requirements. They do so because, as created in God's image, their true nature is "being-as-communion." In their other-centredness, they welcome the Other as Oneself. Hospitality is a matter of being that translates into praxis. Furthermore, Christians are called to practice hospitality because of their new life in Christ, as displayed in the Eucharist. In the Eucharist, worshipers are invited, as guests, to share in the life of the Triune God whose hospitality extends beyond the few to the many. Divine hospitality, as displayed in the Eucharist, is radically missional.

Finally, as hospitality is a matter of being and praxis, Christian hospitality ought to be modelled after the non-hegemonic perichoresis between the persons of the Triune God, whereby unity embraces differences. The three persons are one, yet the Father is neither the Son nor the Holy Spirit, the Son is neither the Father nor the Holy Spirit, and the Holy Spirit is neither the Father nor the Son. Indeed, the church, including its diaspora, still has a long way to go in welcoming otherness in radical hospitality.

---

37. Amos Yong, *Hospitality and the Other: Pentecost, Christian Practices, and the Neighbor* (New York: Orbis, 2008), 135.

38. Arnold L. Cook, *Remembering Those for Whom No Table Has Yet Been Set*, ed. The Christian and Missionary Alliance in Canada (Camp Hill: Christian Publications, 1994).

References

Altez-Albela, Fleurdeliz R. "The Body and Transcendence in Emmanuel Levinas' Phenomenological Ethics." *Kritike* 5, no. 1 (2011): 36–50.

Boersma, Hans. *Violence, Hospitality, and the Cross: Reappropriating the Atonement Tradition*. Grand Rapids: Baker Academic, 2004.

Cook, Arnold L. *Remembering Those for Whom No Table Has Yet Been Set*. Edited by The Christian and Missionary Alliance in Canada. Camp Hill: Christian Publications, 1994.

Derrida, Jacques, and Anne Dufourmantelle. *Of Hospitality*. Palo Alto: Stanford University Press, 2000 [1997].

Douglas, Mary. "Deciphering a Meal." Pages 29–47 in *Food and Culture: A Reader*. Edited by Carole Counihan, Penny Van Esterik, and Alice Julier. New York: Routledge, 2018.

Gauthier, David. "Levinas and the Politics of Hospitality." *History of Political Thought* 28.1 (2007): 158–80.

Greisch, Jean. "Lévinas Emmanuel (1905–1995)." *Encyclopædia Universalis* (2015). https://www.universalis.fr/encyclopedie/emmanuel-levinas/.

Grenz, Stanley J., and John R. Franke. *Beyond Foundationalism: Shaping Theology in a Postmodern Context*. First Edition. Louisville: Westminster John Knox Press, 2001.

Jipp, Joshua W. *Saved by Faith and Hospitality*. Grand Rapids: Eerdmans, 2017.

Kemp, Peter. "Ricoeur between Heidegger and Levinas." *Philosophy & Social Criticism* 21.5-6 (1995): 41–61.

Levinas, Emmanuel. *Totality and Infinity: An Essay on Exteriority*. Translated by Alphonso Lingus. Pittsburgh: Duquesne University Press, 1969 [1961].

Marshall, I. Howard. *Last Supper and Lord's Supper*. Vancouver: Regent College Publishing, 2006 [1980].

McGowan, Andrew. "Changing Courses: Eucharistic Origins." *Westar Institute Seminar Papers* Fall (2017): 35–48.

Moltmann, Jürgen. *The Trinity and the Kingdom: The Doctrine of God*. Minneapolis: Fortress Press, 1993.

Molz, Jennie Germann. "Appropriation, Aspiration and the Aporia of Absolute Hospitality." *Hospitality & Society* 5, no. 2-3 (2015): 109–16.

Newman, Elizabeth. *Untamed Hospitality: Welcoming God and Other Strangers*. Grand Rapids: Brazos Press, 2007.

Osborne, Kenan B. *Christian Sacraments in a Postmodern World: A Theology for the Third Millennium*. Mahwah: Paulist Press, 1999.

Pavey, Emma. "Hospitality as Mission." https://www.academia.edu/9626424/.

Placher, William C. *The Domestication of Transcendence: How Modern Thinking About God Went Wrong*. Louisville: Westminster John Knox Press, 1996.

Redick, Caroline. "Making a Home for Refugees." *International Journal of Public Theology* 13, no. 1 (2019): 40–54.

Ricoeur, Paul. *Oneself as Another*. Translated by Kathleen Blamey. Chicago: University of Chicago Press, 1994 [1992].

Shepherd, Andrew. *The Gift of the Other: Levinas, Derrida, and a Theology of Hospitality*. Eugene: Pickwick Publications, 2014.

Smith, Dennis E. *From Symposium to Eucharist: The Banquet in the Early Christian World*. Minneapolis: Fortress Press, 2002.

Smither, Edward L. *Mission as Hospitality: Imitating the Hospitable God in Mission*. Eugene: Cascade Books, 2021.

Sutherland, Arthur. *I Was a Stranger: A Christian Theology of Hospitality*. Nashville: Abingdon Press, 2010.

Vanderslice, Kendall. *We Will Feast: Rethinking Dinner, Worship, and the Community of God*. Grand Rapids, Michigan: Eerdmans, 2019.

Vanhoozer, Kevin J. *Remythologizing Theology: Divine Action, Passion, and Authorship*. Cambridge: Cambridge University Press, 2010.

Volf, Miroslav. *Exclusion and Embrace: A Theological Exploration of Identity, Otherness, and Reconciliation*. Nashville: Abingdon Press, 1996.

Ward, Graham. "Hosting the Stranger and the Pilgrim." Pages 63–68 in *Saintly Influence: Edith Wyschogrod and the Possibilities of Philosophy of Religion*. Edited by Eric Boynton and Martin Kavka. New York: Fordham University Press, 2009.

Westmoreland, Mark W. "Interruptions: Derrida and Hospitality." *Kritike* 2, no. 1 (2008): 1–10.

Wright, Robin. "The New Tribalism." *Los Angeles Times* (1992): 1.

Yong, Amos. *Hospitality and the Other: Pentecost, Christian Practices, and the Neighbor*. New York: Orbis, 2008.

Zizioulas, John. *Being as Communion: Studies in Personhood and the Church*. Contemporary Greek Theologians. Crestwood: St. Vladimir's Seminary Press, 1985.

15

Hospitality as a Platform for African Urban Migratory Theology

Afolabi Ghislain Agbèdè

Introduction

Africa is highly multicultural and this multiculturalism is increasing at a very accelerated pace due to migratory movements within the continent and into the continent. The urban population is growing at a very rapid rate. In Cotonou, Pretoria, Yaoundé, and Nairobi, in every big city in Africa, it is easy to meet people of several ethnic groups. Migration is one of the great global realities of our era. It is estimated that 281 million people are living outside their countries of origin, voluntarily or involuntarily.[1] The term "diaspora" is used here to mean people who have relocated from their lands of birth for whatever reason.[2] Diasporas in Africa are currently increasing with the agreement between the United Kingdom and Rwanda, which will make it a welcoming place for migrants. Will this not create other conflicts in Africa and particularly in Rwanda which is already struggling to find geographical space for its population?

Kirsteen Kim affirms that: "Although human beings have been on the move since our ancestors migrated within and out of Africa, the current era

---

1. World Migration Report 2022, https://publications.iom.int/books/world-migration-report-2022.
2. Cape Town 2010 Commitment.

especially has been characterized as 'the age of migration.'"[3] That is the reason why, as children of "Issachar," we need to learn to discern this *Kairos* moment (1 Chr 12:32). Let us also raise our spiritual eyes to see the end-time fields already ripening for harvest (John 4:35).

Working on the research project "Urban Africa 2050: Imagining theological education/formation for flourishing African cities" with the Centre for Faith and Community at the University of Pretoria (South Africa), I moved forward in the attempt of elaborating the concept of the Pentecost of the city which theological curricula must take into consideration. The article, named "Pentecost of the city: Towards an African urban migratory theology," focuses on the issue of migration in the city of Cotonou in Benin. In this chapter, I focus on how the church can appropriate and apply the concept of hospitality to urban migrants in Africa – the displaced Africans within Africa and growing Asian diasporas in Africa.

Misunderstanding and ignorance of the biblical perspective about migration have created a lot of conflicts in Africa. This chapter's central question is: How can putting into practice African Urban Migratory Theology bring peace to Africa? The chapter examines the ideas of theologians such as Ray Bakke and Fabio Baggio. It begins by analyzing diaspora in Africa and its consequences, and then focuses on the theological concept of migration, bringing out God's intention about diaspora. It then concludes with a call to the church in Africa to apply African Urban Migratory Theology.

Synoptic Picture of the African Diaspora in Africa

All over Africa there are people from every other region of the continent and this often creates tension between natives and foreigners. "Africa's urbanization has been rapidly increasing. For example, sub-Saharan Africa is regarded as the world's fastest-urbanizing region. This increase in urbanization is related to the increase in people migrating into urban areas. However, urbanization often leads to overpopulation."[4] Because of selfish interests in responding to migratory impacts, the spirit of the conflict between "Cain and Abel" persists in Africa. The foreigner, the migrant, is seen as a *faience dog* (unwanted stray dog) especially when he behaves as a dominator and holder of economic levers.

---

3. Kim, "Los Angeles as an Intersection: Questions of Mobility, Power, and Race in Southern California," 1–2.

4. Uwingabire, "How Infrastructure addresses Urban Overpopulation in Africa."

Indeed, on African soil, the Ivorian has the impression that the Burkinabe appropriates his lands, and his earthly blessings; the Togolese, the Beninese, and the Cameroonians have an apprehension and fear of the Nigerians. The Gabonese, the Equatorial Guineans, and the Chadians panic at the sight of Cameroonian migrants in their respective countries. The South Africans treat other Africans who get by with their small jobs as job thieves. Unfortunately, this leads to xenophobia, violence, hatred, and murder in many parts of the continent. To correct that behavior Julius Malema, a member of the South African parliament, said in one of his speeches:

> Please do not buy into the anti-African agenda. Africans are hated everywhere. Soweto cannot afford to hate Africans. Black people are hated everywhere. When you see a black person, see yourself. When you see a black person, say my brother, my sister, let's work together to build the African continent . . . You hate Africans but you don't hate Chinese. You always said the Africans are taking your jobs. Stop being used on black violence. The top is used on an anti-black agenda. Love yourself and once you love yourself you love another black person.

The exploitation and sale of migrants into slavery in this present century are still happening in Libya, Morocco, Saudi Arabia, Kuwait, and other geographical regions of the earth. The conflict between Rwanda and DRC in the east of DRC for many decades because of the mineral resources is an issue of lack of peace in that part of Africa.

Asianisation of Africa

At the end of the last century, the Chinese began settling by helping African countries in the construction of stadiums, and roads and offering some scholarships to Africans. This present century is witnessing massive Asian migration into Africa without a clear declaration of intent. Africa seems to have become "the Garden of Eden" for the Chinese. "China has become the engine of the world and has chosen Africa in its expansion. Migrants are likely to hold the economy, which would remain informal. Many religions of the world, such as Asian religions, will be found in Africa."[5]

The impact of Asian migration and industrialization, particularly Chinese, in Africa no longer needs to be demonstrated. The Chinese, Indian, and

---

5. Agbèdè, "Pentecost of the city."

Pakistani businesses are damaging Africa's environment with the support of African politicians and administrators. There are contracts that are signed to the detriment of African populations. For example, the approach of the Chinese company Sinsteel in May 2022 regarding the Kribi's iron mining contract was denounced by the Cameroonians.[6] Africans deplore the growing exploitation of their forests and mineral resources by Chinese companies which mistreat African employees. This state of things is a source of crises and latent tensions which seek the opportune moment to hatch. While the infusion of cash by Chinese businesses into Africa has created jobs, brought food, built new roads and made life in Africa better for some, foreign aid has generally failed to promote economic growth or reduce poverty but instead has created a culture of dependency and corruption.[7]

Theological Background of the Diaspora Movement

In the Garden of Eden, God made a migratory act by coming to dialogue with the humanity that he created in his image (Gen 3:8). The incarnation of the Second Person of the Trinity is also a migratory act, a movement of the divinity from heaven to earth to put on humanity and live among humans. On the day of the Pentecost, the Third Person migrated and dwells in us as the temple of the Holy Spirit. It was a voluntary migration for the good of human beings. Therefore, migration is rooted in the trinitarian divine being.

After the fall in the Garden of Eden, humanity experienced exile for the first time in its history and subsequently, people were dispersed all over the world (Gen 3; 4; 11). From Genesis 11:31 to Genesis 12:5, we read about the migration of Terah, Abraham's father, and his family toward Canaan. Abram received the promise of the land of Canaan (Gen 12:7; 13:14–18; 15:13). Abraham, Isaac, and Jacob's descendants migrated through Egypt during the period of famine (Gen 12:10). God protected his servants even in the lands to which they migrated (Gen 12:17; Ps 105:12–15).

> Many books of the Bible were written while their inspired writers lived in diaspora . . . Since the creation of the world, therefore, till today, diasporas have been an indispensable means by which God has accomplished his redemptive purposes through Jesus Christ. The history of the expansion of the Christian Church yesterday,

---

6. Moki E. Kindzeka (VOA), "Cameroonians Villagers Protest China Iron Ore Mining Deal," May 23, 2022.

7. Moyo, *Dead Aid: Why Aid is not Working and How there is a Better Way for Africa*, 152.

today, and tomorrow – past, present, and future – cannot be explained apart from the historical reality of God's Sovereignty, ruling over the nations, and the moving of His people everywhere.[8]

Indeed, "care for the poor is clearly at the heart of the Old Testament."[9] This is why the people were instructed to care for foreigners, widows and orphans who are among the poorest and most vulnerable people often (Gen 18; Exod 22:21–22; 23:9; Deut 10:17–18; Matt 25:35–37; James 1:28). God reminds his people that they were migrants in Egypt and must therefore empathise with all the fears of all migrants and thus come to their aid.

Practices of African Urban Migratory Theology through Hospitality

"Umuntu Ngumuntu Ngabantu" or "I am because you are" is the philosophical concept of *Ubuntu* – the notion of interconnectedness in Africa. *Ubuntu* reminds us how we must welcome and treat others. Abel N'Djerareou rightly asserts that:

> Regarding foreigners, Africa lives in a kind of contradiction between the community nature of society as an African value and the exclusion of foreigners forgetting its recent past from the same communities tragically separated by colonization. The Old Testament creates a space that puts the stranger in a position of vulnerable people to be cared for but is also based on shared common humanity.[10]

This vulnerability can be seen in the reception of the foreigner or the passing visitor, and in the popular African adage that "the foreigner is often very hungry and it is necessary to give him a lot of food to strengthen him." My grandmother always cooked extra food with the expectation that a visitor may come at any moment. Furthermore, in Africa, people don't ask for an appointment before coming. Nelson Mandela once said: "A traveler through a country would stop at a village and he didn't have to ask for food or water. Once he stops, the people give him food and entertain him. That is one aspect of *Ubuntu*." Explaining further, he said, "we are human only through the humanity of others; that if we are to accomplish anything in this world it will

---

8. GDN, *Scattered to Gather: Embracing the Global Trend of Diaspora*, 15–16.

9. Jeong, *Mission from A Position of Weakness*, 17.

10. N'Djerareou, "Politique et Développement : L'Ancien Testament est-il un modèle de développement aujourd'hu," 68.

in equal measure be due to the work and achievement of others."[11] Hospitality is in African DNA. "African hospitality is characterized by the emphasis on interdependence. This calls us to share whatever talents and gifts we have for the sake of God and the general prosperity of our society as a way of encouraging one another."[12] Archbishop Desmond Tutu summarized the concept as:

> Africans believe in something difficult to render in English. We call it '*ubuntu, botho*'. It means the essence of being human. You know when it is there and when it is absent. It speaks about humaneness, gentleness, and hospitality, putting yourself on behalf of others, and being vulnerable. It embraces compassion and toughness. It recognizes that my humanity is bound up in yours, for we can only be human together.[13]

This chapter's thrust on hospitality should take into consideration the condition of the human heart (Jer 17:9). This hospitality must be nuanced. We shouldn't romanticize African hospitality. We need to have the discernment of the Holy Spirit, strategies, creativities and wisdom in that welcoming ministry and have some criteria for hospitality, because it is always risky to welcome a foreigner you never knew before. Other proverbs that clarify that African hospitality should be expressed with prudence: *Ndugu nyingi ithatagia muhuko* meaning, "Having too many friends empties one's pockets" (Kikuyu), and *Kinandu kia mucii gitihakagwo mugeni* means, "The family oil is not to be used on strangers" (Kikuyu). Thus, while acknowledging the need for hospitality they urge that prudence be the guide in its practice. It also shows that hospitality is more than welcoming people, for it also means avoiding being misused or exploited, as the above proverbs have shown.[14]

Practices of African Urban Migratory Theology

According to the Scriptures, our mission as servants of God is to bring blessing to the whole world. All humanity are descendants of Adam and Eve, and Noah (Gen 4:25–26; 7:7, 13; 9:1, 18–19). Therefore, we are a family and need to love one another. A migrant is doubly hungry. First, she is physically hungry. She

---

11. Quoted in Claire Oppenheim, "Nelson Mandela and the Power of Ubuntu," *Religions* 2012 3(2), 369–88.
12. Gathogo, "Some Expressions of African Hospitality," 278.
13. Tutu, *The Words of Desmond Tutu*, 69.
14. Gathogo, "Some Expressions of African Hospitality," 280.

travels to seek to meet the five basic human needs and ensure her protection according to hierarchy of needs pyramid. Second, the migrant is spiritually hungry. He needs God, and an understanding of the Scripture to answer his questions about the multiple causes and consequences of his migration and his destiny. It is with good reason that one of the slogans of the Lausanne Movement affirms that the whole gospel must be presented to the whole person (body, soul, spirit) throughout the whole world.

A migrant is doubly foreign. First, he is a stranger by his presence on earth as a creature of God on pilgrimage. Second, she is a stranger by her departure from a geographical space, her native country in which God placed her, and which she recognized as her own; the land that she is most familiar with, and which she mastered and developed before moving to a foreign land.

> Towards the end of the fourth century, John Chrysostom, the Bishop of Antioch, in his commentary on Romans, rebuked the inhospitable attitude of some members of his community towards foreigners. In his homilies, he reminded the faithful that the duty of hospitality is founded in the presence of Jesus Christ in the foreigner.[15]

African urban migratory theology requires that states and churches in Africa must offer hospitality to the migrants because they are human and created in the image of God. Hospitality is one of Africa's core values. We need to have the mind of Christ (John 13:5) by washing the feet of migrants, and by considering them superior to us. We also need to organize meetings and train church leaders to use African hospitality as a platform for the concept of African urban migratory theology (Heb 13:1–2).

Africa must maintain its hospitality values and properly welcome diasporas in Africa. Since the time of Abraham, Africa knew and practiced hospitality. That is a part of the recommendation of African urban migratory theology. "We are convinced that contemporary migrations are within the sovereign missional purpose of God, without ignoring the evil and suffering that can be involved."[16]

Migrants are tools in God's hand to flourish the land (Joseph) and seek the good of the city (Jer 29:7). Brazil recognizes the great contribution of African slaves in building their country. During the Lausanne Third Congress Cape Town 2010, Rev. Key Yuasa acknowledged this and led the Brazilian delegation to say something about the four hundred years of the slave trade and slavery

---

15. Baggio, *Theology of Migration: Exodus Series, A Resource Guide for the Migrant Ministry in Asia*, 20–21.

16. Cape Town 2010 Commitment.

which built their country. The pardon letter written by Yuasa was signed by fifty-nine of the Brazilian delegation. I met him again in the City of Atibaia in Sao Paulo, Brazil on April 3, 2014, and he gave permission to cite his letter:

> Dear Brothers and sisters of the great continent of Africa . . . Your people have been building our country not only with sweat, toil, and blood. Your people and their descendants have been building with hands, heads, and legs (Pélé, Ronaldo, Robinho, etc., etc.), with heart, mind, faith, hope, and love as many musicians, novelists, artists, or technical skills as doctors, engineers, jurists, politicians, etc. in all walk of life. Many are church members, pastors, bishops, saints, professors, and leaders. Your people and descendants are a blessing to our country.[17]

Implications for Diaspora Missions

We must seize the opportunities of migratory movements to announce the gospel and accomplish the Pentecost of the city by presenting the gospel to all migrants whom God in his mercy and sovereignty brought to us.

> Through today's migrations, God is bringing nations and tribes to us in our cities as Cotonou for discipleship and allows migrants to access the Gospel through the hospitality and life of Christians engaged in society . . . We need to be aware of that and present the Gospel to the migrants from different nations gathered in Cotonou for various reasons as the day of Pentecost (Acts 2:5–11) in Jerusalem. That is what we are calling "Pentecost of the city" It is no longer in Jerusalem, but in a city like Cotonou, where it is essential to preach the Gospel to other nationalities or migrants. "Pentecost of the city" is a process toward a movement back to the centripetal mission method.[18]

It is important to understand that the "city is a place of mission, ministry with vision, creativity, persistence, tolerance, acceptance of others, prayer, and lay ministerial involvement. It is a place needing the best in missions now."[19] So, as Christians, we must not look at the migrant as an invader with hostility.

---

17. Agbèdè, *Le Millénium Transformationnel*, 393–95.
18. Agbèdè, "Pentecost of the city: Towards an African urban migratory theology," 16.
19. Ellison, "Cities, Needs, and Christians," 20.

We must not minimize, flout, or persecute the migrant who has great value before God. Christ is at the centre of our theological mission which entails many sociological dimensions.

The meeting of two, or several cultures and ethnic groups, must therefore produce acceptance and not rejection and contempt for the other. We must avoid ethnocentrism and seize the opportunity of cross-cultural evangelization which offers celestial citizenship. As Sam George demonstrates, migrants can find Christ after going to a foreign land: "many Indian emigrants and their progenies have embraced the Christian faith in their adopted homelands."[20]

Conclusion

Benin has a friendly policy towards migrants. The current immigration policy of Benin provides a free visa for ninety days for all Africans. This will result in Cotonou being a desired destination for migrants. Besides African nations, many Chinese, Indians, Lebanese, and South Koreans are interested in immigrating to Benin and other parts of West Africa. Cotonou attracts foreigners from other regions in search of education, employment, business, and family reunification.[21] I agree with Fabio Baggio who said,

> Economic interests and political and cultural considerations tend to view migration solely as an economic process, where migrants are just factors of production. The challenge for the Church is to present a different perspective, where migration becomes a component of dialogue among cultures and societies, and migrants are viewed as human beings. The challenge is also to question a model of development which ignores inequalities and disparities that uproot people from their environment and heritage. Finally, the challenge is to build a Christian community capable of appreciating differences while celebrating the unity of faith[22]

African migratory urban theology asks that the legendary African hospitality, the welcome, and the attention that is given to the stranger be brought in conformity with the word of God. It demonstrates from Genesis to Revelation that God wants migrants and foreigners to be welcomed and offered the opportunity to encounter Christ. It also shows that migration is rooted in

---

20. George, "Two Diasporas of the Global Indian Christianity," 1.
21. Agbèdè, "Pentecost of the city: Towards an African urban migratory theology."
22. Baggio, vii.

the Trinitarian being, our theology and the doctrine of humanity created in the image of God must take this reality into account. The migration process is a return to the Garden of Eden. May today's migrants find a new Garden of Eden in Africa and meet with their creator and saviour.

References

Agbèdè, A. G. *Le Millénium Transformationnel : L'Eschatologie Engagée pour la présence chrétienne dans la société*. Cotonou: Adonaï-Yireeh House, 2016.

———. 2022. "Pentecost of the city: Towards an African urban migratory theology," *Missionalia*, vol. 50 (2020), 6–22. https://doi.org/10.7832/50-0-390.

Baggio, F. *Theology of Migration: Exodus Series, A Resource Guide for the Migrant Ministry in Asia*. Quezon City: Scalabrini Migration Center, 2005.

Bakke, R. *A Theology as Big as The City*. Downers Grove: InterVarsity Press, 1997.

Ellison, Graig. "Cities, needs, and Christians" in *The Urban Mission*, ed. Craig Ellison. Eerdmans, 1974.

Gathogo, Julius Mutugi. "Some Expressions of African Hospitality" *Scriptura* 99 (2008), 275–87. https://scriptura.journals.ac.za/.

George, Sam. "Two Diasporas of the Global Indian Christianity" in *Desi Diaspora: Ministry among Scattered Global Indian Christians*, ed. Sam George. Bengaluru: SAIACS Press, 1999.

GDN. *Scattered to Gather: Embracing the Global Trend of Diaspora*. Revised Edition. Manila: GDN, 2017.

Jeong, P. Y. *Mission from A Position of Weakness*. New York: Peter Lang Publishing, 2012.

Kim, K. "Los Angeles as an Intersection: Questions of Mobility, Power, and Race in Southern California" in Kirsteen Kim and Alexia Salvatierra, *Migration, Transnationalism, and Faith in Missiological Perspective: Los Angeles as a Global Crossroads*. Minneapolis: Fortress Academic, 2022.

Kindzeka, Moki E. (VOA), "Cameroonians Villagers Protest China Iron Ore Mining Deal," May 23, 2022. https://www.voanews.com/a/cameroonian-villagers-protest-china-iron-ore-mining-deal-/6585546.html.

Moyo, D. *Dead Aid: Why Aid is not Working and How there is a Better Way for Africa*. New York: FSG, 2009.

N'Djerareou, Abel. "Politique et Développement: L'Ancien Testament est-il un modèle de développement aujourd'hui ?" in *Eglises, Elections politiques et Développement en Afrique Contemporaine*. Eds. Rubin Pohor and Issiaka Coulibably. Abidjan: FATEAC, 2016, 51–72.

Oppenheim, Claire. "Nelson Mandela and the Power of Ubuntu," in *Religion* 3, no. 2, 2012: 369–88. See https://www.mdpi.com/2077-1444/3/2/369.

Tutu, N. *The Words of Desmond Tutu*. London: Hodder and Stoughton, 1989.

Uwingabire, Renova. "How Infrastructure Addresses Urban Overpopulation in Africa." (2020). https://borgenproject.org/urban-overpopulation/.

16

Engaging African Diaspora Communities with Media

Rudolf Kabutz

Introducing Media Engagement for Diaspora Peoples

People are on the move around the world, moving from familiar places to distant locations, and media plays a significant role along their journeys. People take elements of their home culture with them as they move into new host cultures, and then frequently connect with those of similar cultural backgrounds to form diaspora communities. They closely monitor media broadcast channels for news from their countries of origin, and to receive familiar linguistic and cultural messages. Media tools are used to broadcast media content from diaspora communities to people in their countries of origin, and vice versa. They also offer unique opportunities for people to hear the Good News at a time and place when they are displaced. Engaging African diaspora communities strategically with media provides unique opportunities for spreading the gospel.

Media ministry has been utilized effectively to engage German-speaking people from Europe who have migrated into southern Africa. Simultaneously, many people from African countries have moved elsewhere in Africa, and many have relocated into Europe. Media tools are being used to engage "people on the move" within Europe, and these tools are also becoming accessible to African diaspora. This chapter explores how "thinking media" can strategically help church and ministry leaders to engage African diaspora with the gospel.

Intentionally Engaging with People through Media

People of the diaspora are influenced through different channels by which they engage with media.[1] Media engagement involves becoming aware of the influence of media messages and considering how to influence through the media.[2] While the cultural expressions of communities are shaped through media, Horsfield emphasized that "Christianity itself is a mediated phenomenon," where the Christian faith becomes shaped through the culture expressed through media.[3] When Christian influencers use media, it shapes the mainstream news, documentary, entertainment, and popular culture by communicating a holistic biblical worldview.

When interacting with diaspora people, three facets of media engagement demonstrate how people relate to the media: a) **Media awareness:** A good understanding of media influences on diaspora people provides insight into different types of messages in varying contexts, including messages from contrasting worldviews. b) **Media presence:** Through Christian influencers in the mainstream media, messages with spiritual depth can address the diaspora people's needs within their cultural media spaces. c) **Media ministries:** Messages crafted for specific ethnic groups aim to communicate the gospel in a contextually relevant way. When these messages of hope are distributed via memory devices, online platforms and radio transmitters, they become accessible to diaspora people in their times of need.

Transformational media engagement with the African diaspora and diaspora communities in Africa can be approached through a set of six mindsets:

1. **See compelling visions:** This concerns gaining a vision of what God can change amongst diaspora people by utilising transformative processes of interactive media tools.

2. **Dwell in authentic communities:** Intentionally nurturing relationships within a community of Christian voices and influences is an effective means of developing a capacity for loving outreach

---

1. Lars Dahle, "Media Engagement: A Global Missiological Task," *Lausanne Global Analysis* 3, no.1 (2014), https://www.lausanne.org/content/lga/2014-01/media-engagement-a-global-missiological-task.

2. Lars Dahle, "Media Messages Matter: Towards a New Missiological Approach to Media Engagement," *Norsk Tidsskrift For Misjonsvitenskap* 2 (2014): 105–21, https://journals.mf.no/ntm/article/view/4311/3628.

3. Horsfield, *From Jesus to the Internet*, 286.

and discipleship to diaspora people,[4] who can then be equipped to help others follow Jesus using media processes.

3. **Know relevant information:** Systematic research is key for understanding the issues and challenges facing dispersed people, so that relevant media messages can be developed to help them on their journey.

4. **Go on strategic journeys:** As media influencers interact with people of the diaspora, focused strategies can help spread media messages widely amongst these people.

5. **Tell contextual stories:** Through accessible media channels, contextualized stories and biblical narratives can be communicated. The diaspora people can receive further personal help through interactive direct messaging platforms in discipling relationships.

6. **Be the envisioned transformation:** Media influencers can themselves experience transformation as God enables them to deeply connect with people on the move and by journeying alongside them through media. As the diaspora people engage with the media, they also contribute value into the groups of Christian communicators.[5]

Engaging German Communities in Africa with Media

Over the past centuries tens of thousands of German-speaking people have moved from Germany to South Africa and Namibia. These German immigrants established churches, schools and clubs that function as German cultural centres. When Trans World Radio (TWR) Africa began broadcasting across southern Africa via shortwave in 1974, German programmes from ERF Medien in Germany were included for reaching the local German population with the gospel.

Local media broadcasts were expanded by developing connections with various German communities across South Africa and Namibia, and personal relationships with the leaders. A close community of friends and supporters of the media ministry was established to shape the direction of engaging Germans

---

4. Rudolf Kabutz and Lars Dahle, "Media Engagement beyond the Coronavirus," *Global Missiology*, Digital Media and Missions 18, no. 2 (April 2021). www.globalmissiology.org.

5. Sam George, *Desi Diaspora: Ministry Among Scattered Global Indian Christians* (Bengaluru: SAIACS Press, 2019), 74–75.

with media. Eventually Christian media programmes were developed amongst the local German communities for broadcasting across the whole region.

Visits to churches, schools and other institutions provided a wide understanding of German communities and their spiritual needs. At times, focused research was done to understand the unique changing needs and challenges amongst German communities, which in turn shaped ministry priorities.

Using this knowledge, plans and strategies were designed to foster meaningful interaction with German people. Activities included workshops, presentations, and sermons at churches, as well as cultural events in schools and other centres. People were informed about media programmes available and encouraged to actively participate in media initiatives.

Media content initially focused primarily on radio, with most audio content contributed from the media partner in Germany. Local media content through interviews and reports was contributed for addressing topics pertaining to people in South Africa and Namibia. Programmes were developed in partnership with Christian organisations and German congregations to broadcast events and musical concerts to the communities.

The ERF German media aimed to contribute as "the extended arm of the local church" through counselling seminars, printed presentations on current topics for pastors, training for radio-preaching for pastors and a Bible correspondence course. In addition, a library of radio programmes on cassette was made available for use in home fellowships and Bible study groups.

Recorded media was widely distributed across the region, sold at events and mailed by post. Produced initially on audiocassette, then on CD and eventually on DVD, the media included spiritual messages, music, children's stories, counselling messages, and Christian films. Regular printed magazines provided counselling articles, information about the media ministry and focused prayer points. These various media devices and channels were aimed at sharing the gospel and providing resources to help people grow in their faith.

Developing a vision for reaching the German communities was not easy for people embedded within this community. Over time, the people involved in this missional media community changed, by making themselves available, by giving of themselves, by investing in relationships, and by listening deeply on their journey with the wider German community. It took time to build relationships with people and to sense God's heart for influencing this German community with the love of God.

Over the past decades through this media ministry amongst the German community, individuals have been challenged by the message of the gospel, were encouraged in their faith through daily devotional radio programmes, have deepened their biblical knowledge through correspondence courses, have been able to use Christian stories as ministry for their own children and the children of their friends, and have been inspired to get involved in various aspects of global missions.

Nowadays the context of the German communities in southern Africa has shifted significantly, with many German speaking people integrating into the English and Afrikaans communities in which they are embedded. While German radio programmes can still be heard daily on FM networks across Namibia, many previous radio broadcasting channels have shifted online. German-speaking people in South Africa can easily access radio and television programmes and other media tools from the ERF Medien partner in Germany directly online. The local media ministry in southern Africa links closely with the media partner in Germany, continuing to make media resources available to the German diaspora community in Africa.

Engaging the African Diaspora with Media

The African diaspora is being engaged with media, as illustrated by experiences from the Horn region, Central Africa, and Burundi, and also from Europe.

Horn of Africa media ministry

People are being displaced and emigrating from countries in the Horn of Africa due to political, social, environmental, and economic problems, as well as bloody conflict. While shortwave radio has been used extensively to reach people in the Horn of Africa, nowadays digital social media platforms such as telegram, WhatsApp, YouTube, and Facebook are used to reach listeners scattered all over the world.

Local media partners have received positive feedback from the diaspora and refugees of countries from the Horn. Consumers of media have expressed appreciation, provided witness of following Jesus, and shared testimonies of spiritual growth from programmes that offer Bible teaching, testimonies, evangelistic messages, and prayers. Furthermore, there are nowadays many Asians in the Horn region, who have never heard the gospel and who would benefit from programmes in their respective languages.

Central African diaspora media

The diaspora from Central Africa uses media communication tools to interact with each other and come together as an immigrant family. This media is essential for them to remain current with information about their home countries. However, most media outlets use the trade languages of English, French, Spanish or Portuguese. Since many diaspora people have not mastered these languages, media ministry will do well to record media messages in the local languages of the people.

Reaching people from Burundi

People from Burundi have moved both to neighbouring countries and also to more distant places, so TWR is utilising media content on social media platforms in order to reach them. These Burundian diaspora people then distribute media content amongst their networks and reply with testimonies, praise reports and prayer requests. FM radio stations in the neighbouring countries broadcast programmes and provide feedback. Christian literature in Kirundi is distributed in distant refugee camps and in initiatives that promote peace. Media ministry is a valuable source of hope and comfort to dispersed Burundians.

Diaspora Peoples in Europe

In 2015 Europe experienced a wave of refugees, mainly from Syria, for which ministry partnerships developed. This collaboration included media resources that were distributed via a mobile phone app, with marketing being done by distributing power banks with a QR code to search for media content.

Amidst the war in Eastern Europe during 2022, TWR has provided hope-filled, gospel-focused content for traumatized people who have become scattered throughout Europe. Collaboration has been key: a local partner in Ukraine has created media content in both Ukrainian and Russian, TWR Europe has provided the broadcast infrastructure for distributing media programmes, and a continent-wide mission organisation has distributed information about these media tools amongst people on the ground. TWR has specialized content for trauma and healing, while local Ukrainian partners have developed content specifically for those suffering from the war.

Greater collaborative media initiatives across Europe, first amongst the wave of Syrian refugees and now amongst Ukrainians, are shaping a mind-shift for ministering to immigrant communities in the future.

Key Insights Gained from Diaspora Media Initiatives

Media is helping diaspora people to have their needs addressed, find their identity in the new communities, and enabling them to contribute towards an emerging culture shaped by media.[6]

TWR media ministry was initially focused on refugees but has now shifted attention to diaspora communities that have become established within Europe. While the focus was first on the crisis of Syrian refugees moving to Europe, and now on Ukrainians moving across Europe, the future focus will also involve significant numbers of Afro-Europeans, who trace full or partial ancestry to sub-Saharan Africa.

While needs, identities, and perspectives are incredibly diverse among the groups, niche media messages and platforms can provide meaningful, comforting, and helpful information that is both general to people on the move, yet unique to a specific people group. Even though diaspora groups are often very small communities amidst much larger host communities, tools of media engagement are ideally suited for linking groups interspersed in many locations, facilitating them to learn to shape their identity, and developing an emerging identity shaped by their own roots, those of their host culture and the virtual spaces of the interlinking media networks.

Perspectives for Future Media Engagement among Diaspora Communities

The experiences of engaging African diaspora and diasporas in Africa with media showed that these tools can be used to nurture faith. In the process the newer media may shape how the identity of communities are shaped, since information and agency become available to the populace.[7] The influence of media messages needs to be seen in the light of the powerful influence of the latest media tools themselves, particularly among the diaspora communities.

The following eight perspectives emerged: first, we want to provide media content created by people from a particular language group and culture with innate understanding of local needs and life issues. Any content translated from another culture is to be verified by local experts. Second, we want to contribute information to shape reliable, attractive, and life-changing content on topics relevant for the audience. Third, we want to distribute media programmes

---

6. C. J. P. Niemandt, "A Network Society, Social Media, Migration and Mission," *Missionalia* 41, no. 1 (April 2013): 22–39, 36.

7. Heidi Campbell, *When Religion Meets New Media* (New York: Routledge, 2010), 241.

over multiple platforms including satellite TV channels, memory cards, social media, and local FM stations where possible. Long-range shortwave programmes can be used for covering large areas over which people are dispersed. Fourth, East Africa is now home to many immigrants from Asia who have never heard about Jesus, but who can now be reached through printed gospel tracts and electronic media. Fifth, media ministry amongst the diaspora needs focus, intentionality, and long-term planning for integration and should not be done spontaneously or haphazardly. Sixth, since there are so many unique diaspora groups, partnerships with ministries on the ground can work together to address this wide need. Media content is best produced in a culturally appropriate way. Even though people who flee from war situations may have experienced similar traumatic events, media messages should be tailored to each culture. Seventh, with the number of displaced people growing, engaging people with media is becoming more crucial than ever. Since Europe is a desired destination for people on the move, ministries in Europe will want to give special focus to creating media tools for future immigrants. Finally, we want to nurture intentional close collaboration between media practitioners and ministry practitioners to develop innovative, relevant, and interesting media messages that can be utilized to interact closely with the diaspora people.

Here are *seven questions* to consider that can be a helpful guide in exploring media engagements with diaspora communities:

1. How can we gain a vision for engaging people of the diaspora through media by transferring aspects of ministry into media spaces?

2. How can we foster unity and trusting collaborative loving relationships amongst networked communities for media ministry amongst diaspora people?

3. How can we deeply understand the needs of people, media preferences, available communication channels, and appropriate media messages and platforms?

4. How can we implement plans and strategies to engage diaspora peoples with media, raise their awareness of media's influence on them, and inspire them to move into media spaces where they can be influencers?

5. How can we listen carefully, interact meaningfully, and shape effective contextualized messages through which God can speak?

6. How can we ourselves transform through our engagement with the people on the move through the media, which God can use as a means of spiritual transformation?

Conclusion

Media interaction has a powerful impact on diaspora peoples. It resonates just as when one string on a musical instrument is plucked, it causes the other strings to vibrate in harmony with each other. Such media engagement begins when a group of trusted friends comes together, giving each other the space for exploring to develop innovative approaches for connecting people on the move with meaningful messages.

Africans in the diaspora and the diasporas in Africa can be engaged using media through intentional collaborative innovative processes using the various tools available to develop relational journeys towards faith. By engaging the diaspora communities in the media, they can become followers of Jesus, and then be equipped to utilize these media tools to reach people within their own and other diaspora communities with the gospel.

References

Campbell, Heidi. *When Religion Meets New Media*. First Edition. New York: Routledge, 2010.

Dahle, Lars. "Media Engagement: A Global Missiological Task." *Lausanne Global Analysis* 3.1 (2014). https://www.lausanne.org/content/lga/2014-01/media-engagement-a-global-missiological-task.

———. "Media Messages Matter: Towards a New Missiological Approach to Media Engagement." *Norsk Tidsskrift For Misjonsvitenskap* 2 (2014): 105–21. https://journals.mf.no/ntm/article/view/4311/3628.

George, Sam. *Desi Diaspora: Ministry Among Scattered Global Indian Christians*. Bengaluru: SAIACS Press, 2019.

Horsfield, Peter G. *From Jesus to the Internet: A History of Christianity and Media*. Malden: John Wiley & Sons, Ltd, 2015.

Kabutz, Rudolf, and Lars Dahle. "Media Engagement beyond the Coronavirus." *Global Missiology*. Digital Media and Missions 18.2 (April 2021). www.globalmissiology.org.

Niemandt, C. J. P. "A Network Society, Social Media, Migration and Mission." *Missionalia* 41.1 (April 2013): 22–39.

Conclusion: Africans in Diaspora and Diasporas in Africa

Sam George

Cape Town and Global Missions

What a delightful experience it had been to convene the Lausanne Diaspora Consultation in Cape Town, South Africa in the last week of August 2022 with the help of the amazing team of leaders of the Global Diaspora Network, and now to compile and edit the proceedings of the consultation into this volume for publication, along with my Lausanne co-catalyst for diasporas. My delight stemmed from two historical antecedents related to the city of Cape Town in the history of the Modern Missionary Movement. First, a recent one just over a decade ago, that I was a part of, and another from a distant past of two centuries ago – both of which have left a decisive imprint on the current state of Christianity worldwide and will continue to shape the trajectory of the expansion and growth of Christianity in the coming decades and centuries.

First, the Third Lausanne Congress on World Evangelization was held in Cape Town between 16 and 25 of October 2010. It brought together four thousand two hundred evangelical leaders from one hundred and ninety-eight countries and was extended to hundreds of thousands more in meetings around the world and online. *Christianity Today* called it "the most representative gathering of Christian leaders in history."[1] It brought a renewed impetus and new momentum for the global church to bear witness to Jesus Christ and all his teachings to all people in every nation and every sphere of society. It was considered the one hundredth anniversary of the well-known World Mission Conference in Edinburgh, Scotland in 1910. The 2010 Lausanne Congress featured a younger, ethnically diverse, and geographically varied consortium of Christian leaders than ever before in its entire history.

---

1. J. W. Kennedy, "The Most Diverse Gathering Ever," *Christianity Today* (Sep 1, 2010): 66, https://www.christianitytoday.com/ct/2010/september/34.66.html.

I had the distinct privilege to be one of the delegates of the Cape Town 2010 Congress and was invited to be part of a global team of subject matter experts on migration and diaspora missions. At that time, I was pursuing my doctoral research at the Andrew Walls Center of the Liverpool Hope University in Liverpool, UK, and was in the middle of intense research and writing on the same topic. At first, I was a little hesitant to take time off to write research documents and go to another "mission conference." However, at the insistence of my professors and other Christian leaders I had known, I decided to be part of the congress. I consider it one of the significant moments in my entire Christian life and ministry because of the unique opportunity to meet so many wonderful leaders from numerous nations under one roof. While I was well-acquainted with mission concepts and well-read on the topic, including the writings of some of the speakers, my highlight of the congress was walking through the hallways and hearing so many languages and kingdom spirit throughout the congress. I was powerfully reminded of John's heavenly vision of "a great multitude that no one could number, from every nation, from all tribes and peoples and languages" (Rev 7:9a ESV).

Second, as mentioned earlier, one of the rationales for convening the above congress in 2010 was to commemorate the centenary anniversary of the renowned Edinburgh Mission Conference in Scotland. Many mission conferences were held in the year 2010 by different mission networks in diverse locations and a wide range of publications were brought out. At the pinnacle of the Great Christian Century (1800–1910) when most Christians lived in Europe and North America, this gathering, though it had many lacunae and lacked diverse representation, had a noteworthy impact on global missions for the rest of the twentieth century. Several international mission conferences were held earlier in different places such as Liverpool (1860), Berlin (1884), and New York (1900) as well as later such as Jerusalem (1928), Tambram, India (1938), Whitby, Ontario (1947), Amsterdam (1948), Willingen, Germany (1952), Accra, Ghana (1958), Wheaton (1966), Berlin (1966), and others.[2]

The idea of a conference of missionaries from around the world in 1910 has an earlier precedent that can be traced back to the Father of the Modern Missionary Movement – William Carey, the English cobbler turned Bible translator, social reformer, and educator. His ship docked at Table Bay, near Cape Town in South Africa en route to the mission field in Colonial India, which he considered to be the "uttermost parts of the Earth." He dreamed of

---

2. Scott Moreau, ed., *Evangelical Dictionary of World Missions* (Grand Rapids: Baker Books, 2000), 1029.

the southern tip of Africa as an ideal location for a world missionary conference as it was halfway between Europe and Asia. Remember, this was the early nineteenth century, and Christians in the Americas or the Oceania regions were not significant players within global missionary consciousness or involvement.

William Carey wrote from Calcutta on 15 May 1806 to Andrew Fuller, the secretary of the Baptist Missionary Society:

> The Cape of Good Hope is now in the hands of the English; should it continue so, would it not be possible to have a general association of all denominations of Christians, from the four quarters of the world . . .let the first meeting be in the year 1810 or 1812 at farthest. I have no doubt, but it would be attended with very important effects; we could understand one another better, and more entirely enter into one another's views by two hours conversation than two or three years epistolary correspondence.[3]

Carey wanted such conferences to be held every ten years or so. Kenneth S. Latourette claimed that

> Carey seems to have been the first to propose that Christians take concrete steps to bring their Gospel to the whole human race. It was one of the distinguishing marks of Carey that he dreamed persistently of the needs of the entire human race and called upon his fellow Christians to make the dream come true.[4]

When William Carey proposed to convene an international mission conference, he suggested a place and time that would be convenient for all to participate and an accessible stop on then-known shipping routes, namely the British colony in the city of Cape Town in South Africa in 1810. While he gave three years of lead time to plan and organize such an event and the location was ideally suited, it never materialized, and this idea was eclipsed in the annals of the history of British missions. William Carey was an exceptional visionary mission leader, centuries ahead of his time, to conceive a need for such a conference. He realized how such an event could provide an increased momentum for mission work globally. However, it took nearly two centuries

---

3. S. P. Carey, *William Carey* (London: Hodder and Stoughton, 1934), 268–69. Also, P. G. J. Meiring, "William Carey's Pleasing Dream," 219–28; and Ruth Rouse, "William Carey's Pleasing Dream," *The International Review of Missions* 38 (1949): 181–92.

4. K. S. Latourette, *A History of the Expansion of Christianity, vol. IV* (London: SPCK, 1929), 69.

to gather global mission leaders to express their unity and renew their commitment toward world evangelization in this new era of global Christianity.

Another reason that made the Lausanne Diaspora Consultation special was that it was a long-awaited event in which the Lausanne Diaspora team had been working for nearly three years, though I must admit it was frustrating at times. The issue of migration and diaspora mission featured prominently on the Lausanne's radar at the Cape Town Congress in 2010, and it was launched as a new issue network of the Lausanne Movement with the appointment of a new catalyst (then known as senior associate) a few years prior to it. At that time, I was entrenched in finishing my doctoral research and never imagined that I would take on the mantle of leadership for this issue network. Upon completion of my studies and when the ministry term of the former catalyst ended, I was invited to take on the role of the global catalyst for diasporas. At first, I was uncertain what it would entail as the task was enormous. In 2016, I agreed and was appointed as the catalyst of the Lausanne Movement at the Lausanne Younger Leaders Gathering in Jakarta, Indonesia, and dedicated to this ministry at the Biblical Seminary of the Philippines in Manila.

In the summer of 2019, as we wrapped up the annual diaspora consultation in the UK, the core team decided to convene the next diaspora mission consultation in 2020 in Cape Town, South Africa to celebrate ten years of the issue network and to envision the diaspora agenda for the ensuing decades. We identified a local team of leaders in South Africa, including a local seminary and various church and mission leaders in Cape Town and other parts of South Africa and across Africa. We had finalized the venue, theme, program, and speakers for the consultation. The website and promotional material were ready, and everything was set to launch. And then the COVID pandemic hit and the world shut down. We were forced to pivot to new realities and hosted an online diaspora consultation with the same theme and speakers. Only in August 2022 were we able to return to Cape Town to host the consultation we had been planning since 2019. Waiting does make the heart grow fonder, I guess.

Africans are Going All Over the World

Africans are on the move. They are going places. A record number of people are migrating from Africa to foreign lands. This outflow is only gathering momentum and the volume is sure to exceed what has happened in the past centuries. Today, Africans can be found in every continent and in nearly every nation. They have unshackled from the parochial tribal tendencies to stay put within their geographical confines and among one's own clans, to explore worlds far beyond. In the past, they were taken forcibly, but now many are volitionally seeking out better avenues in foreign lands with their distinctive knowledge, skills, and passion. Many are recruited to work in global multinational corporations while others have built global companies based out of the continent itself. Others are escaping unfavorable circumstances and for sheer survival. The ecological crises in many parts of Africa are driving millions to flee to other places. The extreme poverty, civil wars, religious persecution, and strict religious laws imposed by governments in Northern Africa particularly will force many more to emigrate to safer locales.

The African outmigration could be broadly categorized into three: a) migration of people out of the continent, b) out of their native country but within the continent, and c) those who migrate internally within their own nation-state. African urbanization has drawn millions in recent decades into nearby cities and given birth to many new cities entirely. The concentration and uneven distribution of resources, opportunities, capital, etc., will continue to drive the migration of people from their villages into towns and cities. For many urban centres are a launching pad to explore better opportunities outside of their country, mostly to neighbouring lands or other economic centres on the continent. Cities also provide access to information and services needed for migratory travels and act as a conduit to reach other destinations. The urban centres facilitate migratory processes of obtaining passports, learning about foreign opportunities, obtaining necessary skills or education, and access to travel to foreign destinations. They provide vital connections with middlemen agents and other migrants who have gone abroad. The pan-African identity and continental business entities are causing people to move across many states. A policy proposal by the African Union to allow the free movement of people within the continent will be a great boon to intra-continental migration and movement of Africans beyond their countries. Migration out of the continent is the most demanding and risky and it remains small compared to the other two categories. Migrants are more likely to migrate again as they become aware of still better opportunities and encourage and help others in their family and homelands to migrate.

The cardinal rule in migration studies that Westerners need to realize is that *they are here because we were there*. Africans are going to migrate to countries from which people had come to them in the past. Just as Westerners went to Africa for a plethora of reasons over the recent centuries, Africans are tremendously mobile, travelling beyond their homelands and continents all over the world. The trends of globalization, newer technologies of transportation and telecommunication, the surge of youth demography, lack of adequate economic prospects and gainful employment as well as geo-political conflicts will propel many more to look for greener pastures and security elsewhere. The accomplishments and success stories of those who have gone abroad earlier in addition to positive media portrayals in ancestral homelands will fuel the aspirations of more young Africans to venture out.

However, not everyone will realize these migrant dreams. While pursuing them, for many those dreams turn into nightmares as they fall through the cracks of the global migration system, and they become victims of human greed, exploitation, unjust policies, and regulations along the migratory routes. Their own ignorance, vulnerability, and naivety, and others' racism, may be contributory factors. Desperation and survival instinct force many to take extreme risks to escape their current realities, hoping against all odds to make it safe and secure in their new destinations.

The World is Coming to Africa

The other side of the story of a growing number of Africans going all over the world is the fact that people from all over the world are coming to Africa with renewed enthusiasm and in greater numbers. In the past, it was Jews, Arabs, Indians, and most prominently the Europeans who came to Africa for various reasons such as trade, natural resources, slavery, colonial rule, religious propagation, etc. The new migrants to Africa are optimistic and bring fresh vitality to work with and for locals, yet some are merely repeating the mistakes of the past of exploitation in new ways.

The growing market potential, natural resources, new opportunities, latest technologies, global investments, and the growing middle class in Africa are drawing a new generation of workers and entrepreneurs to the continent. Thousands of African Americans, Caribbeans, Black Britons, and others have moved back to Africa in recent years. Governments are taking new initiatives, for example, Ghana had a campaign called the "Year of Return" in 2019 to mark the four hundredth anniversary of the transatlantic slave trade (now extended to 2030 on account of COVID-19 disruption) to attract Africans in the West to return to their ancestral land.[5] Some are pushed out of the West by growing

---

5. See DW News, "Back to Roots: Why African Americans are flocking to Ghana" (Jan 16, 2023), https://www.dw.com/en/back-to-roots-why-african-americans-are-flocking-to-ghana/a-64403580.

racism, while others are pulled by novel possibilities in Africa, and yet others live in both places, making the most of both worlds.

The demographic realities of Africa will force more out of their homelands than ever before to other African nations. The African continent is young and vibrant, while population projections of sub-Saharan Africa are estimated to cross two billion by 2050.[6] The youthful population of the continent (those below the age of thirty) is expected to reach unprecedented levels, over several hundreds of millions. The declining mortality and increased life expectancy will squeeze young people to migrate to neighbouring cities, countries, and overseas. Without any viable options in pursuing education or gainful employment, millions will look beyond their current habitations. The current economic models or natural resources will not be able to create enough employment or contribute meaningfully to national economies. The uneven distribution of natural resources and economic disparities across African nations will realign its human resources to a greater measure than before. The rampant corruption, political instability, local conflicts, the impact of global warming, and religious persecution will keep national leaders from developing progressive policies or competing in the globalized market economies to fully realize the potential of their resources or personnel.

After finishing Western education, many African international students are returning to Africa to start new businesses or work in the private sector with their global links and knowledge of new business models. Even those who stay back to work in advanced economies, unlike their forerunners, are bringing their know-how, connections, and capital to develop new ventures in their homelands or elsewhere in Africa. Chinese universities have provided a record number of scholarships to African students in recent years and their education included Mandarin language proficiency; they were later employed by Chinese companies to work in Africa. Many African enterprises and nations are attracting talent globally and new economic policies are making it lucrative to invest in the continent. Some of the people who are coming to Africa include China, India, Brazil, South Korea, United States, and others. These trends are likely to proliferate to record levels in the coming decades.

---

6. United Nations, *World Population Prospects 2022* (New York: DESA Population Division, 2022).

Globalizing of African Christianity

Since the dawn of the twentieth century, over the last one hundred and twenty years, Africa has experienced the most remarkable religious transformation demographically and has become the largest Christian continent in the world. This has profound implications for global Christianity of the twenty-first century and beyond. According to the latest *World Christian Encyclopedia*, by 2023 Africa accounts for nearly seven hundred million Christians.[7] The numerical shift in the centre of Christianity from the global North to the South corresponds to a correlated shift in migration, mission-sending capacity, mission resources, spirituality, denominational leadership, and theology. Among them, migration will play a strategic and indispensable role in determining most other aspects of missionary engagements in the coming decades. Andrew Walls claimed that "migration [is] an essential theme of world Christian history, and . . . a vital factor for the future of World Christianity."[8]

The explosive growth of Christianity in Africa coincided with the waning of the church in the former missionary-sending countries as well as a reduction in their burden and giving for missions. While Western-led missionary endeavors and colonial exploits were inextricably intertwined in the past, non-Western missionary activities are closely tied to migratory movements.[9] The presence of non-Western Christians in the West is particularly de-Westernizing Western Christianity and metamorphosing the face of Christianity by diversifying its constituents. In other words, global migration is globalizing Christianity and re-invigorating its missionary impulse with new linkages from every corner of the globe. When the West overshadowed the Christian mission space, it made Christianity look like a Western religion as most of the personnel leading it were Westerners. Euro-American theologies and ecclesial practices became normative, eclipsing the contributions of several centuries and continents in its development.

Historically it can be deduced that where and when Christianity had grown in any part of the world, people in those locales became mobile and explored lands far beyond their places of birth, either for survival or for better livelihood. They are more aware of opportunities outside of their homelands highly

---

7. See Todd Johnson and Gina Zurlo, *World Christian Encyclopedia* (Edinburgh: University of Edinburgh Press, 2020); and Gina Zurlo and Todd Johnson, "World Christianity 2023," *International Bulletin of Mission Research* 47, no. 1 (2023):11–22, 11.

8. Andrew Walls, *Crossing Cultural Frontiers: Studies in the History of World Christianity* (Maryknoll: Orbis Books, 2017), x.

9. This is Hanciles' thesis. Jehu Hanciles, *Migration and Making of Global Christianity* (Grand Rapids: Zondervan, 2022).

motivated to avail themselves of educational prospects abroad and eager to climb new economic ladders by finding better employment and renumeration beyond what is offered in their native economies. With Christians in every country, regions with a large number of Christians tend to connect with other Christians elsewhere and explore potential ventures together, now made easier with new technologies of connectivity that are affordable and accessible. Countless are displaced under duress to seek shelter in nearby nations or cross seas and oceans to escape from wars, ethnic cleansing, economic collapse, or climatic catastrophes; most of them still go to neighbouring nations. Across the entire spectrum of socioeconomic categories and nationalities, an increasing number of Africans, many of whom are Christians or become Christians along the migratory routes or destinations, will find themselves residing in lands far from their places of birth.

When African Christians arrive at new places, they are found to carry a distinctive spirituality, worldview, and missionary passion with them. They are quick to connect with others from their part of the world to form ethnic congregations in their host nations as well as share their faith with other immigrants and hosts. This is evident from the fact that some of the largest churches in the UK and many cities in Europe are now headed by Africans.[10] They have steadily become visible and risen in the ranks of the Western churches, Christian organizations, institutions, and mission agencies. For example, the World Council of Churches is now headed by a South African, and many of the leaders of the Anglican churches are Africans. Several Nigerian, Ghanaian, Kenyan, and other denominations started in Africa have established their diaspora congregations in North America. Some African denominations have planted churches in more than one hundred countries. Though most tend to cater to the needs of African immigrant Christians, some have diversified beyond their own people to include other people, races, and nationalities.

However, over a period of time, especially when the population of the next generation reaches a critical mass, and with the generational differences on account of the loss of cultural frames of reference and language, churches are forced to start services in the dominant languages of the host countries. Church members also begin to attract their friends and colleagues to the church or are forced to look for other multi-ethnic churches where they could fit in. Others birth churches that are not ethnocentric or affiliated to denominations

---

10. Harvey C. Kwiyani, "Blessed Reflex: African Christians in Europe," *Missio Africanus* 3, no. 1 (2017):41–49, 45. Also Jehu Hanciles, *Beyond Christendom: Globalization, African Migration and Remaking of the West* (Maryknoll: Orbis Books, 2015).

back in Africa but intentionally create pan-African congregations that may appear homogeneous to host Christians who cannot distinguish the differences of tribal, ethnic, national, or originations of Black Christians. Some are intentionally focused to reach all and impact the host nations, as is the case of one of the largest churches in Canada now that is based in Vancouver British Columbia which was started by a Ghanaian and has grown remarkably.

The growth of Christianity in Africa and the growing migration out of Africa will globalize African Christianity through the establishment of migrant churches and the emergence of African leaders in non-African organizations. It will not be monolithic, but will show great diversity within and great momentum for the cause of Christ globally. Neither will this trend continue without any challenges or controversies. No matter what, African Christians and their growing migration to the ends of the earth will be a major part of the story of Christianity in the twenty-first century. Walls reminds us, "We may need to look at Africa today in order to understand Christianity itself."[11]

References

Carey, S. P. *William Carey*. London: Hodder and Stoughton, 1934.
DW News, "Back to Roots: Why African Americans are flocking to Ghana." (Jan 16, 2023). https://www.dw.com/en/back-to-roots-why-african-americans-are-flocking-to-ghana/a-64403580.
Hanciles, Jehu. *Migration and Making of Global Christianity*. Grand Rapids: Zondervan, 2022.
———. *Beyond Christendom: Globalization, African Migration and Remaking of the West*. Maryknoll: Orbis Books, 2015.
Johnson, Todd, and Gina Zurlo, *World Christian Encyclopedia*. Third Edition. Edinburgh: University of Edinburgh Press, 2020.
Kennedy, J. W. "The Most Diverse Gathering Ever." *Christianity Today* (Sep 1, 2010): 66. https://www.christianitytoday.com/ct/2010/september/34.66.html.
Kwiyani, Harvey C. "Blessed Reflex: African Christians in Europe," *Missio Africanus* 3.1 (2017): 41–49.
Latourette, K. S. *A History of the Expansion of Christianity*, vol. IV. London: SPCK, 1929.
Meiring, P. G. J. "William Carey's Pleasing Dream." *Missionalia* 21:3 (November 1993): 219–28.
Moreau, Scott, ed. *Evangelical Dictionary of World Missions*. Grand Rapids: Baker Books, 2000.

---

11. Andrew F. Walls, *The Cross-Cultural Process in Christian History* (Maryknoll: Orbis, 2005), 119.

Rouse, Ruth. "William Carey's Pleasing Dream." *The International Review of Missions* 38 (1949): 181–92.
United Nations. *World Population Prospects 2022.* New York: DESA Population Division, 2022. www.un.org.development.desa.pd/files/wpp2022_summary_of_results.pdf.
Walls, Andrew F. *Crossing Cultural Frontiers: Studies in the History of World Christianity.* Maryknoll: Orbis Books, 2017.
———. *The Cross-Cultural Process in Christian History.* Maryknoll: Orbis, 2005.
Zurlo, Gina, and Todd Johnson. "World Christianity 2023." *International Bulletin of Mission Research* 47, vol. 1 (2023):11–22.

Author Profiles

Bulus Galadima, PhD serves as a catalyst for diasporas of the Lausanne Movement and associate pastor of West Shore Baptist Church, Pennsylvania, USA. He was dean of the Cook School of Intercultural Studies at Biola University in California and Provost/President of Jos ECWA Theological Seminary (JETS) in Nigeria. He studied at JETS, Wheaton, University of Edinburgh, and Trinity International University, USA. Originally from Nigeria, now lives in Camp Hill, Pennsylvania.

Sam George, PhD is the director of Global Diaspora Institute at the Wheaton College Billy Graham Center and a catalyst for diasporas of the Lausanne Movement. Originally from India, he has lived and worked in five countries, currently making home in the northern suburbs of Chicago, Illinois, USA. He holds degrees in mechanical engineering, business management and has studied at three seminaries in the US and UK. He is author/editor of a dozen books, including a recent three volume series on *Asian Diaspora Christianity* for Fortress Press.

Jehu J. Hanciles, PhD is the D.W. and Ruth Brooks professor of world Christianity and director of the world Christianity program at Candler School of Theology, Emory University, Georgia, USA. Originally from Sierra Leone, he has lived and worked in Sierra Leone, Scotland, Zimbabwe, and the US, and has been a visiting professor at schools around the world. Previously, he was an associate professor of the history of Christianity and globalization, and director of the Center for Missiological Research at Fuller Theological Seminary, California, USA. He is the author of *Migration and Making of Global Christianity* (Eerdmans, 2021), *Beyond Christendom* (Orbis Books, 2009), and other books.

Harvey Kwiyani, PhD is a Malawian theologian currently serving as CEO of Global Connections and leading a master's program exploring diasporas in world Christianity at Church Mission Society, Oxford, UK. He is involved with *Missio Africanus*, an intercultural mission training initiative that seeks to equip and empower the African church for missions in Europe. Having served in Europe and North America for a long time, he writes a great deal on issues to do with cross-cultural mission and leadership. He has authored and edited several books including *Africa Bears Witness* (Langham Global Library,

2024), *Sent Forth: African Missionary Work in the West* (Orbis Books, 2014) and *Multicultural Kingdom: Ethnic Diversity, Mission and the Church* (SCM Press, 2020). His blog is harveykwiyani.substack.com.

Moses O. Biney, PhD is professor of religion and society, and African diaspora studies at New York Theological Seminary, USA. He holds ThM and PhD degrees in social ethics from Princeton Theological Seminary, New Jersey, USA, and other degrees from universities in Ghana. He is the pastor of Bethel Presbyterian Reformed Church in Brooklyn, NY as well as the current moderator of the Presbytery of New York City, and moderator of the Conference of Ghanaian Presbyterian Churches in North America. He is a member of the editorial board of the World Christianity Journal. He is the author of *From Africa to America* (NYU Press, 2011) and co-editor of *World Christianity, Urbanization, and Identity* (Fortress Press, 2021).

Tharwat Wahba, PhD is professor of missions. He earned his PhD in 2009 from the London School of Theology, UK. His dissertation was on the history of Presbyterian Mission in Egypt and Sudan. He is also Egypt's mission coordinator for Frontier Fellowship. As an ordained Presbyterian minister, he served for nine years as the chairman of the Pastoral and Outreach Ministries Council of the Presbyterian Church of Egypt. He also served with Campus Crusade for Christ in Egypt as a staff member and a campus directorfor twelve 12 years. He has written several articles and chapters as well as his book, *The Practice of Mission in Egypt: A Historical Study of the Integration between the American Mission and the Evangelical Church of Egypt, 1854–1970* (Langham Academic, 2015). He has a vision for evangelism, church planting, and missions in Egypt, the Middle East, and the diaspora.

André Jonas Chitlango, PhD studied theology in Mozambique, Ghana, and holds a doctorate in theology from University of KwaZulu-Natal, South Africa. André lived and worked in South Africa and is originally from Mozambique. He is the executive director of More than a Mile Deep (MMD), an organization that trains leaders for the church in Africa using an African curriculum. MMD was a key partner in the publishing of the Africa Study Bible. André is an ordained minister and past president of the United Baptist Church Mozambique (IUBM). He currently lives in Maputo, Mozambique.

Dr. Yaw Perbi is a physician, pastor, and principal at the global executive leadership education company PELÉ. He served as pastor of a Chinese church in Canada (2012–2016), where he was also president of International Student

Ministries Canada (2013–2021). Yaw has been the Lausanne Movement catalyst since 2015 and is the international director of Kwiverr, providing thought leadership and catalyzing movements among internationals. Dr. Perbi is the author of about 20 books including *Thinking Outside the Window* (Xulon Press, 2015) and *Africa to the Rest* (Xulon Press, 2023). As global CEO of The HuD Group, he champions holistic leadership development on all six continents and has physically served in over fifty countries. He has been the toast of media groups worldwide including CNN, the National Press Club (Washington, DC), VOA, CBC, and BBC. Yaw and Anyele have seven delightful children and make their home between Montreal, Canada, and Accra, Ghana.

Harshit Gudka serves as an associate lecturer in theological and intercultural studies at the International Leadership University, Kenya (formerly known as The Nairobi International School of Theology). He is also an elder with New City Fellowship, Nairobi, a multicultural church plant with a focus on South Asians in Kenya. He is an associate teacher with Naya Jeevan Project, a ministry of Cru focusing on South Asian diaspora ministries. Harshit is a PhD candidate in intercultural studies at the Cook School of Intercultural Studies, Biola University, California, USA.

G. John Daniel, PhD serves as the academic dean and professor of intercultural studies at South Asia Institute of Advanced Christian Studies (SAIACS), Bangalore, India. He was a church planter and pioneered a couple of Bible schools. He is a church-growth consultant and conducts workshops and seminars. John researched the Tamil diaspora in the UK and his PhD research was on the diaspora Sri Lankan Tamils in the city of London. John mentors young pastors and provides leadership to a couple of churches.

Wenhui Gong, PhD is a diaspora Chinese and has worked as a peasant, immigrant worker, electronics engineer, business entrepreneur, church pastor, missionary, and missiologist. During his rich and colourful life, he had various desires fulfilled but never satisfied until he met Jesus Christ and was saved by him in 1999. His life was then turned inside out. He has become all things to all people for the sake of the gospel so that by all means he may share with them in its blessings (1 Cor 9:23). He planted house churches in China, started campus ministries and Chinese diaspora church pastoring in the USA, and discipled church leaders with iTM in Africa. In 2016, he founded Chinese Diaspora Mission (CDM) with a mission field in Kenya and headquarters in the USA. CDM seeks to help Chinese churches mobilize, equip, and send out missionaries who will make disciples among diaspora Chinese and beyond.

Elizabeth Mburu, PhD is the Regional Coordinator of Langham Literature in Africa. She is also an associate professor of New Testament and Greek at Africa International University, Kenya. She pursued her doctoral studies at Southeastern Baptist Theological Seminary, North Carolina, USA. She serves as the coordinator of the Africa Bible Commentary revision project and is the New Testament theological editor. She is also an editor on several projects and serves on several editorial boards, both in Africa, as well as internationally. Her research and publishing interests are primarily in the areas of New Testament, Bible translation, intercultural hermeneutics, and culture and worldview studies. She is from Kenya.

Godfrey Harold, PhD holds two doctoral degrees in theology and presently serves as the principal at Cape Town Baptist Seminary as well as on the executive council of the Baptist Union of Sothern Africa. He serves as a distinguished fellow at BH Carol Theological Institute, USA, and a postgraduate supervisor at The South African Theological Seminary and the University of Forth Hare. He has published numerous peer-reviewed articles in national and international theological journals and serves as the chief editor of the South African Baptist Journal of Theology. He is author of *The Apostolic and Prophetic Reformation* (Lambert Academic Publishing, 2017) and several book chapters. Godfrey is a research associate at Stellenbosch University and an associate minister at Athlone Baptist Church, Cape Town. Godfrey is married to Patricia and they have a daughter, Odelle Amy.

Mitch Hamilton, PhD, DMin is a pastor, diaspora missiologist, and migration strategist for the International Mission Board and numerous faith-based organizations. Together with his wife, Teresa, they seek to understand diaspora culture and the challenges sub-Saharan Africans face as they follow the perilous routes to a perceived better life. Networking with indigenous, immigrant, and international churches, they are committed to developing better methodologies to engage moving people with the gospel. Over the past four decades, Dr. Hamilton has served in leadership positions across his own denomination while continuing to write, lead conferences, and teach in globally diverse academic settings. He served as senior pastor in urban contexts for nearly thirty years before transitioning to the Sahel in 2015. Their background has allowed them to consult with pastors on five continents and over thirty countries. They currently make their home along the Mediterranean and divide their time between Africa and Europe.

Anne Abok has an associate of arts degree in communication arts and media from the University of the Nations, a bachelor's in theology from Faith Bible College, South Africa, and a master's degree in social rehabilitation from the University of Abuja, Nigeria. She is a screenwriter and filmmaker. She is also an astute development worker, passionate speaker, media trainer, and accredited facilitator with the South African qualification framework. Anne's passion for social change and godly transformation of society led her to pioneer Media Village in Nigeria (www.mediavillageng.org) in 2005. Anne also pioneered Media Campaign Against Human Trafficking (MeCAHT) in 2008 where she acquired experience in anti-trafficking work leading her to write and produce more than a dozen anti-trafficking films. She has won several awards for her work locally and internationally. Anne has published on issues related to COVID-19 and anti-trafficking. Anne currently lives in the UK and is pursuing ordination within the Church of England.

Clene Nyiramahoro is a Rwandan and married with six children. She works for SIL International on the Global Diaspora Services team. She has trained mother-tongue Bible translators and has worked as a translation consultant. Currently, she is working as a trauma healing master facilitator and coordinator. She has lived and worked in cross-cultural contexts for the last twenty-eight years. She is currently working among refugees mostly living in Africa, but hoping to expand her ministry to refugees living outside Africa as well. She has led trauma healing workshops in different countries hosting refugees in East and Southern Africa and she has seen first-hand the impact of that life-changing ministry in the lives of people. She is the author of *Beyond the Tears: A Story of God's Faithfulness* (Integrity Publishers, 2010). She believes God uses our brokenness to encourage others in the Kingdom, and to give hope to the hopeless.

Mabiala Justin-Robert Kenzo, PhD was born and raised in Maduda, in the Democratic of Congo (formerly known as Zaire) where he still holds strong ties. Currently, he is serving as the District Superintendent of the Saint Lawrence District of the Alliance in Canada, while at the same time teaching as an associate or visiting professor at the École de Théologie Évangélique au Québec (Université Laval), Ambrose Seminary (Ambrose University), and Regent College. In the past, he served as National Church President of the Evangelical Community of Alliance Churches in the DRC as well as teaching theology at Trinity Divinity School in the USA (sessional), Ambrose Seminary in Canada, FATEAC in Côte d'Ivoire (sessional), CFTEAC (Gabon), and the Alliance University in Congo.

Afolabi Ghislain Agbèdè, PhD is the President of Foundation Adonaï-Yireeh House, a growing ministry of teaching, seminars, theological consultation, radio broadcasts, evangelism, editing, and publication of theological works (www.adonaiyireeh.org). He is a professor of systematic theology and holistic development and a theological consultant. As a researcher, teacher, leader, and visiting lecturer in various theological faculties in Africa, he has a creative mind. He is the founder of the online Faculty of Holistic Theology and Applied Missiology (FAHTAM) and a research associate of the Centre for Faith and Community at the University of Pretoria in South Africa and Nagel Institute. He is married to Eveline and together they have four children.

Rudolf Kabutz is a Catalyst for Media Engagement for the Lausanne Movement and a media research strategist of Trans World Radio (TWR) Africa based in South Africa. After training in nuclear physics and working as a medical physicist, he joined TWR to utilize media for equipping communities in Southern Africa. He is engaged with various ministry and media networks in Africa, promoting cooperation between media practitioners and networks of impactful local initiatives. Rudolf is passionate about reaching people globally through strategic collaborative media networks on multiple levels for shaping and transforming society with the hope of Christ.

Index

A
Adelaja, Sunday 68
Adogame, Afe 64
African Christianity 2, 25, 29, 32, 107–8, 204, 206
African church 31–32, 64, 68, 71–72, 75, 87, 100, 104–5
African diaspora *See* diaspora, African
African Independent Church 28
African Union 3, 64, 201
Akrofi-Christaller Institute of Theology, Mission and Culture 107
Aladura 28
Alexandria 1–2, 46, 49, 105, 172
Algeria 45, 48, 136, 138, 152
Arabs xiii, 2, 202
Asian 7, 52, 75–82, 178, 191
Asians 75, 77–82
Augustine 2, 106

B
Barth, Karl 126
Benin 2, 7, 60, 151, 178, 185
Bible 1, 10, 72, 95, 99–100, 106, 122–23, 153, 164, 180
Brazil 5, 55–61, 183, 203
Brazilian 57–61
Brazilians 55, 59–61
Brem-Wilson, Thomas Kwame 26
British 27, 29–32, 56–57, 76, 79, 199
Burundi 149, 191–92

C
Carey, William 198–199
Carthage 46
Central African Republic 149, 192
Chad 136, 138
Chinese xiii, 5, 93–101, 179, 185, 203
churches 19–20, 27–32, 35–36, 38, 40, 42, 46, 48–51, 60, 69, 81–82, 84, 88, 93–95, 99–100, 104, 107, 121, 141, 155, 159, 169, 183, 189–90, 205–6
colonial xi, xii, 30, 47, 79, 106, 120, 128, 133, 202, 204
community 2, 12, 48–49, 56, 58–60, 71, 77–80, 82, 88, 95–97, 104, 121, 124–25, 127, 139–40, 147, 154, 162–63, 165–66, 188–91
compassion 16, 120–21, 123, 127, 153
conflicts 96, 108, 133, 147, 150, 163, 177–78, 202–3
Coptic Orthodox Church 46, 48, 50, 105
cross-cultural 10, 65, 70, 72, 98, 101, 185
Crowther, Samuel Ajayi 26, 106
cultural 17, 36–37, 40, 71, 79–80, 82–83, 95, 97–98, 113, 115, 148–50, 174, 187–88, 190
culture 1, 7, 10, 12, 20, 38, 41, 52, 60, 70, 75, 78–80, 94, 97, 100, 103, 106, 109–10, 127, 140, 171, 180, 187–88, 193–94
Cugoano, Ottobah 26
Cyril of Alexandria 172

D
destination xiii, 6, 40, 68, 83, 85–86, 116, 132–33, 135, 140–41, 146–47, 152, 155, 185, 194, 201–2, 205
diaspora 1–4, 12, 30, 32, 39–40, 45, 47, 49–52, 55, 61, 78–79, 84, 94–96, 98, 101, 105–6, 109–10, 115–16, 174, 177–78, 180, 183–84, 187–89, 191–95, 197–98, 200, 205
African 3, 5, 15, 25, 36

40–41, 50, 59, 61, 64, 105, 108, 134, 178, 187–88, 191, 193
Chinese 97–99, 101
communities 51, 88, 114, 116, 187, 193–95
Indian xiii
mission 6, 20, 36, 61, 65, 75, 81–83, 88, 94, 200
disciple 25, 31, 71, 94, 103
discipleship 31, 51, 97–98, 100–101, 184, 189
displaced 14, 16, 21, 47, 178, 187, 191, 194, 205
diversity xi, 7, 78, 82, 116, 206

E
East Africa 5–6, 75–77, 79, 82, 107, 194
economic xii–xiii, 12–14, 37, 45, 52, 65, 76, 80, 86, 105, 116, 120, 124, 132–33, 149–50, 160, 178, 180, 191, 201–3, 205
education 1–3, 7, 27, 30, 50–51, 66, 83, 95–96, 99–100, 147, 162, 185, 201, 203
Egypt 1–2, 45–50, 84, 180–81
Ekarte, Daniels 27
environmental crises xii, 150–51
Equiano, Olaudah 26
Eritrea, Eritrean 49, 149
Ethiopia 2, 49
ethnic 2, 16, 20, 31, 39, 50, 79, 82, 177, 185, 188, 205–6
Europe 2, 11, 13, 16–19, 27–31, 38–39, 45–48, 50, 64, 68, 103, 106, 131, 133–35, 139, 141, 145, 151–52, 187, 191–94, 199, 205
evangelical 6, 65, 121–22, 127–28, 165, 197
evangelicalism 120–21, 125, 128
evangelism 32, 35, 38, 50–51, 97, 99, 101, 120–23

F
FATEAC 108
Fourah Bay College 106

G
Gambia 134, 136
German, Germany 39, 116, 126, 151, 189–91, 198
Ghana 2, 5, 28, 35, 37, 41, 60, 69, 71, 107, 198, 202
Ghanaian 5, 26, 28, 31, 35–40, 42–43, 205–6
gospel 12, 21, 49–52, 68, 70–72, 84, 88, 93–94, 96, 103, 105–6, 110, 113–14, 119–24, 127–28, 132, 140–41, 183–84, 187–92, 194–95, 199

H
Hausa 1, 60
healing 6, 161–66, 192
Hippo 46
Holy Spirit 52, 71, 174, 180, 182
hospitality 4, 6, 16, 94–95, 154, 169–74, 178, 182–83, 185
human rights 145, 150, 153

I
illegal 47, 50, 135, 140, 151, 153
immigrant 15–20, 36, 39, 41, 43, 48, 50, 52, 64, 77, 79, 81, 94–95, 114, 134, 189, 194, 205
  anti-immigrant 15
  illegal 83, 115
immigration xiii, 15, 18, 41, 77, 83, 85, 95, 115, 169, 185
  illegal 48
independence xii, 77, 79, 100, 107
India 5, 11–12, 65, 68, 75, 79, 82–88, 198, 203
Indian xiii, 5–6, 75–76, 79, 81, 83, 86–87, 185
Indians 76, 83, 88, 202
integration 75, 77, 79–82, 194
internally displaced persons (IDP) 160
  See also displaced
International Association for Refugees 163
International Organization on Migration (IOM) 146, 151

international students, African Christian 63, 65, 67–68, 70–72
Islam 46–47
Islamic 2, 49, 68, 148
Israel 1, 124, 153
Israelites 115, 153

J
Jea, John 26
Jesus Christ 2, 7, 70, 72, 113, 123–25, 197
Jewish 2, 105, 171
justice 111, 120–21, 123, 125, 127, 153, 155, 159

K
Kanyemba 58
Kenya xiii, 5–6, 75–82, 160
Kenyan 77–78, 80–81, 205
kingdom of God 125–26
Kiswahili 76, 80

L
labour xii, 27, 76, 95, 135, 139, 146–47, 149, 151
Lausanne Congress 197
Lausanne Covenant 125–26
Levinas, Emmanuel 170–71
liberation xi, 124–25, 128
Liberia 4
Libya 2, 45, 47–48, 136, 152, 179

M
Malawi 28, 41, 56–57, 59, 161, 163
Mali 2
Mandela, Nelson 181
Mauritania 136, 140, 149
Mark, apostle 105
marriage
  forced 147, 149
McKnight, Scott 127
Mediterranean 45, 47–48, 51, 135–38, 151–52
media 187–95
medical 84–86, 95, 101
mental health 161

migrant xiii, 6–7, 10–15, 19, 37, 39, 45, 47, 50–51, 64, 71, 75, 80, 114, 133–37, 139–41, 151, 153, 160, 177–79, 181–82, 184, 201–2, 206
  African 16
  economic xiii, 131
  illegal 47
  Indian 76
migration 9–14, 16, 21, 36, 55, 64, 68, 71, 75–76, 81–83, 88, 114, 132, 134–36, 140, 145, 150, 153, 155, 177–78, 180, 183, 185, 198, 200–202, 204, 206
  African 16, 132
  Asian 179
  biblical theology 9
  climate 151
  control xiii
  economic xii
  forced xiii
  global 14–16, 18, 204
  illegal 51
  irregular 145–46, 152
missio Dei 21, 72, 121–23, 125–28
mission 9–10, 12–14, 20–21, 25, 32, 35, 37–41, 43, 46–47, 50, 60–61, 64, 66, 68, 71–72, 84, 93–94, 98, 101, 103, 108, 120–22, 124, 126–27, 182, 184, 192, 198, 204
  African 64
  church's 126
  drive 40, 43
  holistic 127
  of God 46, 65, 67, 100, 123, 125–26, 128, 153
  reverse 39–40, 43
missionaries 11–12, 101, 116, 121
missionary 10, 12–14, 20–21, 37, 39–40, 48–49, 64, 70–71, 93, 95, 174, 199, 204
  God as 126
missions xiii, 5–7, 9, 11, 17, 20, 55, 65, 69–71, 93, 95, 98, 101, 105, 184, 191, 198, 204
  worldwide 37
mobility 2, 9, 11, 15, 21, 109, 132

Moltmann, Jürgen 173
Mansa Musa More than a Mile Deep (MMD) 107, 109
Morocco 45, 116, 136–37, 152, 179
Mozambican 56, 58, 61
Mozambique 55–61
Muslim 3, 45, 49–51, 78, 84, 151

N
Nairobi Evangelical Graduate School of Theology (NEGST) 107
nationalism
  White 17
  White Christian 17
Newbigin, Lesslie 71, 128
Nigeria xiii, 1, 4, 6, 12, 26, 55–56, 59–60, 68, 82–84, 107, 147, 151–52
Nigerian 5, 7, 26, 28–29, 31, 49, 151, 205
Nigerians 179
North Africa xiii, 1–3, 5–6, 45–48, 50–52, 105, 133, 152
North America 18, 28, 35–43, 45, 50, 64, 93, 198, 205
Nova Scotia 106

O
Oden, Thomas 2, 105
Owusu, Sam 69
Origen 105

P
Padilla, Rene 121, 124
partnership xiii, 42, 49, 88, 97–98, 100, 115, 154, 163, 190, 192, 194
Paul, apostle 10, 103, 110–14, 140, 174
Pentecostal 26, 28, 30, 36, 60, 107
persecution 14, 45, 52, 150, 201, 203
Portugal 56
Portuguese xiii, 55–58, 82, 192
postcolonial 120, 172
poverty xii, 11, 47, 133, 139, 150, 180, 201

R
race 30, 199, 205
racism 25, 30, 48, 59, 202–3
refugees 48–52, 114, 146, 159–61, 163, 165–66, 191–93
religion 9, 12, 29, 36, 39, 78, 80, 109, 111–12, 119, 124, 179, 204
religious 3–4, 9–10, 18, 20, 28, 36–38, 50, 70, 75, 78, 109–10, 114–15, 148, 150, 153, 170, 201–4
Ricoeur, Paul 170

S
Sahara Desert 137
Said, Edward 120
Sider, Ron 125
Sierra Leone 12, 106
Simon of Cyrene 2, 105
slaves 3, 55–60, 106, 183
  former 5, 26, 58, 60
  freed 26, 60
  modern 6
  sex 151
  trade 3, 5, 25–26, 56–59, 61, 106, 183, 202
slavery 79, 183, 202
  modern 146–49
smuggle, smugglers, smuggling 11, 51, 135–37, 139, 145–46, 152
South Africa xiii, 4–6, 15, 56, 93, 116, 120, 152, 178, 189–91, 198–200
southern Africa 163, 187, 189, 191
South Sudan, Sudanese 49, 149
spiritual 37, 40, 48–49, 51, 95–96, 120–21, 128, 140, 154, 160, 178, 188, 190–91
Stott, John 125
sub-Saraha 12, 19, 47, 85, 133–34, 137–40, 149, 178, 193, 203
Swahili 163

T
theological education 5, 51, 103–11, 114–16, 178
  by Extension (TEE) 107

the Other 7, 120, 169–71, 174
the Self 170–71
trafficking xiii, 6, 146–49, 152–55
   child 148, 154
   child sex 149
   drug 86–87
   human 48, 51, 135, 145–47, 149, 151, 153–55
   sex 149–53
transform 98, 100, 128
Trans World Radio (TWR) 189, 192–93
trauma 154–55, 159, 192
   healing 161–64
tribal 75, 77–78, 81, 200, 206
tribe 1, 77
Trinity 6, 108, 172–73, 180
Triune God 126, 171–74

U
ubuntu 7, 181–82
Uganda xiii, 82
UK 5–6, 16, 25–26, 28–32, 68, 75, 94, 198, 205
Universal Declaration of Human Rights 145
urban xiii, 7, 77, 133, 141, 162, 177–78, 183, 185, 201
urbanization 178, 201

W
Walls, Andrew 4, 11, 107–8, 204, 206
West Africa 26, 56–57, 59, 86, 94, 107, 148–49, 152, 185
White superiority 31
World Council of Churches 205
worship 31, 38–39, 41, 46, 50, 78, 110, 172
worshipping 88, 114
Wright, Christopher J. H. 122–23, 127

Y
Yoruba 31, 60, 106

GLOBAL DIASPORA NETWORK

www.GlobalDiasporaNetwork.org

"Fulfilling God's Redemptive Mission for the People on the Move"

GDN's Vision
To empower the global church and respond effectively to the missional opportunities arising out of global migration and diaspora communities worldwide.

GDN's Mandate
1. To catalyze the global Church to demonstrate and proclaim the whole gospel to, through, and beyond diasporas everywhere.
2. To foster theological thinking on diaspora through dialogues and consultations with reflective practitioners and scholars for the development of relevant resources.
3. To network with local churches, denominations, mission agencies, NGOs, theological institutions, and other mission networks.
4. To accelerate the development and adoption of diaspora missiology in leading seminaries, universities, and institutions worldwide.

Global Diaspora Network
4th Floor, Back to the Bible Bldg., 135 West Ave
Bungad, Quezon City, Philippines 1104.

Global Diaspora Institute
Wheaton College Billy Graham Center
500 College Ave, Wheaton, IL 60187.

https://lausanne.org/network/diasporas

Langham Literature and its imprints are a ministry of Langham Partnership.

Langham Partnership is a global fellowship working in pursuit of the vision God entrusted to its founder John Stott –

> *to facilitate the growth of the church in maturity and Christ-likeness through raising the standards of biblical preaching and teaching.*

Our vision is to see churches in the Majority World equipped for mission and growing to maturity in Christ through the ministry of pastors and leaders who believe, teach and live by the word of God.

Our mission is to strengthen the ministry of the word of God through:
- nurturing national movements for biblical preaching
- fostering the creation and distribution of evangelical literature
- enhancing evangelical theological education

especially in countries where churches are under-resourced.

Our ministry

Langham Preaching partners with national leaders to nurture indigenous biblical preaching movements for pastors and lay preachers all around the world. With the support of a team of trainers from many countries, a multi-level programme of seminars provides practical training, and is followed by a programme for training local facilitators. Local preachers' groups and national and regional networks ensure continuity and ongoing development, seeking to build vigorous movements committed to Bible exposition.

Langham Literature provides Majority World preachers, scholars and seminary libraries with evangelical books and electronic resources through publishing and distribution, grants and discounts. The programme also fosters the creation of indigenous evangelical books in many languages, through writer's grants, strengthening local evangelical publishing houses, and investment in major regional literature projects, such as one volume Bible commentaries like *The Africa Bible Commentary* and *The South Asia Bible Commentary*.

Langham Scholars provides financial support for evangelical doctoral students from the Majority World so that, when they return home, they may train pastors and other Christian leaders with sound, biblical and theological teaching. This programme equips those who equip others. Langham Scholars also works in partnership with Majority World seminaries in strengthening evangelical theological education. A growing number of Langham Scholars study in high quality doctoral programmes in the Majority World itself. As well as teaching the next generation of pastors, graduated Langham Scholars exercise significant influence through their writing and leadership.

To learn more about Langham Partnership and the work we do visit **langham.org**

www.ingramcontent.com/pod-product-compliance
Lightning Source LLC
Chambersburg PA
CBHW050441240426
43661CB00055B/2470